Daniel Crouch Rare Books Ltd
4 Bury Street, St James's
London
SW1Y 6AB

+44 (0)20 7042 0240
info@crouchrarebooks.com
crouchrarebooks.com

Daniel Crouch Rare Books New York LLC
PO Box 329
Larchmont
NY 10538-2945, USA

+1 (212) 602 1779
info@crouchrarebooks.com
crouchrarebooks.com

ISBN 978-1-9196418-5-0

Catalogue edited by Daniel Crouch, Kate Hunter,
Elena Napoleone, Mia Rocquemore, Qi Sun and Nick Trimming
Design by Ivone Chao
Photography by Louie Fasciolo and Marco Maschiao
Cover: item 2

Terms and conditions: The condition of all books has been described. Each item may be assumed to be in good condition, unless otherwise stated. Dimensions are given height by width. All prices are net and do not include postage and packing. Invoices will be rendered in £ sterling. The title of goods does not pass to the purchaser until the invoice is paid in full.

MIX
Paper from responsible sources
FSC® C001785

Printed by Park Communications on FSC® certified paper. Park is an EMAS certified company and its Environmental Management System is certified to ISO14001. 100% of the inks used are vegetable oil based, 95% of press chemicals are recycled for further use and, on average 99% of any waste associated with this production will be recycled. This document is printed on Galerie Matt made of material from well-managed, FSC®-certified forests and other controlled sources. The pulp used in this product is bleached without the use of chlorine (ECF).

The Art of the Deal

DANIEL CROUCH RARE BOOKS

Porte de Ville
QUOTIDIENNE
As de Pique

Introduction

'Life is not always a matter of holding good cards, but sometimes, of playing a poor hand well.'
– Jack London

Playing cards is, in many ways, a hallmark of civilisation. Like maps and money, a deck of cards is a way of representing an entire value system and an understanding of human nature on paper. A game of cards embodies the inherent unpredictability of life, allowing us to grapple with the uncertainties, directing them towards our own ends. At the card table, when the hands are dealt, all men are temporarily equal; it is how they choose to play those cards that determines who will draw ahead. The players are required to practice both strategic and emotional discipline, and one's reaction to a bad hand or a sudden windfall can reveal much about his temperament and priorities. As in cards, so in life.

Nothing illustrates the intuitive nature of cards more clearly than the idioms that have been adopted in modern English. Nobody needs to be told what it means to 'keep your cards close to your chest', to 'follow suit' or to be 'dealt a bad hand'. With separate origins in China, the Middle East and North Africa, and a long history in Europe, cards are one of the most universal and timeless forms of interaction. Played by nomads and emperors, parlour maids and Lords, cards form a shared pastime that connects all levels of society across the ages.

The basic concept is always the same: a set of symbols representing a range of values and subgroups. The execution, however, can take on a myriad of different forms, many of which are illustrated by the cards within these pages. Not only do their designs reflect the market, from unique silk cards fit for a king (item 2) to mass-produced cards for general use, but they also offer valuable insight into their contemporary societies. From satire (items 10, 11, and 40, for example) to propaganda (such as items 131-134, 141, 142, and 148), many of the decks take on overtly political positions, while the images on others reveal much about the fashion (like items 11 and 39), entertainment (see items 59 and 149) and events (items 29 and 50) of the day. Some are not used for playing games at all, but instead for sending messages (such as items 13 and, poignantly, 16), promoting products (numerous examples such as items 105, 111, 114, 122, and 124) or even teaching music (item 57).

Spanning four centuries and two continents, the cards within this collection represent a wealth of potential. These palm-sized pieces of paper have the power to enrich, educate, reunite, advertise or entertain. They can record the social, political and cultural movements of a nation's history, while still remaining a light-hearted way to pass the evening. The artistic and technical innovations of the generations of card-makers represented in these pages have ensured that, even if you get dealt a bad hand, you are still holding good cards.

The Collector

Frank van den Bergh was born in 1961 in the Dutch city of Nijmegen. He fell in love with the game of bridge at fifteen years old, and quickly became a fanatical player. Recognising this, his parents gave him an uncut sheet of old Dutch playing cards for his eighteenth birthday. He received a second when he turned 21, and a third when he graduated from the School of Economics. Despite this early start, things then became dormant on the playing card front for a number of years until a fateful visit to Paris with his wife, Annelies, in 1989.

In a tiny bookshop, so small that its one customer had to leave before another could enter, Frank found and bought a book about nineteenth century playing cards by Jean Verame. The cards in this book fascinated him so much that he decided to start his own collection. Back in the Netherlands, he visited Harry Kenter, a famous Dutch dealer and collector of playing cards, who helped him build a small but beautiful collection. His motto: "Building a beautiful collection of playing cards is the art of saying "no"".

Frank and Harry decided that only rare, beautiful, and exceptional decks, in mint or excellent condition, could enter the collection. In the years that followed, enthusiastically supported by Annelies, Frank visited many playing card fairs, auctions, and conventions, and adhered to the original plan of compiling a high-quality collection of choice decks.

In 2011, Frank decided to write a book so that he could share his collection with the rest of the world, and, seven years later, in November 2018, "Collected Playing Cards, the Frank van den Bergh collection" was presented to family, friends and other enthusiasts.

In 2023, after more than 30 years of collecting, and in close discussion with Annelies, the decision was made to sell the collection.

GRABADA EN MADRID P.OR
MAN.L ALEGRE EN
1811

Glossary

Court cards
The court cards, or picture cards, are the three highest-value cards in a deck apart from the Aces. They are typically represented as a King, Queen and Jack in each suit, although this can vary from system to system. In German decks, for instance, we find a King, Knave and Under-Knave.

French system
The French system has been widely adopted as the standard format of a 52-card deck. It uses the familiar four suits of Clubs, Diamonds, Hearts and Spades, and three court cards of King (Roi), Queen (Dame) and Jack (Valet). Under the French system there were many regional variants, the most dominant being the Paris pattern. The Paris pattern was published in the form of both a 52-card and 32-card deck, the latter with the pip cards from Two to Six omitted.

German system
The German system is one of the earliest distinct European systems, having emerged in the mid-fifteenth century. The four suits are represented by Acorns, Bells, Hearts and Leaves; it was from these that the more common French system developed. The court cards show a King (König), Knave (Ober) and Under-Knave (Unter), and its Ace cards (Daus) are valued not as One, but as Two, meaning that the standard deck had 48 cards. In some variants, this was further reduced by the removal of the Three, Four and Five, perhaps due to paper shortages.

Italian system
The Italian system was developed in the northeastern region around Venice during the fifteenth and sixteenth centuries. It consists of 52 cards, but some of the local variants that emerged in other areas omit the Eights, Nines and Tens, leaving only 40 cards. The most common Italian deck uses the four suits of Clubs, Coins, Cups and Swords, which also feature in the Spanish system. The majority of Italian decks have three court cards consisting of a King (re), Knight (cavallo) and Knave (fante), although tarock decks also include an additional Queen (regina or donna) between the Knight and King.

Pip cards
Pip cards, or number cards, refer to the cards in a deck which represent a numerical value from two to ten in a standard 52-card deck. They are known as pip cards because of the 'pips' on the front of each card: the small, easily countable symbols that correspond to its value. Some pip cards also show a Roman or Arabic numeral to clarify the value.

Spanish system
The Spanish system is similar to the Italian system, in that it uses the four suits of Clubs, Coins, Cups and Swords. It also uses the three court cards of King (rey), Knight (caballo) and Knave (sota), but again some decks contain an additional Queen (reina). Although it is thought that the decks introduced into Spain during the Moorish invasion consisted of 52 cards, the removal of the Tens at some point in the fifteenth or sixteenth century leaves the standard Spanish deck with only 48 cards. A particularly popular game named Ombre uses an even more reduced deck of 40 cards, with the Eights and Nines omitted.

Suit marks
The suit marks, also known as 'pips', refer to the symbols used to represent the various suits. In the standard French system, this means the familiar forms of Clubs, Diamonds, Hearts and Spades, but in other variations, they are represented by Acorns, Bells, Coins, Cups, Leaves and Swords.

Tarot
Tarot cards emerged in western Europe during the mid-fifteenth century for use in specific games such as Italian tarocchini, French tarot and Austrian Königrufen. The decks varied in size between reduced 22-card decks and expanded decks of 78 cards. In the eighteenth century, tarot cards began to be used for cartomancy, the attempts to divine one's future or fortune by selecting and analysing cards.

Transformation deck
Transformation decks, which emerged in the nineteenth century, are innovations on the traditional pip cards. The artist incorporates the card's suit marks into its design, thus 'transforming' them into part of the image. This often makes for questionable results, with strangely spade-shaped faces or bodies modelled in the form of the club symbol.

Trappola
Trappola is a card game that emerged in Venice during the sixteenth century and subsequently became popular across Europe. Played with an Italian deck, the game uses only 36 cards, with the pip cards from Three to Six omitted. The game fell out of fashion in the twentieth century, with the last known deck published in 1948.

Value

Quite straightforwardly, the value of each card refers to what it is worth in any given game. The pip cards are fairly self-explanatory, as they each represent a number, while the court cards rely on the shared understanding of rank to convey their value. It is common knowledge, for example, that the King ranks higher than the Queen, who in turn ranks higher than a Jack. Although their value is technically one (or two in the German system), the Ace cards are generally held as the most valuable card in the deck.

"Mr. Blome hath got nothing but scandal and evil will by his bad accompts and great mistakes"

1 BLOME, Richard

[Heraldic playing cards].

Publication
[London, Richard Blome, c1675].

Description
52 engraved playing cards with text, versos blank.

Dimensions
92 by 63mm (3.5 by 2.5 inches).

References
Baynton-Williams pp.90-92; British Museum Schreiber English 52; Hargrave pp.173-174; van den Bergh pp.18-19; Yale 2240/ENG93.

The Maker

Richard Blome (1635-1705) was an English engraver, cartographer and publisher. He was born to bookseller Jacob Bloome and used this surname in certain registries; his work, however, was exclusively published under the name 'Blome'. During his career, he successfully published and sold a large number of maps, none of which were original. In fact, he was even accused of plagiarism, since he often failed to credit the original sources.

Despite being embroiled in several conflicts that led one critic to remark that "Mr. Blome hath got nothing but scandal and evil will by his bad accompts and great mistakes", Blome won the favour of Charles II. The newly-restored king granted the publisher a royal privilege and recommended his work to friends and officials alike.

In addition to his cartography, Blome also published written works on heraldry, and was among the first to fund his work by taking advance subscription and including the heraldic arms of his patrons in the final publications.

The Cards

The accession of Charles II to the English throne in 1660 ushered in the Restoration period, during which the ascetic and austere values of the Interregnum were replaced with a more liberal and indulgent culture. As a result, playing cards once again came into fashion. Blome's deck of cards, ornamented with heraldric crests and descriptions, is similar in style to a deck produced in France by the Marquis de Brianville in 1655.

On each card, the suit mark is shown in the upper right-hand corner with either a numeral or portrait to identify its value. Each card has an armorial crest in the upper left-hand corner, which is accompanied by French text explaining the heraldic devices and design. Among these are the crests of Charles II, the Marquess of Dorchester, Lord Berkeley and the Duke of Albemarle, to whom the game is dedicated. Along the lower edge of the Three of Hearts is printed:

"To whose patronage these Armorial Cards are humbly dedicated by his Grace most humble & obedient servant Ric: Blome".

This is likely the only complete deck in private ownership (van den Bergh).

VI

The Achievement of a viscount.

The R.t Hon.ble Thomas Needham L.d viscount Killmurrey of y.e Kingdome of Ireland beareth 2 Coates quaterley first pearle a bend engrailed saphir between 2 bucks heads cabosed diamond 2.dly pearle, on a cheife emerald a Taw between 2 mullets Topaz. above y.e same on a Crown & Helmet befitting his degree, a wreath of his Colours a phenix in her flames q.y. mantled Ruby, doubled Er. supported on y.e dexter side by a horse purple & on y.e sinister by a buck q.y. & for his motto in a scrole NVNC AVT NVNQUAM.

The saltier was made y.e hight of a man and was driven full of Pinns, and served to scale y.e walls of a City

(1) A. a saltier G. (2) B. a saltier quarterly quartered O. & A. (3) G. a saltier O. surmounted of a nother S. (4) p. pale A. & B. a saltier counter changed.

This ordinary as y.e rest is born engrailed, wavy or the like. & between, or charged w.th a charge as y.e ordinary.es are.

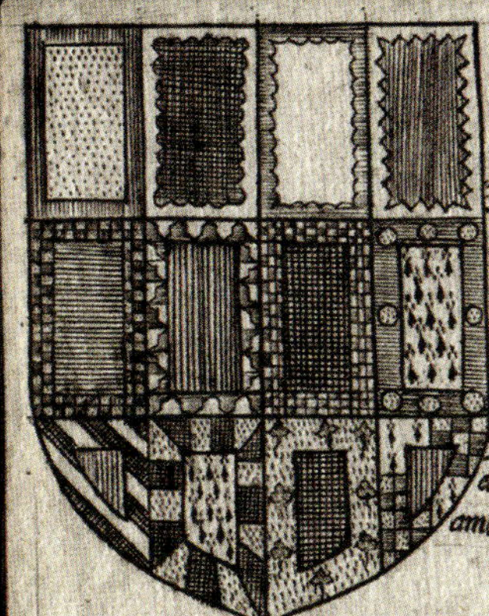

1

Bordurs were devised for y.e distinguishing of Coates armour of particular persons of one & y.e same family each from other amongst themselues.

(1) O. a bordure G. (2) S. a bordure engrailed A. (3) A. a bordure invected B. (4) G. a bordure indented A. (5) B. a bordure counter compone'd O. & G. (6) G. bordure vayre, (7) S. a bordure checky A. & B. (8) er: a bordure B. charged with 8 besants. (9) G. a bordure S. charged with 3 bendlets A. (10) Er: abordure Gobonated O. & S. (11) S. a bordure O. charged w.th verdoy of trefoiles slipped PP. (12) G. a bordure quarterly composed of purflew. Er. & countercompony O. & B.

Beasts, or fower footed Animalls

(1) G. a Elephant passant A. (2) er. a Bull passant G. (3) A. on a mount q.y. a stagg lodged G. (4) A. a stagg triping q.y. attired O. (5) vt. a stagg springing forwards O. (6) A. a Unicorn seiant S. armed O. (7) A. a Bear rampant S. musled O. (8) B. a wolfe saliant A. (9) vt. a grey hound currant A. collored O. (10) A. 3 conies S. (11) A. 3 catt a mountaines in pale passant S. (12) A. a cheveron B. between 3 squerills seiant G.

A luxury silk and brocade deck

2 [ANONYMOUS]

[Silk and brocade playing cards].

Publication
[?Germany, c1680].

Description
36 playing cards, coloured silk and brocade laid between paper, bound in calf book.

Dimensions
88 by 56mm (3.5 by 2.25 inches).

References
Hargrave p.108; van den Bergh pp.36-37.

The Maker
There is no information on the present deck of cards about its maker, but the nature of the materials used demonstrate that he or she must have been working for some extremely wealthy clients.

The Cards
The present cards are uniquely luxurious, each one being comprised of layers of coloured silk and brocade laid between two sheets of paper. The different layers of fabric give the images added depth, which reinforces the sense of meticulous craftsmanship.

The janiform eagle, which had been a symbol of the German emperors since the fifteenth century, points towards a German origin for these cards. Indeed, Hargrave records another deck of silk trappola cards from the seventeenth century which appear to have been made in Germany.

These handmade cards are apparently unique.

Mortier follows suit

3 MORTIER, Pieter

[Heraldic playing cards].

Publication
[Netherlands, Pieter Mortier, c1690].

Description
52 engraved playing cards with text, versos blank.

Dimensions
86 by 55mm (3.5 by 2.25 inches).

References
Hargrave pp.61-62, van den Bergh pp.46-47; for similar see Yale 2584/FRA284.

The Maker

Pieter Mortier (1661-1711) was an engraver from Leiden. In 1685, Pieter Mortier founded a map publishing group in Amsterdam, and in 1710 he produced a set of cartographic playing cards. The four suits of this deck each featured a different continent, with the individual cards displaying a map of various countries or regions. After travelling to Paris in the early 1680s, he was awarded the right to publish the maps of French cartographers in Amsterdam. On his death, Mortier's business was inherited by his sons and continued in partnership with another publisher until the 1780s, by which time the company had a monopoly over the production of cartographic playing cards.

The Cards

Possibly one of the most copied decks of playing cards is the heraldic deck made by Claude Oronce Fine de Brianville in 1655. After the original deck was published, many versions were produced across Europe, including the present deck by Pieter Mortier. Although de Brianville's original deck was issued with an explanatory manual, Mortier does not appear to have published such a document.

The cards bear the coats of arms of Europe's royal and aristocratic families, along with text that explains and describes them in French. The Prince of Spades, for example, shows the English Royal family represented by the Order of the Garter, one of the oldest orders of the knighthood in Europe. The order's motto of 'Honi soit qui mal y pense' ('Shame to those who think badly of it') is prominently displayed around the crest. The Papal coat of arms displayed on the King of Clubs is that of Pope Clemens IX, who held the office from 1667 until 1669. The value of each card is contained within a suit mark in the upper left corner.

P
Le Roy de La Grand Breta-gne
HONI SOIT QUI MALY PENSE
Escartelé au 1 et 4 contres cartelé, de France et d'Angleterre qui est de gueules a trois Leopards d'or l'vn sur l'autre. Au 2 d'or au Lyon de gueules en fermé dans vn trescheur de mesme qui est d'Escosse. Au 4 d'Irlande. qui est de gueules a la harpe d'or.
L'Ordre de la Iartiere autour de l'Escu.

R
LE PAPE
Porte Escartelé d'Or et d'Azur a quatre Lozanges de l'vn en l'autre.
l'Escu tymbré de la Thiare et orné des deux Clefs du St. Siege.

P
Castille et Leon
Escartelé au 1 et 4e de gueules au Chasteau d'or qui est de Castille. au 2 et 3 d'argent au Lyon de pourpre qui est de Leon. armé lampassé d'or. La croix d'Alcantara. et les entraues de Calatraua.

R
MONTIOYE S.T DENY
Le Roy de France
Porte deux Escus ioints et accolez le 1er d'azur a trois fleurdelys d'or. deux en chef et vne en pointe qui est de France. Le 2. de gueules aux chaines d'or posées en croix. en sautoir et en double orle qui est de Nauarre.

...masked players, harlequins and lecherous old men...

4 SH

[Commedia dell' Arte].

Publication
[?Netherlands, c1690].

Description
51 engraved playing cards, without the Three of Clubs.

Dimensions
86 by 56mm (3.5 by 2.25 inches).

References
Van den Bergh pp.30-31.

The Maker

The lower right-hand corner of the Queen of Spades shows the monogram 'SH'. Apart from this, there is nothing to identify the maker of this deck.

The Cards

Commedia dell'Arte was a theatrical movement that originated in Italy during the sixteenth century and soon became popular across the continent. Its farcical plotlines revolved around a cast of stock characters, and it was one of the earliest forms of theatre that permitted women to perform on stage in public. The widespread success of Commedia dell'Arte is evidenced by the present deck of playing cards, which depicts the artists, musicians and characters associated with the genre, including masked players, harlequins and lecherous old men.

Van den Bergh has suggested that the Kings and Queens found in the deck may have been intended as personifications of the four continents. As typical of such allegorical representations, they are shown wearing exotic dress and surrounded by distinctive animals. In this case, however, it is difficult to distinguish whether such designs are supposed to evoke the idea of the continents, or the characters from Commedia dell'Arte.

The value of each card is contained within the suit mark, although an error appears on the Ten of Hearts, where the 1 and the 0 have been switched.

This is likely the only deck in private ownership (van den Bergh).

The four seasons personified

5 **GOLE, Jacob**

[Bi-lingual educational playing cards].

Publication
[Netherlands, Jacob Gole, c1700].

Description
52 engraved playing cards with fine original hand-colour.

Dimensions
75 by 47mm (3 by 1.75 inches).

References
British Museum Schreiber Dutch 15; van den Bergh pp.38-43.

The Maker
The imprint of Jacob Gole is shown on both the Ace of Hearts and the Ace of Spades. Jacob Gole (1660-1737), son of the esteemed French cabinet-maker Pierre Gole, was a Dutch draftsman, engraver and publisher who was best-known for his portraits. Over the course of his career, he engraved and printed portraits of highly influential figures, including Pope Innocent XI, Louis XIV and Rembrandt.

The Cards
Each card in the present deck shows a highly detailed depiction of a different figure, the majority of them labelled in both French and Dutch. The Aces are allegorical personficiations of the four seasons, and the King and Queen cards show monarchs from each of the four continents, while the Jacks are figures from the Commedia dell'Arte. The pip cards represent a variety of different categories:

10 – the continents
9 – the elements
8 – parts of the day
7 – the senses
6 – the arts
5 – the sciences
4, 3, 2 – the months

L'Europe
Reine
Une Reine
d'Afrique
Reine.
Une Reine de L'Asie
Roy
Koning
Le Roy d'Albion
en Amerique
La Musique.
Reine
Une Reine de
L'Amerique

The game theory of warfare

6 MORTIER, Pieter

Jeu de la Guerre.

Publication
[Netherlands, Pieter Mortier, c1700].

Description
52 engraved playing cards with text, versos plain, housed within printed paper box with engraved battle scene above publisher's name and place to side.

Dimensions
85 by 56mm (3.25 by 2.25 inches).

References
Hargrave 62-68; Yale 778/HOLsheet264; van den Bergh pp.44-45.

The Maker
For a decription of Pieter Mortier, please see item 3.

The Cards
The art of war and military strategies are explained in this educational deck of cards. Each card displays and describes a different aspect of warfare, with a highly detailed illustration on the upper half of the card, and French text on the lower half, in which financial, foreign and military laws are addressed. In the upper right-hand corner the cards are numbered from one to 52, and the value of the card is contained within the suit mark in the upper left-hand corner. The court cards are designated with "R[oi]" for the King cards, "D[ame]" for the Queen, "C[hevalier]" for the Knight and "P[rince]" for the Jack.

The designs for the Jeu de la Guerre were created by French draftsman Gilles de la Boissiere in the seventeenth century and engraved by Pierre le Pautre. Both the illustrations and the text on Boissiere's original cards are identical to those found in the present deck, with the exception that the present cards have been re-ordered with the numbers changed. Both Pieter Mortier and another Dutch publisher, Peter Schenck, published their own editions of the Jeu de la Guerre around 1700.

CHAMADE

EXERCICE,

L'Exercice est linstruction quon fait aux Soldats qui entrent dans le seruice pour les dresser au maniement des armes et leur apprendre tous les temps et toutes les mesures qui s'obseruent dans la discipline militaire. cette instruction se fait par un Sergent habile en presence des Officiers: tant pour imprimer plus de respect aux Soldats. que pour obliger le Sergent a se mieux acquitter de sa fonction.

FOURAGE.

Le Fourage est tout ce qui peut faire subsister un cheval comme la paille le foin l'auoine Fourage se dit encor de l'action des Caualiers qui vont faucher et enleuer la paille et les foins qui sont dans la Campagne: elle se fait quelquefois par toutte la caualerie; d'autrefois par une partie seulement. on fait touiours escorter les fourageurs par de l'Infanterie. pour les soutenir contre les efforts et les surprises de l'Ennemy.

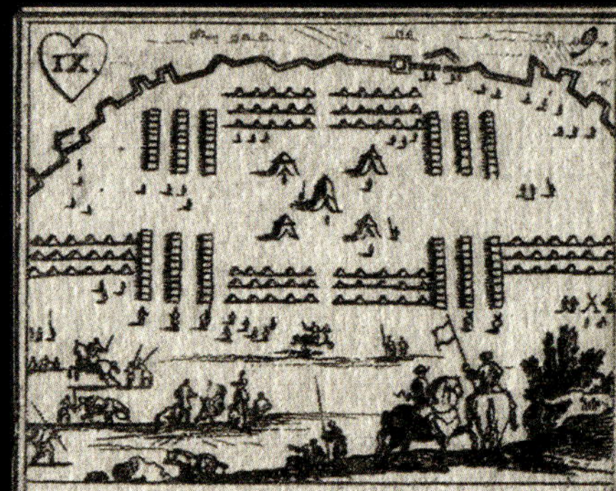

CAMPEMENT,

Le Campement est le choix que le General fait d'un lieu auantageux pour y disposer son armée et la mettre a couuert des insultes des Ennemys. ce lieu doit estre fortifie par des Lignes et par des Redoutes qu'on y construit de distance en distance. l'ordre qu'on garde dans le Campement. est que l'Infanterie couure la Caualerie; parce que les fantassins sont plus tost sous les armes si l'Ennemy est en presence. on loge le canon de son coste; si l'armée est en marche on le place a la teste du Camp

CONVOY,

Le Convoy, est un secours de munitions de guerre et de bouche quon jette dans un Camp ou dans une place, et que lon conduit sous une bonne escorte d'Infanterie et de Caualerie pour empescher l'Ennemy de l'enleuer. Quelquefois on conduit le Convoy sur une riuiere dans des bateaux quon apelle Pontons.

ASSAULT

Assault, est une Attaque violente pour emporter de vive force une Place, ou quelque poste considerable

BATTERIE.

Batterie, est le lieu ou lon place le Canon pour le faire tirer: Batterie se prend aussi pour le canon mesme qui est en batterie. On se sert de batteries pour demonter le canon des assiegés dans l'attaque d'une place, pour appuyer les pionniers et pour ruiner les murailles et les autres pieces de deffence. On en fait de simples, de hautes et d'enterrées selon que les occasions le demandent.

CONSEIL DE GUERRE,

Conseil de Guerre, est une assemblée qui se tient dans la tente du General. On y appelle les principaux officiers de l'armée et l'Ingenieur en chef, pour donner leur avis sur ce qui est proposé par le General. Il est alors de la prudence du General sur tout dans les affaires d'importance de faire signer a chacun son avis.

VICTOIRE,

Victoire, est l'auantage qu'on remporte sur l'ennemy dans une battille; la victoire est entiere lorsqu'on demeure Maitre du champ de battaille, qu'on oblige l'ennemy d'abandonner son artillerie et son bagage, et qu'on l'empesche de tenir la campagne le reste de l'année.

JUSTICE MILITAIRE,

Iustice militaire est la punition qu'on fait des Soldats coupables, de desertion ou de quelqre autre faute contre le devoir de la discipline. un des Prevosts de l'armée est chargé de les interroger, d'instruire leur procés, de le raporter dans le conseil de guerre de dresser la Sentence et de la faire executer. Toutte la procedure se termine en tres peu de temps et l'executeur pour l'ordinaire est quelque voleur au quel on aura fait grace.

CONTRIBUTIONS,

Contributions, sont des Taxes que payent les places et le pays de la frontiere pour se rachepter du pillage et des insultes de l'ennemy. Elles se payent en argent, en bled, ou en d'autre denrées equiualentes dans un temps limité moyenant des ostages, qu'on donne pour assurer le payement.

BOMBARDEMENT

Bombarder, c'est battre une ville ou une place auec des bombes, la bombe est une grosse boule de fer creuse; qu'on remplit de feux d'artifice et de cloux: elle a deux anses a costé du trou ou tient la fusée qui y doit mettre le feu, et est placée sur un mortier monté de son affust.

SIEGE

Siege, ce sont les trauaux et les attaques qu'une armée campée deuant une place fait pour la prendre. On comence le Siege par des lignes de circonuallation, qui sont des fossés creusés du costé de la campagne auec des redoutes de distance en distance pour asseurer les quartiers et empescher le secours: ensuitte on trauaille aux lignes de contreuallation du costé de la place pour arrester les sorties de la Garnison.

A fortifying game

7 SCHENCK, Pieter

Festung Baues Spiel.

Publication
[Netherlands, Pieter Schenck, c1700].

Description
52 engraved playing cards with text, printed in sepia, versos blank, housed within orange paper slipcase, decorated in blind.

Dimensions
80 by 52mm (3.25 by 2 inches).

References
Van Den Bergh p.51; Yale 779/HOLsheet265.

The Maker
Pieter Schenck (1660-1711) was a German engraver and cartographer who worked in Amsterdam and Leipzig. Schenck became best-known for his maps, after acquiring the plates of Johannes Janssonius, but he also published a number of other prints. Among these were two decks of playing cards. Schenk had three sons who all followed in his footsteps to become engravers, with two of them continuing his business after his death.

The Cards
In 1700, Schenck published a deck of cards entitled 'Das Festung Baues Spiel' ('The fortress building game'). Each card shows an illustration of a different European fortress, accompanied with an explanation of its construction. The images had originally been designed by Gilles de la Bossière and published in Paris in 1668. Schenck copied these cards, replacing the French text with his own native German. The suit and value of the cards are shown in miniature in the upper right corner, and each one is numbered from one to 52. As a result, they form a fully functioning deck of playing cards, as well as an informative and educational tool.

ARCENAL
47

ZUG-BRUCKE
48

MUNSTER PLATZ
38

STREB MAUR
32

5

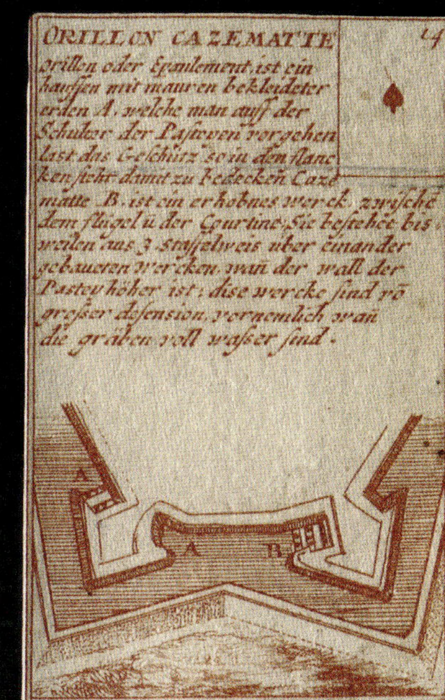
ORILLON CAZEMATTE

Amsterdam street characters: Castanago, Kats de preeker, Ootmarser, and Non datur vacuum

8 [GOLE, Jacob] [attributed to]

[Amsterdam street character playing cards].

Publication
[Netherlands, Jacob Gole, c1710].

Description
52 engraved playing cards with fine original hand-colour.

Dimensions
55 by 32mm (2.25 by 1.25 inches).

References
Van den Bergh pp.32-35; for similar see British Museum Schreiber Dutch 16; Yale 1034/HOL33 and 1035/HOL34.

The Maker

For a description of Jacob Gole, please see item 5.

In 1690 and 1700, Gole also published two decks of playing cards that are almost identical to the present example. The Jack of Spades in both these decks is imprinted with the words "J. Gole exc. cum Priviegio Ordin. Hollan. et West Frisiæ", which does not appear on any of the present cards, making it unclear whether they were made by Gole or in imitation of him.

The Cards

The pip cards in the present deck display a combination of characters from the Commedia dell'Arte, such as the Harlequin, and familiar figures from the streets of Amsterdam, such as a police officer. The court cards show full-length depictions of the kings and queens of Spain, France, England, the Holy Roman Emperor, and his consort in elaborate dress. Each card shows the name of the character depicted, making it easy to identify them.

Clubs:
Ace – Koele Jabob
King – La Roy d'Espagne
Queen – La Reine d'Espagne
Jack – Le Fasicieux Crispin
10 – Girige Geraard
9 – Castanago
8 – Kats de preeker
7 – Ootmarser
6 – Non datur vacuum
5 – Uylenspiegel
4 – Jantje wat droomje
3 – Koddige snaphaan
2 – Arlekyn

Servitori.
2 I.
Weesperstudent.
2 II.
Kodige Joris.
3 III
Aardige Piet.
4 IIII
Jantje Roen.
5 V.
Sokeratus.
6 VI.
Scheyt Fontansjes.
7 VII.
Lubert Lubertse.
8 VIII
Chapin.
9 IX.
Oro pro Vobis.
10 X.
Jan Girar.
La Reine d'Angleter
Le Roy d'Angleter

Diamonds:
Ace – Brille koop volk
King – La Roy de France
Queen – La Reine de France
Jack – Mesetin le Drole
10 – Wie wilder wie selder
9 – Dat gaat na Rome
8 – Camper Markure
7 – Lello
6 - Leert wel broeder
5 – Scharmoesje
4 – Hans Beuling
3 – Hans Pos Pas
2 – Sa kivala

Hearts:
Ace – Seryitori
King – Le Roy d'Angleter
Queen – La Reine d'Angleter
Jack – Jan Girar
10 – Oro pro Vobis
9 – Chapin
8 – Lubert Lubertse
7 – Scheyt Fontansjes
6 – Sokeratus
5 – Jantje Roen
4 – Aardige Piet
3 – Kodige Joris
2 – Weesper student

Spades:
Ace – Captain of the gang
King – Le Empereur des Romai
Queen -L'Imperatrice
Jack – Le Pai ïsant Hollandais
10 – Diogenes
9 – Esopus
8 – Mesetin
7 – Kiekeboe
6 – Sta vast den bruy
5 – Zoo zoo
4 – Politionelle
3 – Dat gelt jou
2 – Crispyn Medezyn

Koele Jacob.
Arlekyn.
Koddige Snaphaan.
Jantje wat droomje.
Uylenspiegel.
Non datur Vacuum.
Ootmarser.
Kats de preeker.
Castanggo.
Girige Geraard.
Le Faticieux Crispin.
La Reine d'Espagne
Le Roy d'Espagne

An Ovidian deck

9 MORTIER, Pieter

Jeu des Metamorphoses d'Ovide.

Publication
[Netherlands, Pieter Mortier, c1710].

Description
52 engraved playing cards with text, versos blank.

Dimensions
85 by 55mm (3.25 by 2.25 inches).

References
British Museum Schreiber Dutch 5; van den Bergh pp.48-49; for similar see Yale 695/ FRAsheet182.

The Maker
For a description of Pieter Mortier, please see item 3.

The Cards
In the first century AD, the Roman poet Publius Ovidius Naso (better known as Ovid) composed fifteen books of verse entitled 'The Metamorphoses'. The poem describes the creation and history of the world according to Greek and Roman mythology, with all of the stories concluding in a physical transformation. The hunter Actaeon, for instance, transforms into a deer and the nymph Daphne changes into a laurel tree, as famously captured in a sculpture by Bernini. 'The Metamorphoses' would go on to become one of antiquity's most influential pieces of literature, inspiring Shakespeare in particular.

In 1705, Nicolas de Fer, a maker of playing cards based in Paris, published a deck on the theme of the poem. On each card is a detailed illustration of one of the stories, accompanied by a short description of the scene in French. The upper centre of the card bears the suit mark, which contains within it the value. The court cards are designated with "R[oi]" for the King cards, "D[ame]" for the Queen, "C[hevalier]" for the Knight, and "P[rince]" for the Jack.

The present deck by Pieter Mortier was published five years later, and seems to be an exact copy of de Fer's. An example in the Printroom of the British Museum in London still has the original wrapper, which shows an image of the most important gods on top of a cloud.

IUPITER.

Fut Roy des Dieux, et des hommes, fils de Saturne et de Rhea et frere de Neptune et de Pluton. Il chassa Saturne son pere qui l'auoit voulu deuorer: il tira au sort auec ses freres, le Ciel lui echut l'Empire des Mers à Neptune et celui des Enfers à Pluton.

VULCAIN.

Fils de Iupiter et de Iunon, fut Dieu du feu et des forges. Les Poëtes ont feint que sa Boutique étoit sous le Mont Ætna en Sicile, où il trauailloit auec les Cyclopes. Il á fait des armes pour Mars et pour quelques grands Capitaines.

BACCHUS.

Fils de Iupiter et de Semelé fut Dieu du Vin il étoit ordinairement dans vn char trainé par des Tygres Suiuis des Baccantes, des Satyres, des Faunes et du bon Vieillard Silene qui l'auoit instruit à bien boire.

IUNON.

Fille de Saturne et de Rhea fut soeur et femme de Iupiter, dont elle eut plusieurs enfans Iamais Deesse ne fut plus Ialouse qu'elle, et elle a persecuté impitoyablement, non seulement, toutes les Maitresses de Iupiter, mais aussi tous les enfans qui en sont Venus.

A trick for winning the lottery

10 [ANONYMOUS], after Lautje van Schotten

[1720s Bubble playing cards].

Publication
[Netherlands, c1720].

Description
60 engraved playing cards, versos blank.

Dimensions
65 by 52mm (2.5 by 2 inches).

References
Van den Bergh p.26; for similar see Yale 1027/HOL26.

The Maker
The present deck of cards does not give the name of its maker, and nor are there any references to him or her in the literature. The deck, however, is stylistically very similar to cards produced by Lautje van Schotten in Amsterdam in 1720.

The Cards
The financial failures and bad investments of many in the early sixteenth century are ridiculed in this satirical deck of cards. The Ace of Spades, for instance, presents a woman holding up an advertisement for lottery tickets priced at 100,000 guilders. At roughly the same time, a successful book was published under the title 'The Big Scene of Foolishness regarding the rise, the progress and the demise of action, bubble and wind trade, in France, England, and the Netherlands, committed in the years of MDCCXX'. This book ridiculed the dubious financial practices that had occurred throughout Europe in the recent years, disasters which had also been portrayed on playing cards in England and France (see item 11).

The cards in this deck are numbered from one to 60. The first 52 cards form a standard deck of playing cards, and with the additional eight cards, they make up the lottery deck. Often lottery decks included text-cards, but it is not clear whether these were ever included in the present deck.

1
4

10
29

8
37

Vrouw
52

Knegt
3

58

"Come all ye gen'rous husbands with your wives, Insure round sums on your precarious lives, That to your comfort, when you're dead and rotten, Your widows may be rich when you're forgotten"

11 BOWLES, Thomas

[South Sea Bubble playing cards].

Publication
[London, Thomas Bowles, 1720].

Description
52 engraved playing cards with text, suits coloured by hand, stamp to one, versos blank.

Dimensions
95 by 63mm (3.75 by 2.5 inches).

References
Baynton-Williams pp.103-104; Hargrave pp.197-199; van den Bergh pp.20-21.

The Maker

Thomas Bowles (II) (1688-1767), followed his father into business in 1714. He went on to become a leading, and highly successful, London print seller and publisher. As a retailer, he also catered to map buyers; he published what might be termed "good shop stock": separately published plans of London and environs, including an early pocket plan of the city, maps of England and Wales, Scotland, the British Isles, the world and so on. He was also a partner in a number of atlas projects, notably Owen and Bowen's road-book, the 'Britannia Depicta' (1720), Moll's 'New Description of England and Wales' (1724), 'The World Described' (1726 onward) and the 'Large English Atlas' in the 1750s.

Then, often working in conjunction with his brother John, he published numbers of interesting broadsheet maps depicting important events of the period, such as theatre of war maps, siege-plans and battle-plans that would interest and inform his customers, in order to supplement the brief accounts in the news-sheets of the day, which were mostly unillustrated.

A newspaper advertisement from 12 March 1720 states that the Bowles firm was shortly to publish a deck of playing cards, depicting the effects of the 'South Sea Bubble'.

The Cards

The South Sea Bubble is the most notorious episode in the history of eighteenth-century financial speculation. It was a fevered attack of mass madness, which affected all levels of society, as a significant proportion of the British population became convinced that their fortunes would be transformed by investing in the South Sea Company. The Company was formed as early as 1711, and was promised a monopoly on all trade to the Spanish colonies in South America, in return for taking on and consolidating the national debt. Unfortunately, the Treaty of Utrecht, which ended the War of Spanish Succession, severely restricted the trading rights of the Company, since it confirmed Spain's sovereignty of its colonies in the New World. However, that did not stop the Company from attempting to convert their 'assets' (i.e. the National Debt) into shares, which they mis-sold on the basis of wildly exaggerated profits from their South Sea trading. Between January and May of 1720, shares in the South Sea Company soared from £128 to £550 each.

Encouraged by this apparent success, hundreds of smaller "Bubbles", or joint-stock ventures, were created, and gained similar momentum. In an attempt to ward off competition, the South Sea Company put its weight behind The Bubble Act, passed in June of 1720, which required all joint-stock companies to have a Royal charter. Once the Company had received its own Royal seal of approval this way, its shares almost doubled in price to an astronomical and unsustainable £1050. Consumer confidence waned,

BUBBLES.
River Douglas

then collapsed, and by September the share price had returned to £175, and the bubble was well and truly burst. Fortunes won were now largely lost. By 1721, investigations revealed a tangled web of corruption and fraud, involving company and government officials.

In this complete, and very rare as such, pack, each playing card is assiduously dedicated to satirizing actual companies, individual "Bubbles" associated with the larger fraud, and ridiculing those foolish enough to invest in them. Many famous, and some not so, seemingly madcap schemes are cruelly illustrated and then renamed in rhyme: beginning with the Ace of Spades, and the 'River Douglas', a canal scheme in Lancashire that foundered; and including the failed York Buildings insurance scheme, 'Puckle's Machine' gun, 'Raddish Oil', Holy Island Salt,… Some schemes attempted to sanitize the mean streets of Britain, by employing the poor, looking after orphans, and clearing out brothels, and no opportunity to be bawdy has been missed. At an early date the most offensive rhymes have been expurgated, affecting the Queen of Spades 'Bastard Children', Six of hearts 'Errecting Houses of Office in N. Britain for Strangers & Travellors' [ie toilets], Three of Diamonds, 'Office for cureing the Grand Pox or Clap', and the Ten of Clubs which is about 'Bleeching of Hair'.

As expected, many of the cards depict Bubbles associated with America: the 'Pensilvania Company' (with contemporary corrective paste-over), the Bahama Islands, and 'Settling Collonies in Accadia North America' (complete with cannibalism); numerous Fisheries: 'Royal', 'Grand', and 'Whale'; and 'Cureing Tobacco for Snuff'.

Scotland, having just about weathered the collapse of the Darien Scheme, and John Law's Mississippi venture, was also greatly affected by the South Sea Bubble. Scottish money flooded into London, investing heavily in three of the companies depicted in Bowles' cards: the York Buildings insurance scheme, and the Grand Fishery of Great Britain, as well as house fire insurance companies, like the 'Rose Insurance from Fire' company, on the 7 of clubs. Other Scottish industries that come under fire include: 'Correcting Houses [ie outdoor loos] of Office in N. Britain for Strangers & Travellors'; 'Hemp & Flax'; 'Drying Malt by the Air'; and 'Stockings' manufactory.

St. Jn L———ts Improvement of Land
An Act against Bubbles
The Famous Knight that is the Sole Projector
Of this New Bubble, is a South Director,
But twould be better taken at his Hands,
To raise Poor South Sea than Improve Poor Land

Insurance on Horses
You that keep Horses to preserve your Ease,
And Pads to please your Wives, and Mistresses;
Insure their Lives, and if they Die we'll make
Full Satisfaction, or be bound to Break.

River Douglas
Since Bubbles came in vogue, new Arts are found,
To cut thro' Rocks, and level rising Ground,
That murm'ring Waters, may be made more Deep,
To drown the Knaves, and lul the Fools asleep.

Insurance on Lives
Come all ye Gen'rous Husbands, with your Wives.
Insure round Sums, on your precarious Lives;
That to your comfort, when you're Dead & Rotten
Your Widows may be Rich when you're forgotten

The Ace of Spades, which shows the industry expanding around the River Douglas, bears the lines:

"Since bubbles came in vogue, new arts are found
To cut thro' rocks, and level rising ground;
That murmuring waters may be made more deep,
To drown the knaves and lull the fools asleep".

The Six of Spades, which shows the newly established life insurance companies, reads:

"Come all ye gen'rous husbands with your wives
Insure round sums on your precarious lives,
That to your comfort, when you're dead and rotten,
Your widows may be rich when you're forgotten".
The Five of Clubs, entitled 'Sugar', is accompanied by the rhyme:
"Fair tattling gossips, you that love to see
Fine sugar blended with expensive tea,
Since you delight in things both dear and sweet,
Buy sugar shares, and you'll be sweetly bit."

As is usual for the date, the Ace of Spades bears the red ink Tax Stamp, which was obligatory on packs of cards from 1711, and is why the Ace of Spades is traditionally the leading card in any pack. It is known that Bowles created two sets of playing cards to commemorate the South Sea Bubble disaster, and both are very rare, especially when complete. The companion set depicts domestic scenes of despair, and is more common. As well as providing a scathing social commentary, these cards form fully functioning decks, with the suit mark and value of each card shown in miniature in the upper left corner.

This rare and entertaining deck of cards offers valuable contemporary insight into the feverish atmosphere, trades and fashions of the day.

Hemp & Flax
Here Hemp is Sow'd, for Stuborn Rogues to Die in,
And Softer Flax, for tender Skins to Lye in;
But Should the usefull Project be defeated;
The Knaves may prosper but the Fools are cheated.

Coal Trade from Newcastle
Some deal in Water, Some in Wind like Fools,
Others in Wood, but we alone in Coals;
From Such like Projects, the declining Nation,
May justly fear a fatal inflamation.

Buying Seamen's Tickets
As the Case Stands the Wapping Ale Wives buy,
The Seamen's-Tickets for a small Supply;
But t'is no matter whether Spendthrift Slaves,
Are Chous'd by Wapping Whores or Bubbling Knaves

Sugar
Fair Tattling Gossips, you that Love to See,
Fine Sugar blended, with Expensive Tea,
Since you Delight in things, both Dear & Sweet,
Buy Sugar Shares, and you'll be Sweetly Bit.

“Unprecedented and incredible” (Pope)

12 **BOWLES, John**

[The Beggar’s Opera playing cards].

Publication
[London, Carington Bowles, c1730].

Description
52 engraved playing cards with text, suits coloured by hand, versos blank.

Dimensions
95 by 64mm (3.75 by 2.5 inches).

References
Columbia University Library GB0121; Hargrave pp.197-201; van den Bergh pp.24-25.

The Maker
John Bowles (1701-1779) was the son of Thomas Bowles, who founded a publishing house in the early eighteenth century, which flourished under the leadership of his brother, also named Thomas Bowles. Since his older brother had inherited their father’s stock, John was forced to produce his own maps and prints, which he continually updated with the latest developments. In 1753, he was joined in partnership with his son Carington, and they worked together for about ten years as John Bowles & Son.

The Cards
John Gay premiered his first full-length opera in London on January 29, 1728. ‘Beggar’s Opera’ was so well-received that Alexander Pope, who had been in attendance, later wrote that “the vast success of it was unprecedented and incredible”. The prima donna, Lavinia Fenton, made such an impression on the 3rd Duke of Bolton that he immediately fell in love and began an affair with her. Gay’s opera, a satire of Italian opera, became the second longest running production in theatre history to date, and was even performed in America.

Later that year, perhaps while the performances were still running, John Bowles produced a deck of playing cards carrying the lyrics and musical scores of some of the opera’s most popular songs. For instance, one card entitled ‘Tune of Cold and Raw’ bears the lyrics:

> “If any wench Venus’ girdle wear,
> Though she be never so ugly;
> Lillys and roses will quickly appear,
> And her face look wondrous smugly.
> Beneath ye left ear so fitt but a cord,
> (A rope so charming a zone is!)
> The youth in his cart has ye air of a lord
> And we cry there dies an Adonis”.

The suit mark and value of each card is shown in miniature in the upper left corner, with the court cards showing the standard full-length figures used on playing cards at the time. The imprint is found on three of the cards: the King of Clubs, Ten of Spades and Ace of Hearts.

There appear to be only two complete examples of this deck in private ownership (van den Bergh).

Tune of Cold and Raw.
Sung by Mrs. Peachum
If any Wench Venus's Girdle wear,
Though she be never so ugly;
Lillys and Roses will quickly appear,
And her Face look wondrous Smugly.
Beneath ye left Ear so fitt but a Cord,
(A Rope so charming a Zone is!)
The Youth in his Cart hath ye Air of a Lord,
And we cry, There dies an Adonis.
Flute.

Tune of If Love's a sweet Passion &c. – Sung by
Lucy Lockit.
Flute.
When young at ye Bar you first taught me
And bid me be free of my Lips, & no more;
I was kiss'd by ye Parson, ye Squire & ye Sot.
When ye Guest was departed ye Kiss was forgot
But his Kiss was so sweet & so closely he prest,
That I languish'd & pin'd till I granted ye rest.

Tune of Bony dun Dee
Sung by –
Mackheath.
Flute.
The Charge is prepar'd ye Lawyers are met
The Judges all rang'd (a terrible Show!)
I go, undismay'd. —— For Death is a Debt,
A Debt on demand. —— So, take what I owe,
Then farewell, my Love – Dear Charmers, adieu
Contented I die —— 'Tis ye better for you.
Here ends all Dispute the rest of our Lives,
For this way at once I please all my Wives.
Printed for Carington Bowles, No. 69 in
St. Pauls Church Yard, London.

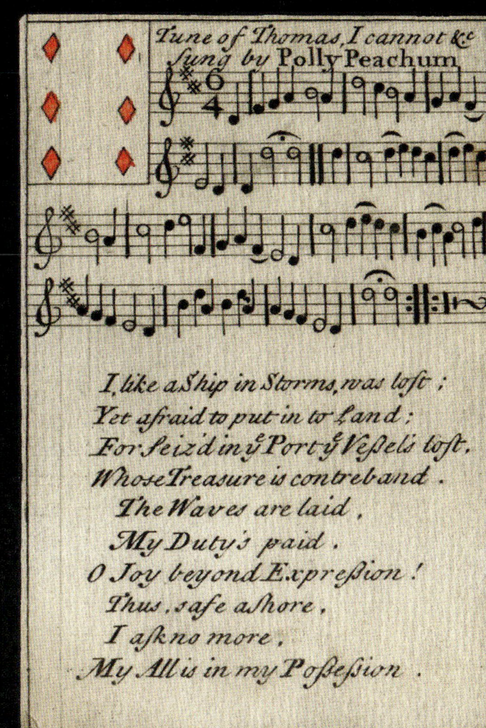

Tune of Thomas, I cannot &c.
Sung by Polly Peachum
I, like a Ship in Storms, was lost;
Yet afraid to put in to Land;
For seiz'd in ye Port ye Vessel's lost,
Whose Treasure is contreband.
The Waves are laid,
My Duty's paid.
O Joy beyond Expression!
Thus, safe ashore,
I ask no more,
My All is in my Possession.

“A la Licome couronnée”

13 MONS, Pierre

[Collection of Court Cards from the standard Paris pattern].

Publication
[France, Pierre Mons, c1730].

Description
Five playing cards only.

Dimensions
87 by 57mm (3.5 by 2.25 inches).

The Maker
The Jack of Clubs bears the name “Pierre Mons”, along with the letter “M” on the figure’s battle-axe. We have been unable to find any evidence of a card-maker working under this name, but the inscriptions on the cards indicate that he was active in France around 1730.

The Cards
Historically, cards have not only been used to play games, but also to serve numerous other purposes, such as sending messages, acknowledging contracts and performing magic tricks. The present group of cards represents one such alternative use, being part of the archive of a French military school. Manuscript notes on the back of each card appear to record some of the school’s domestic arrangements from the year 1735. Each one has a small hole in the centre so that they could be collectively piled up on a paper spike.

The present examples are exclusively court cards; it is not known whether pip cards were also used in the archive. They show the Paris pattern that emerged in the early eighteenth century and swiftly became the dominant design. A distinguishing feature of French playing cards is that the court cards are often associated with specific historic or mythical figures. The present cards show the personages found in the Paris pattern, namely:

King of Diamonds – Caesar
King of Clubs – David
King of Hearts – Charlemagne
Prince of Clubs – Lancelot
Prince of Spades – Hogier

The suit mark appears in an upper corner, and the Kings and Jacks are depicted as the traditional full-length figures ubiquitous at this time. The letters “A” and “LC” appear on the shield of the Jack of Clubs, and may stand for ‘A la Licorne couronnée’ (‘To the crowned unicorn’), a reference to the displayed unicorn.

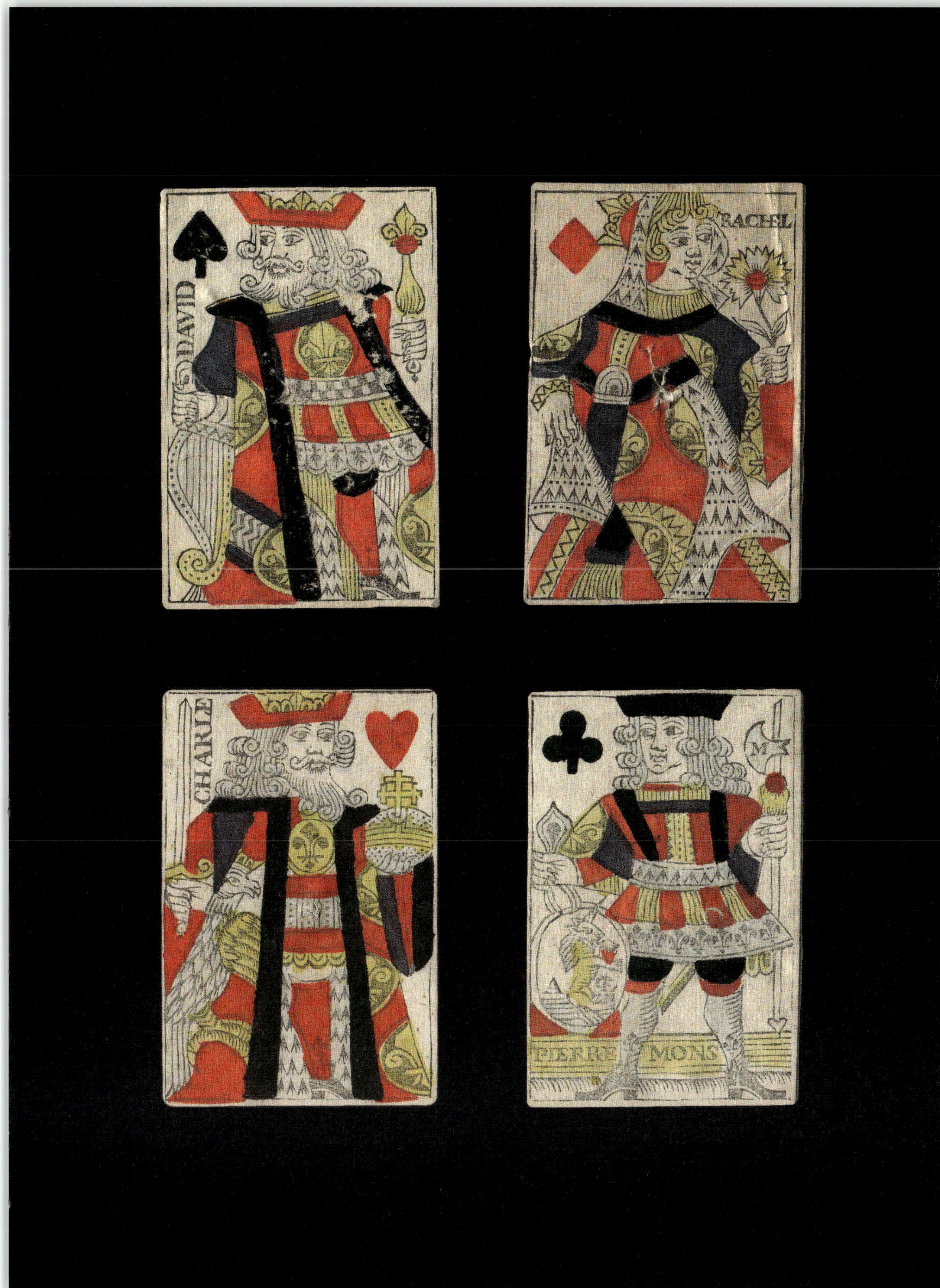
DAVID
RACHEL
CHARLE
PIERRE
MONS

Standard-pattern Lyon with the original wrapper

14 [DESVIGNES, Pierre] [attributed to]

Cartes fines de piquet à Lyon.

Publication
[?Lyon, ?Pierre Desvignes, c1765].

Publication
32 woodcut playing cards with fine original hand-colour, versos blank, original printed paper wrappers.

Dimensions
83 by 56mm (3.25 by 2.25 inches).

References
Hargrave pp.85-86; van den Bergh p.27; Yale 2381/FRA81.

The Maker
Hargrave suggests that the present deck is the work of Pierre Desvignes (1718-1782). Desvignes was active in Lyon from 1754 to 1782, where he made and sold playing cards in the Saint-Pierre parish. His wife was also from a family of Lyonnais card-makers, and both his daughters married card-makers too!

The Cards
In France there exist several regional patterns for playing cards, of which the patterns of Paris and Lyon are most well-known. The Lyon pattern is characterised by the Jack of Spades smoking his pipe, and the banner at the feet of the Jack of Clubs reading the city's name. The shield of the King of Diamonds bears the mark of the golden sun with the fleur de lys in the centre, both symbols of French national pride.

In contrast to these elaborate court cards, the 16 pip cards are fairly plain; their value is indicated by the number of suit marks, shown in their respective colours. The wrapper in which the deck was originally contained identifies the contents as 'Cartes fines de piquet a Lyon'.

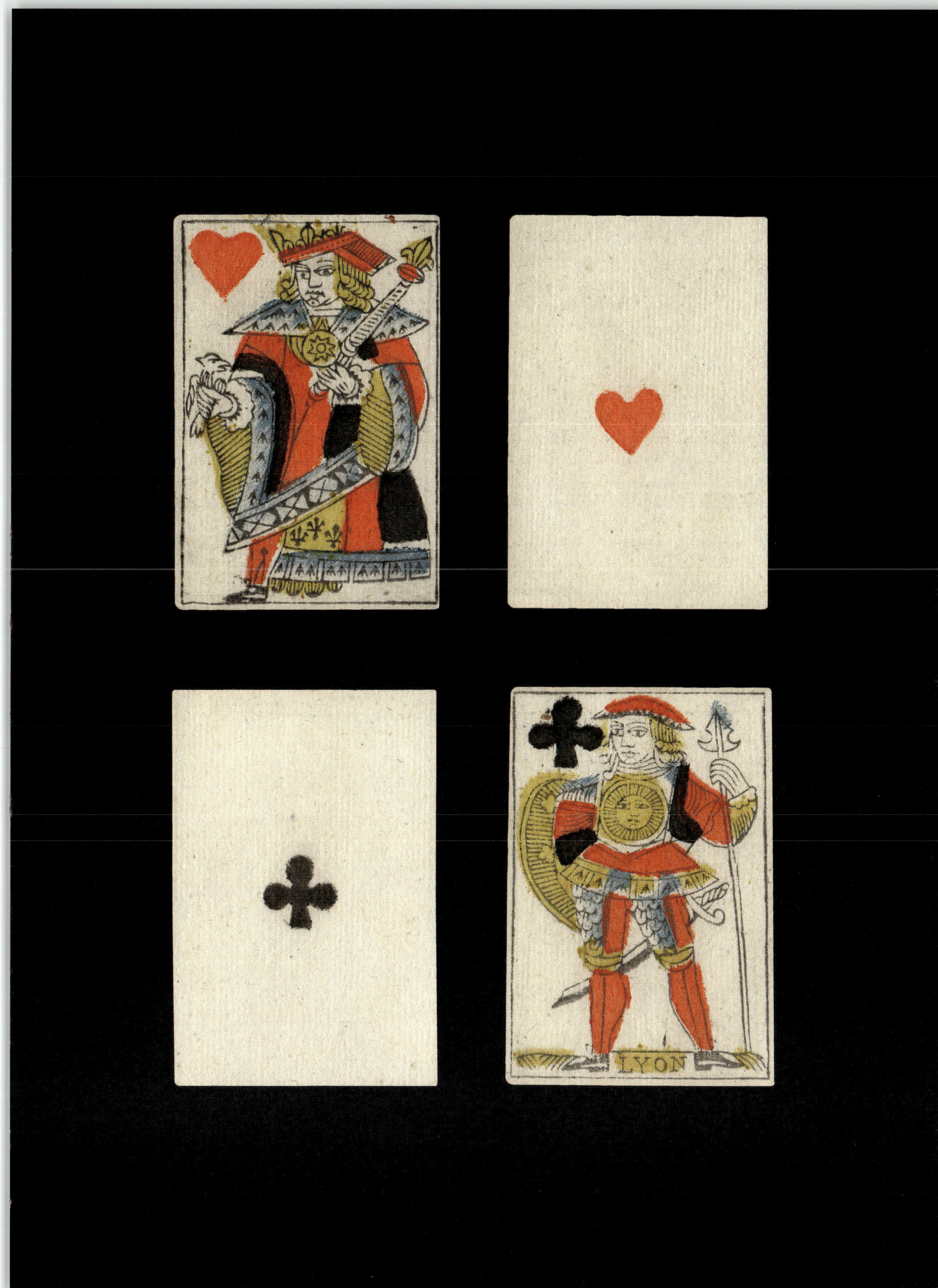
LYON

Unrecorded example of an early pioneer of the double-figured court card that has since become universal

15 GÖBL, Andreas Benedic

Bayerische Karten

Publication
[Munich], Andreas Benedic Göbl, [c1780].

Description
52 woodcut playing cards with fine original hand-colour, blue woodblock pattern to versos.

Dimensions
112 by 59mm (4.5 by 2.25 inches).

References
Hargrave pp.132-133; van den Bergh pp.22-23; for similar see Yale 1954/GER27 and British Museum Schreiber German 26, 77, 137-141, 186, 240-242, 275, 289 and 322.

The Maker

Andreas Benedic Göbl (fl. 1748-1786) was a publisher and printer who operated from Munich during the late eighteenth century. He is known to have produced sets of tarot cards decorated with a range of themes, from weddings to historical battles to animals. Towards the end of his career, Göbl became notable as an early pioneer of the double-figured court card that has since become commonplace.

The Cards

The present deck does not appear in the literature, although it shares numerous features with other cards published by Göbl. The Jack of Clubs, for instance, shows the maker's name, although here his surname is misspelled as "Gebl". His initials also appear on the Jack of Hearts, while text on the King of Hearts reads "Bayerische Karten: Fabric". The court cards in this deck display the double-figured design for which Göbl later became known, but unlike in other examples of his work, the figures are exclusively shown holding weapons.

Since there are no other recorded examples of this deck, van den Bergh has questioned whether it is, in fact, an incomplete deck of tarot cards. This idea is supported by Sylvia Mann 'Collecting Playing Cards', 1966, page 93.

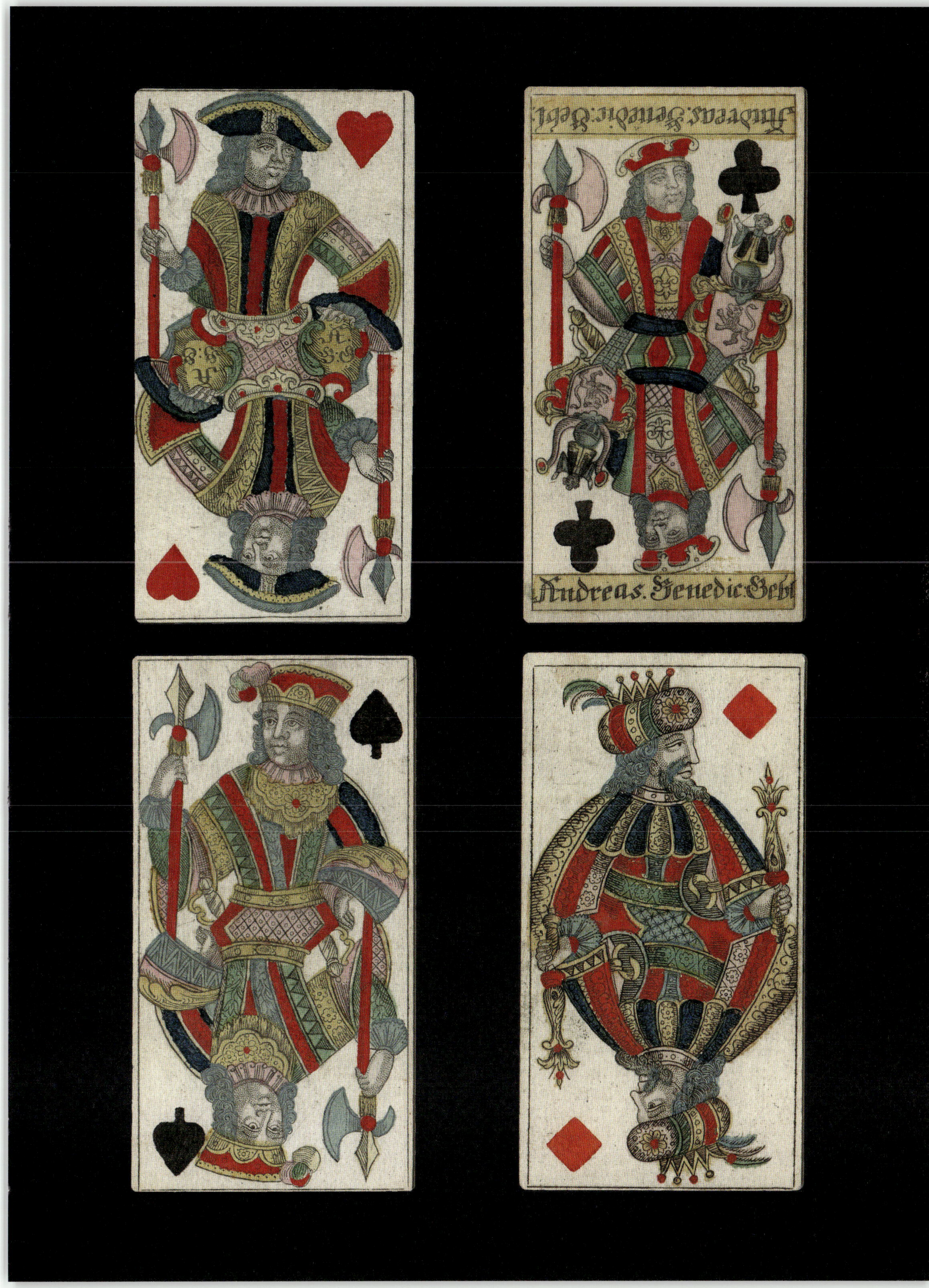
Andreas. Benedic: Gebt
Andreas. Benedic: Gebt

“My burden is heavy…”

16 [ANONYMOUS]

[The Foundling card].

Publication
[Netherlands, c1795].

Description
One woodcut playing card with original hand-colour, manuscript inscription to verso.

Dimensions
81 by 55mm (3.25 by 2.25 inches).

References
Van den Bergh p.50.

The Maker

The standard double-figure design on this card makes it difficult to distinguish the deck or maker, although it is clear that it was manufactured in the Netherlands prior to 1795.

The Card

The foundling card has a tragic background. A mother who was no longer able to care for her newborn child would lay the card to be found alongside her abandoned baby. On the back of a playing card she would write an assignment, a message, or simply the child’s name and its date of birth. Often these are imaginably heartbreaking messages.

The present example is carefully cut, suggesting that the mother was keeping the second part of the card with the intention of finding and reuniting with her child later in life. If a child was found with a complete card, it meant that the mother had renounced the child indefinitely. It may be significant that she chose the Jack of Hearts to leave with her baby, since it is the only card with filial connotations.

On the verso of the card her message reads:

“My burden is heavy, goodbye my dear Femke, Born 1st September 1795”.

It is noteworthy that “Femke” is both a Dutch girl’s name, and also an affectionate name for a girl (mijn femke = my little girl).

Manuscript Dutch street characters: Kees, Bloem/Snujif and Flip

17 [ANONYMOUS]

[Dutch street character playing cards].

Publication
[Netherlands, c1800].

Description
52 manuscript playing cards executed in ink with watercolour, star pattern printed in red to versos.

Dimensions
87 by 60mm (3.5 by 2.25 inches).

References
Van den Bergh pp.28-29.

The Maker
We have been unable to trace any information about the maker and origins of the present deck, although the style of the characters indicates that it was likely designed and produced in the Netherlands.

The Cards
A series of Dutch street characters, who were probably familiar figures to the contemporary audience, appear on the present cards. They range from women selling flowers to beggars at the roadside; similar types of characters appear on other Dutch prints from the same period. The King of each suit is represented by a standing man, the Queen by a woman, and the Jack by a seated man. Each of the court cards is labelled, although the significance of the names remains a mystery. They may perhaps refer to stock characters from Dutch popular culture:

Clubs – Kees, Bloem/Snuijf, Flip
Diamonds – August, Therees, Bestebeentje
Hearts – Fluijtje, Hob Za, Sijme
Spades – Arij, Lulla, Flaas

AUGUST
KEES
HOB, ZA
KLAAS

"I believe Bonaparte stands his chance"

18 [ANONYMOUS]

[Collection of original Transformation cards].

Publication
[England, c1804].

Description
17 manuscript playing cards with original hand-colour.

Dimensions
92 by 67mm (3.5 by 2.75 inches).

References
Van den Bergh pp.154-155.

The Maker
The artist behind the present cards is unknown, but he may have taken inspiration from the contemporary work of John Nixon, who was the first Briton to experiment with transformation cards.

The Cards
These hand-drawn cards represent a preliminary study for the production of a deck of transformation cards. These early sketches highlight the difficulties of convincingly incorporating suit marks into an image. It may be for this reason that a complete deck was never made from the present designs, as it is too difficult to quickly identify the value of each card.

Perhaps the most remarkable feature of these drawings, however, appears on the Five of Spades. The image shows a game of chess being played by the 'Chess Automaton'. This was a "machine" developed in the second half of the eighteenth century that seemed capable of playing the perfect game of chess, an apparent forerunner of artificial intelligence. The whole thing was a trick, however, as a highly skilled player would be stationed inside the machine, controlling its movements.

The device was first exhibited at Schönbrunn Palace in Vienna in 1770, where it was said to have challenged Napoleon to a game. Accordingly, the text on the Five of Spades reads:

"I believe Bonaparte stands his chance".

Hearts become cupids' wings, diamonds books, spades windowframes and clubs a beetle's carapace

19 [JENNISON-WALWORTH, Countess von] [attributed to]

[Cotta 1805].

Publication
Tübingen, J. G. Cotta, 1805.

Description
52 engraved playing cards with fine original hand-colour, here together with printed almanack.

Dimensions
97 by 68mm (3.75 by 2.75 inches).

References
Hargrave p.145; van den Bergh pp.132-135.

The Maker
On the ace of clubs the name of the maker appears: 'À Tubinge chez J.G. Cotta libraire'.

The Cotta family were famous German publishers, closely connected with the history of their country's literature. The firm was established by Johann Georg Cotta in the 1660s, before passing it on to his son, also named Johann George, in 1692. After him, it was taken over by his son, another Johann Georg, and upon his death, his eldest son, this time Christoph Friedrich, became the head of the publishing house.

Under Christoph Friedrich, the Cotta firm was moved to the court at Stuttgart, where the business slowly went into decline. It was eventually rescued by the efforts of his son, Johann Friedrich, and became the publisher for the likes of Goethe, Jean Paul and Hegel. The firm remained in the family until 1889.

The Cards
The Cotta publishing house made its first foray into the field of playing cards with the present deck. They use the standard French system, and are centred around the theme of French history. The court cards are a reminder of the firm's literary connections, with depictions of figures from Schiller's 1801 'Die Jungfrau von Orleans' ('The Maid of Orleans'), a tragedy about Joan of Arc:

Club – René d'Anjou, la couronne de Sicile à ses pieds; Louison, Soeur de Jeanne d'Arc; Montgomeri
Diamond – Philippe de Bourgogne; Agnes Sorel; Raimont, villageois
Heart – Charles VII; Isabeau de Bavière; La Hire
Spade – Talbot, mourant; Jeanne d'Arc; Lionel, enlevant l'épée de Jeanne d'Arc

The pip and the Ace cards are of particular interest due to the novel way in which the suit marks have been incorporated into the design. This style emerged in the early nineteenth century, with the decks becoming known as "transformation playing cards". Here, heart symbols become cupids' wings, diamonds books, spades windowframes and clubs part of a beetle's carapace.

Although often attributed to a Countess Charlotte von Jennison-Walworth, the present cards seem to have been designed and drawn by Countess Mary Day von Jennison-Walworth, the illegitimate daughter of an artistocratic artist mother, who proceeded to evoke huge public scandal by embarking on an incestuous affair with her half-brother.

Roi
René d'Anjou,
la couronne de Sicile à ses pieds.

Dame
Louison,
Soeur de Jeanne d'Arc.

Roi
Charles VII.

Dame
Isabeau de Baviere.

Roi
Philippe de Bourgogne.

Dame
Agnes Sorel.

Roi
Talbot, mourant.

Dame
Jeanne d'Arc.

Spades become jugs, diamonds dogs' collars, inverted hearts as hats and clubs as the base of a wagon

20 [JENNISON-WALWORTH, Countess von] [attributed to]

[Greek Myths and Legends playing cards].

Publication
Tübingen, J. G. Cotta, 1806.

Description
52 engraved playing cards with fine original hand-colour, here together with printed almanack.

Dimensions
98 by 70mm (3.75 by 2.75 inches).

References
Hargrave p.145; van den Bergh pp.136-139.

The Maker
For a description of the Cotta publishing firm, please see item 19.

The Cards
The Cotta firm followed up its successful first edition of transformation cards with the present deck, focused on the theme Greek and Roman mythology. The court cards show caracters from the ancient Epic Cycle:

Club – Pirrhus, Ester, Arcas
Diamond – Agamemnon, Agripine, Oreste
Heart – Ulisse, Iphigenie, Mardochee
Spade – Assuerus, Andromaque, Burrhus

Just as in the deck published the previous year, the Ace and pip cards are distinguished by the way in which the suit marks blend into the background image. Some new designs appear here, with spade symbols forming jugs, diamonds dogs' collars, inverted hearts as hats and clubs as the base of a wagon.

Roi
Aſsuerus

Dame
Eſter

Clubs become balloons, diamonds books, spades a rotund belly and inverted hearts a pig's head!

21 FABER DU FAUR, Christian Wilhelm von

[History of the Thirty Years' War playing cards].

Publication
Tübingen, J. G. Cotta, 1806.

Description
52 engraved playing cards with fine original hand-colour, versos plain, with almanac.

Dimensions
97 by 68mm (3.75 by 2.75 inches).

References
Hargrave p.145; Guiard 217, van den Bergh pp.140 -143; Yale 2905/GER503.

The Maker
The Ten of Clubs gives the name of the designer as Christian Wilhelm von Faber du Faur, while the Ace of Clubs bears the publisher's imprint. For a description of the Cotta publishing firm, please see item 19.

The Cards
The third deck published by the Cotta firm in the early nineteenth century, like the first, revolves around the drama of Friedrich Schiller, this time a triology of plays collectively entitled 'Wallenstein'. The plays trace the decline of the famous German general Albrecht von Wallenstein, and effectively serve as a history of the Thirty Years' War. The court cards show characters from the trilogy:

Club – Octavio Piccolomini, Fräulein Neubrunn, Deveroux
Diamond – Max Piccolomini, Theckla, v. Rosenberg
Heart – Wallenstein Herzog zu Friedland, Herzogin zu Friedland, Seni
Spade – Illo, Grafin Terzky, Neumann

As was becoming a trademark of Cotta playing cards, the pip and Ace cards have the suit marks as a key part of their design. On this deck, club symbols come to represent balloons, diamonds books, spades a rotund belly and inverted hearts a pig's head!

The deck is accompanied by an almanac made up of 16 pages, which include a fictional letter of an unknown Adolf C. to an even lesser-known Julie.

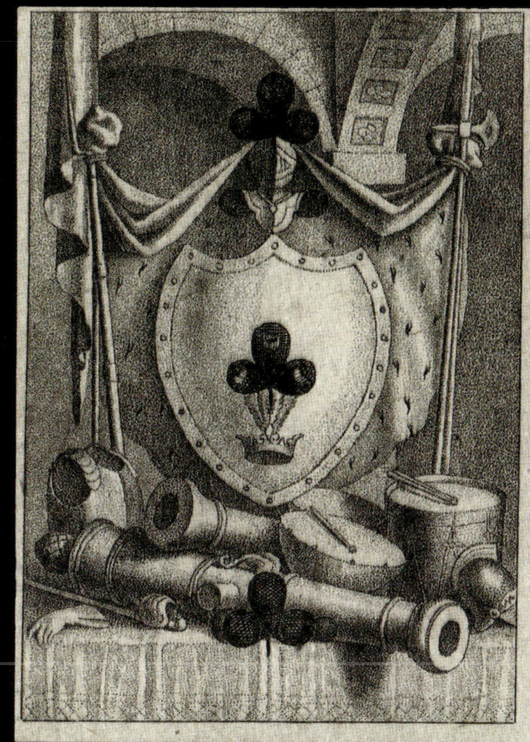

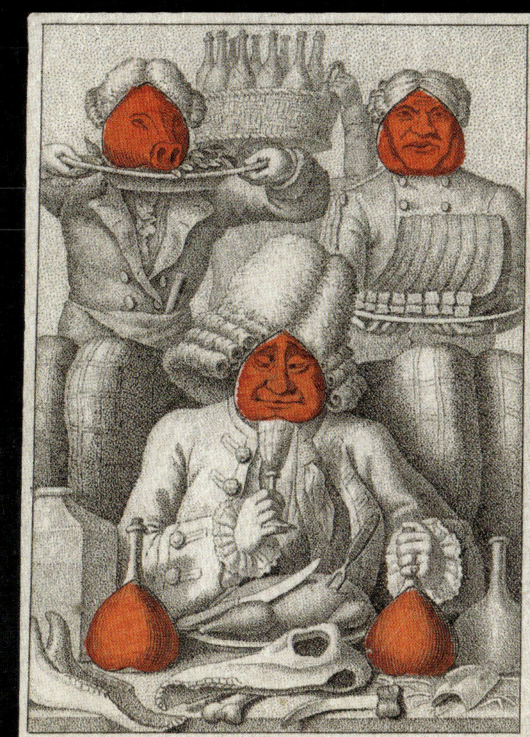

Prototypes for transformation cards

22 **NIXON, John**

[Collection of four proof playing cards].

Publication
[London], 1808 [and] 1811.

Description
4 engraved playing cards with text, fine original hand-colour.

Dimensions
73 by 116mm (2.75 by 4.5 inches) - and smaller.

References
Van den Bergh pp.150-151.

The Maker
John Nixon was a caricaturist and amateur actor who worked with several of London's publishers to produce stage prints and proofs. Nixon is known to have served as a special juryman at the Guildhall court, and as a captain in the Guildhall Volunteers, where he no doubt picked up inspiration for his satirical caricatures.

The Cards
In 1803, Nixon was among the early card-makers to experiment with "transformation playing cards". The suit marks were not always easy to incoporate into designs and sometimes produced interesting results, as can be seen here.

On the first two cards, both Three of Diamonds, Nixon has attempted to form the gentlemen's heads in the shape of the suit mark. The second example is more sophisticatedly executed, but it was the first which was adopted into a later deck published by Fores five years later. The second was never included in any complete deck.

Nixon again attempts to transform the diamond symbol into faces on the Five of Diamonds, another example of a design that was made into a card, but never published as part of a deck. However, once he had modified it by changing the diamonds to hearts, his Five of Hearts founds its place in his 'Metastasis' deck of 1811 (see item 28).

These early sketches and experiments provide valuable insight into the development of English playing cards during the early nineteenth century.

Buy my live Sprats
Past 10 o Clock
Parisot

Frogs. what the Devil have I been swallowing Frogs.
Green Owls! Damme their nothing but Frogs.
ils sont les veritable Grenouilles Monsieur.

and rouse him and rouse him and rouse him
With a rattling peal of Thunder.

Buy my live Sprats
Past 10 o Clock
Parisot

Spades as hats, clubs as chandeliers and hearts as faces

23 MÜLLER, Heinrich Friedrich

[Colloquial character playing cards].

Publication
[Vienna, H. F. Müller, c1809].

Description
52 engraved playing cards with fine original hand-colour, pink marbled paper versos.

Dimensions
91 by 66mm (3.5 by 2.5 inches).

References
Hargrave p.156; van den Bergh pp.168-169.

The Maker

The name of Heinrich Friedrich Müller (1779-1848) is shown on the King of Clubs and King of Diamonds, while the Five of Diamonds bears his initials. Müller was a Viennese innovator in printing technology and publisher who produced the first German picture-books.

He also printed musical scores, tickets and games, as well as cards, publishing tarot, transformation, trappola and standard decks. Müller was the co-founder of the Vienna Art Association and head of the board of Viennese art dealers.

The Cards

Similar to Cotta, Müller used several popular themes for his cards, including military, religious and domestic scenes. Noticeable is the almost rustic way in which the court cards are portrayed with little of the formal imagery common at this time. Instead, the single figures are dressed in quaint theatrical costumes, more akin to those shown on the cards of the previous century.

The Ace and pip cards are fine examples of the transformation style that was emerging at the time of publication. The suit marks take on key roles in the images, with spade symbols serving as hats, clubs as chandeliers and hearts as faces.

Very few examples of the present deck are known.

Wien bei H.F. Müller.

An impossible deck

24 [ANONYMOUS]

[Greek Myth and Legend playing cards].

Publication
Tübingen, J. G. Cotta, 1810.

Description
52 engraved playing cards with fine original hand colour, bound in booklet, text on facing pages.

Dimensions
118 by 86mm (4.75 by 3.5 inches).

References
Hargrave pp.145-146; van den Bergh pp.144-145.

The Maker
There are no details about the artist who designed or drew the cards for the present deck. For a description of the Cotta publishing firm, please see item 19.

The Cards
After it had successfully published four decks of playing cards, the Cotta firm decided to produce its fifth deck with a different design. Rather than issuing playing cards accompanied by a separate almanac, the 1810 edition came in the form of a booklet.

The cards themselves returned to the classical theme of the 1806 deck, this time showing Greek and Roman gods rather than mythological characters:

Club – Jupiter, Junon, Momus
Diamond – Bacchus, Ceres, Paris
Heart – Apollon, Venus, L'Amour
Spade – Vulcain, Minerve, Mercure

Paris and Momus do make two strange additions to the pantheon otherwise shown on the court cards, neither being gods. In keeping with the previous Cotta decks, the pip and Aces are "transformation cards", showing the suit marks merging into the design: spade symbols stand as hats, diamonds as frames, clubs as gables and hearts as various elements from an urn to a rotund stomach. Text on the facing page provides a description and explanation of each card.

Perhaps predictably, the 1810 edition was not a success. The cards were presented somewhat chaotically in the booklet and, more importantly, were actually impossible to play with!

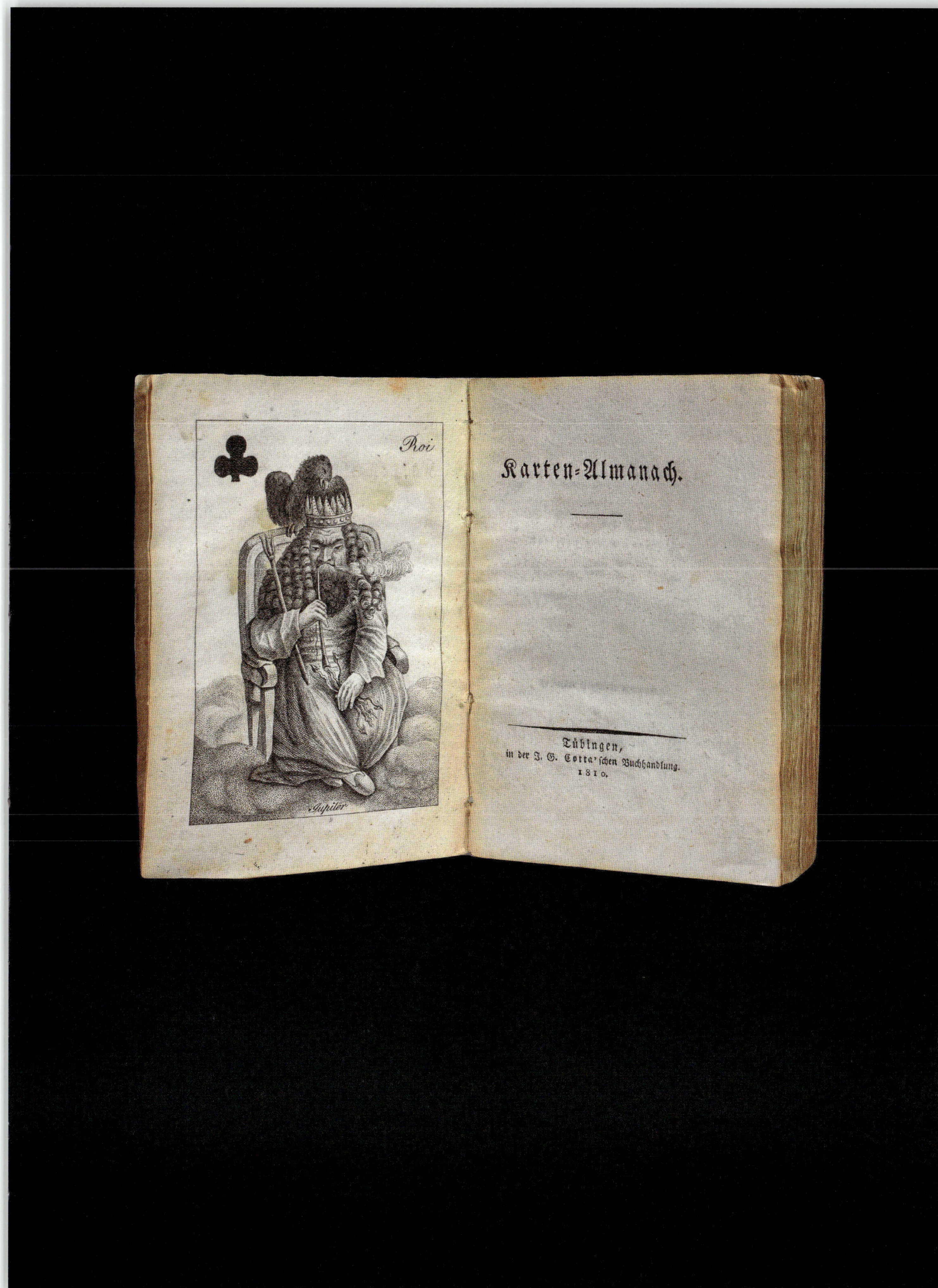
Roi
Jupiter
Karten-Almanach.
Tübingen,
in der J. G. Cotta'schen Buchhandlung.
1810.

The standard pattern of Neuchâtel

25 **FURST, Urs**

[Swiss playing cards].

Publication
[Flumenthal, Urs Fûrst, c1810].

Description
52 engraved playing cards with fine original hand-colour, versos blank.

Dimensions
86 by 55mm (3.5 by 2.25 inches).

References
Van den Bergh p.267.

The Maker
The name of the maker, Urs Fûrst, is found on the wrapper of another example of the present deck. Fûrst was a small-scale card-maker active in Flumenthal, in the Swiss canton of Solothurn during the early nineteenth century. We have not been able to trace any further information about him or his firm.

The Cards
Shown is the standard pattern produced in Neuchâtel, another Swiss canton with a number of prominent card-makers, such as Rochias, although with full-length rather than double-figure court cards. Nevertheless, the images on the court cards show the same design that is commonly found on "standard" playing cards today. These stylised Kings, Queens and Jacks in blue, yellow and red would become increasingly prominent across playing cards until they became customary.

The Aces of all suits have the same floral motif and colour framing the central suit mark, and the value of the pip cards is indicated by the number of suit marks shown on each one.

Heart as cupid's wings, a club as the top of a bird cage, an inverted spade as an urn, and a diamond as a sleeping cap

26 [ANONYMOUS]

[Chivalric code playing cards].

Publication
Tübingen, J. G. Cotta, 1811.

Description
52 engraved playing cards with fine original hand-colour, here together with printed almanack.

Dimensions
97 by 69mm (3.75 by 2.75 inches).

References
Hargrave p.146; van den Bergh pp.146-149.

The Maker
There are no details about the artist who designed or drew the cards for the present deck. For a description of the Cotta publishing firm, please see item 19.

The Cards
Following the failure of its 1810 playing cards, the Cotta firm returned to standard form the next year with a deck more akin to their earlier products. The court cards are focused on the theme of orders of knighthood, and are among the most visually appealing produced by the company.

Club – Prince ou Chef de l'Ordre du Croissant; Chevalière de l'Amaranthe; Chevalier de l'Ordre de St George
Diamond – Ordre de l'Elephant de Dannemarc; Chevalière de la Hache; Chevalier de l'Ordre de St Lazare
Heart – Templier en Habit de Guerre; Amazone; Chevalier de l'Ordre du Porcepic
Spade – Ordre de l'Amaranthende Suede, institue par Christine de Suede; Chevaliere de l'Echarpe; Chevalier de L'ordre de St. Catherine du Mont Sinai

Like all Cotta decks, the pip and Ace cards are distinguished by their novel designs that incorporate the suit marks into the background image. Here, we see heart symbols serving as a cupid's wings, a club as the top of a bird cage, an inverted spade as an urn and a diamond as a sleeping cap.

Roi.
Templier en Habit de Guerre.

Clubs, coins, cups and swords

27 ALEGRE, Manuel

[Peoples of the Continents playing cards].

Publication
Madrid, Andres Castellanos, 1811.

Description
40 engraved playing cards with fine original hand-colour, lattice and asterisk pattern to versos.

Dimensions
83 by 53mm (3.25 by 2 inches).

References
Van den Bergh p.72; Yale 132/SPA58.

The Maker
The engraver's name is found on a caption on one of the Ace cards, which reads 'Grabada en Madrid por Manl Alegre en 1811'. Manuel Alegre was active in Madrid in the early years of the nineteenth century, mainly producing portraits and landscape views; these appear to have been his only foray into the field of playing cards.

The Cards
The present deck is the result of a collaboration between Manuel Alegre and publisher Andrés Castellanos. The four standard Spanish suits are here each associated with a continent:

Clubs - Africa
Coins - America
Cups - Asia
Swords - Europe

Each card is intricately illustrated, with appropriate flora and fauna inhabiting the landscape backgrounds. The court cards show full-length figures representing the natives of their respective continents, while the number cards follow the Spanish suits of clubs, coins, cups and swords, with their value represented by illustrations of their respective objects. Some also have additional vignettes, such as Four of Clubs, which shows Hercules fighting a lion with his own club.

Only one other copy, which is uncoloured, is known to be in private ownership (van den Bergh).

The Queen of Hearts making tarts

28 NIXON, John

[Metastasis].

Publication
London, S. & T. Fuller, 1811.

Description
52 engraved playing cards with fine original hand-colour, versos plain.

Dimensions
95 by 65mm (3.75 by 2.5 inches).

References
Van den Bergh pp.152-153; Yale 2280/ENG134.

The Maker
The present deck of cards was designed, drawn and possibly painted by John Nixon. For a description of Nixon, please see item 22.

The deck was published by Samuel and Joseph Fuller, brothers who ran a publishing firm that operated from 34 Rathbone Place, London, during the first half of the nineteenth century. In 1862, the premises were sold, along with all their stock; an advertisement for a local auction house ran:

"Extensive, Interesting, and Valuable Collection of Modern Engravings, and Illustrated Books, principally the Stock of Messrs. Fuller (sold in consequence of the retirement of the senior partner)".

The Cards
The images on the present deck consist of light-hearted cards that are part illustration, part satire, of day-to-day life in contemporary Europe.

There was no accompanying booklet with either explanation or description of the characters shown on the court cards, meaning that some of them remain rather ambiguous. One recognisable figure is Napoleon, while the King of Spades seems to feature Joseph Bonaparte, short-lived king of Spain from 1808 to 1813. The female figures are less specific: the Queen of Hearts is shown contentedly making tarts, while the Queen of Spades gazes at herself in a mirror, ominously attended upon by a skeleton.

The pip cards exhibit some examples of the "transformation" style that was beginning to emerge, in which the suit marks become a key part of the central image. For instance, on the Eight of Spades, the spades symbols form the soldier's helmets as they march in ranks. Similarly, on the Two of Diamonds, the heads of the two cribbage-players take on the shape of the diamond symbol. Cribbage was a game that emerged at the beginning of the seventeenth century and involved keeping score on a wooden board.

A reproduction of this deck was published for the occasion of the 25th anniversary of the English Playing Card Society.

Private Drills

Robin Goodfellow

Blücher's "Belle Alliance" beats Napoleon at 'Loo

29 [BAUMGARTNER, Friedrich Gotthelf]

[Jeu de Allies].

Publication
Leipzig, Industrie Comptoir, c1815-1820.

Description
36 engraved playing cards with fine original hand-colour, blue star and dot pattern to versos.

Dimensions
90 by 53mm (3.5 by 2 inches).

References
Klaus-Jürgen Schultz, 'Sieges-Karte von Friedrich Gotthelf Baumgärtner'; Parlett, 'The Penguin Book of Card Games', pp.141; Van den Bergh p.92-93; for similar see Yale 2166/GER234.

The Maker
The Seven of Hearts bears the name of the manufacturer, "Industrie Comptoir". The Industrie Comptoir operated in Leipzig between roughly 1815 and 1850 under Friedrich Gotthelf Baumgartner. During this period the company published books and prints on a variety of themes and subjects, as well as cards. In addition to standard playing cards, the firm also produced cartomancy cards, which promised to help the user predict his or her future.

The Cards
The victorious German spirit in the aftermath of Napoleon's defeat at the Battle of Waterloo in 1815 is the inspiration behind the publication of this deck. The Industrie Comptoir also produced another deck celebrating the allied victory (see item 30), but while those use the French suits, the present edition shows the unique German suits: Acorns, Bells, Hearts and Leaves. This indicates that the deck was designed exclusively for the domestic market.

Another distinction is made in the name of the battle. In the aftermath, the leader of the Prussian army, Field Marshal Blücher, proposed that the conflict should go down in history as the 'La Belle Alliance', while the Duke of Wellington preferred the 'Battle of Waterloo'. Consequently, the Knave of Acorns shows Blücher with a scroll reading "Belle Alliance" while the Knave of Hearts shows Wellington reading 'Waterloo'.

The rulers of the most important countries of the Seventh Coalition are displayed as the four Kings:

Acorns – King Wilhelm I of Prussia
Bells – Tsar Alexander I of Russia
Hearts – Emperor Francis I of Austria
Leaves – King George III of Britain

Some of the pip cards show various other military personel from the supporting armies, while others depict symbols of the triumph and glory of the allied countries. Interestingly, the collection of Klaus-Jürgen Schultz contains a deck of cards simultaneously published by the Industrie Comptoir, which shows the same design but different engraving.

'Napoleon', or 'Nap' was a popular English card game in the nineteenth century. With 'Nap, 'Wellington', and 'Blücher' all appearing as 'bids': "... Wellington may only be called against a player who has already bid Nap, and Blücher against one who has already bid Wellington... Blücher is only worth introducing with seven players..." (Parlett). 'Nap' was famously played by Jerome K. Jerome's young voyagers in 'Three Men in a Boat'.

FRIEDE!
la Rothière
d. 1 Febr.
1814.
Belle Alliance
18 Jun. 1815.
PARIS
d. 31. März
1814.
WATERLOO
d. 18 Jun
1815.
Wieder erkämpft.

Napoleon meets his Waterloo

30 [BAUMGARTNER, Friedrich Gotthelf]

[Kongress Karten].

Publication
Leipzig, Industrie Comptoir, c1815-1820.

Description
52 engraved playing cards with fine original hand-colour, blue printed pattern to verso.

Dimensions
86 by 57mm (3.5 by 2.25 inches).

References
Van den Bergh pp.90-91; Yale 2802/GER399.

The Maker
On the Queen of Clubs appear the words "Industrie Comptoir in Leipzig", identifying the manufacturer of the deck. For a description of Baumgartner and the Industrie Comptoir, see Item 29.

The Cards
Published under the title 'Kongress Karten', the key players are engaged in the defeat of Napoleon in 1815. On June 18, the French forces met with the armies of the Seventh Coalition at the battlefield of Waterloo in Belgium, and after a full day's fighting, were defeated by the combined strength of the United Kingdom, Netherlands, the German states, Russia and Sweden. Following the battle, the leader of the Prussian army, Field Marshal Blücher, proposed that the conflict should go down in history as the 'La Belle Alliance', while the Duke of Wellington preferred the 'Battle of Waterloo'. Both men appear as Jacks of the suits representing their native countries, alongside their monarchs:

King, Queen, Jack:
Clubs – Russia: Tsar Alexander I, Elizabeth Alexeievna, Field Marshall Prince Barclay de Tolly
Diamonds – Prussia: Wilhelm I, Augusta of Saxe-Weimar-Eisenach, Field Marshall Blücher
Hearts – Great Britain: King George III, Charlotte of Mecklenburg-Strelitz, Duke of Wellington
Spades – Austria: Emperor Francis I, Maria Ludovika of Austria– Este, Field Marshall Schwarzenberg

The pip cards and Aces in the present deck are simply represented by the number of suit marks shown on each card.

'Napoleon', or 'Nap' was a popular English card game in the nineteenth century. With 'Nap, 'Wellington', and 'Blücher' all appearing as 'bids'. It was famously played by Jerome K. Jerome's heroes in 'Three Men in a Boat'.

SCHWARZENBERG
SCHWARZENBERG
WILHELM
WILHELM

"Play them with cards other than those used and that everyone found hideous"

31 HOUBIGANT, Armand-Gustave

[Cartes historiques].

Publication
Paris, Veuve Danbrin, 1817.

Description
52 engraved playing cards with fine original hand colour, versos white.

Dimensions
80 by 53mm (3.25 by 2 inches).

References
Guiard 135; van den Bergh pp.120-121; Yale 2593/FRA293.

The Makers
Armand-Gustave Houbigant (1790-1863) was the son of famous French perfumer Jean-Francois Houbigant, supplier to the court of Napoleon. Armand-Gustave trained in the arts from a young age, and produced his first series of scenic engravings while still in his teens. His sense of aesthetic refinement led him to strike a deal with his friends, declaring that "he would play them with cards other than those used and that everyone found hideous". Perhaps finding none to his liking, Houbigant proceeded to make his own playing cards, producing several decks during the early nineteenth century.

Nicolas Dabrin was a card-maker with a workshop on the Rue Saint-Avoye, Paris. After he died, his widow continued to produce cards, but appears to have moved the firm to No. 27, Rue Michelle Comte.

The Cards
A range of historical figures, mainly European monarchs, appear on the court cards in this deck.

King, Queen, Jack:
Clubs – François I, Marguerite de Valois, Bayard
Diamonds – Saint Loys, Blanche de Castille, Jean de Joinville
Hearts – Henry IV, Jeanne D'Albret
Spades – Charlemagne, Hildegard, Roland

The personages shown on the Jacks are among the most interesting. Pierre Terrail le Vieux was a French knight of the sixteenth century who came to be known as Chevalier de Bayard. His exceptional bravery distinguished him in many battles across Europe. His motto, "sans peur et sans reproche" ("without fear or blame") appears on the column beside him.

The Jack of Diamonds is Jean de Joinville, one of the great chroniclers of medieval France. He became famous for his biography of Louis IX, which recounted his participation in the Seventh Crusade. He is shown holding this book, entitled 'Chronique de St. Louis' in his hand, and wearing the costume of a crusader.

The Ace and pip cards in the present deck are simply presented, with the number of suit marks indicating their value.

Between 1815 and 1818, three versions of this deck were published, of which this is the second one.

CRILLON
Marguerite de Valois
sainct Loys
ROLAND
sainct Loys
francois I.

Pets at the gaming table

32 INDUSTRIE COMPTOIR

Des Gourmands.

Publication
[Leipzig, Industrie Comptoir, c1818].

Description
32 engraved playing cards with fine original hand-colour, red printed pattern to versos.

Dimensions
86 by 54mm (3.5 by 2.25 inches).

References
Van den Bergh p.219.

The Maker
The Jack of Clubs bears the maker's imprint: 'Industrie Comptoir in Leipzig'. For a description of the Industrie Comptoir, please see item 29.

The Cards
The title 'Des Gourmands' under which the present deck of cards was published fits perfectly with the displayed images. Kings, Queens and Jacks all feast on extravagent meals, and interestingly, the women have brought a variety of pets along to dinner, anything from cats to parrots. This theme also appears on the decks of other card-makers. The suit marks are shown in the upper left- and lower right-hand corners.

The Ace and pip cards are presented simply, with the number of suit marks shown corresponding to the value of each card.

Industrie Comptoir
in Leipzig

Cartes à Rire

33 [ANONYMOUS]

Des théâtres et des journaux.

Publication
[France, c1819].

Description
52 engraved playing cards with fine original hand-colour, plain white versos.

Dimensions
90 by 60mm (3.5 by 2.25 inches).

References
BnF PET FOL-KH-384; Van den Bergh pp.166-167.

The Maker
Although this deck of cards clearly originated in France, we have been unable to trace any information about its maker.

The Cards
Two versions of the 'Cartes à Rire' deck exist, both characterised by their sense of humour.

The title of the present deck, 'des théâtres et des journaux', is not surprising, considering that the court cards show the popular newspapers and magazines of the day. The figures representing these publications are deliberately hyperbolic and satirical, mocking the politics of each one. The name "Figaro" on the Jack of Hearts is not the newspaper that we know today, but a short-lived earlier publication of the same name. The theme of the court cards changes on the second version, the 'Jeu de cartes à rire de Thalia', to focus on theater, dance and opera.

The pip cards in both decks are identical, displaying bizarre, tongue-in-cheek caricatures and images in which the suit marks play a key role. Many of these transformation cards show club, diamond, heart and spade symbols as various cheeky body parts.

Facsimile editions later appeared in Italy and the United States, but the present original deck is extremely rare.

Concert de Ganaches.

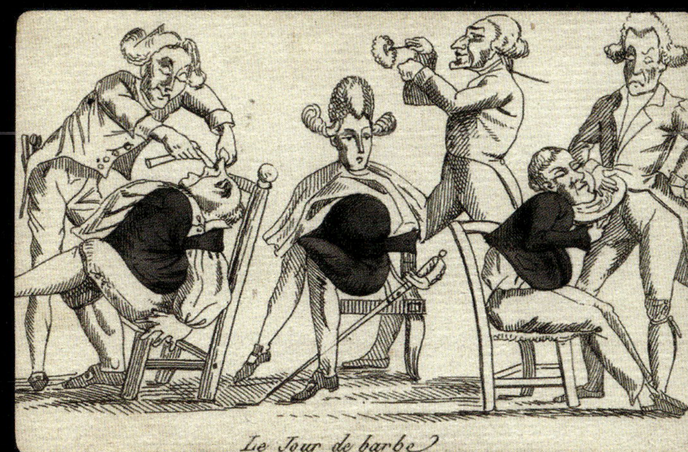
Le Jour de barbe

Les Vélocipèdes.

GAZETTE
D

QUOTIDIENNE
D

A man could no longer pick up a pencil without card-makers flocking to him to demand new designs

34 BELLANGE, Hippolyte

Cartes Recréatives 1819.

Publication
Paris, A. G. H[oubigant], 1819.

Description
32 engraved playing cards with fine original hand-colour, with additional title card and extra card, versos white.

Dimensions
89 by 60mm (3.5 by 2.25 inches).

References
Giuard 222; Van den Bergh pp.160-161.

The Maker
The present cards were designed by Hippolyte Bellangé. Bellangé was best-known for his paintings and prints of French battles, particularly during the Napoleonic era.

The extra card shows the initials "A.G.H.", allowing the deck to be attributed to Armand-Gustave Houbigant. A caricature portrait of the publisher also appears on the box. For a description of Houbigant, please see item 31.

The Cards
With few known copies and deviations in the size of the existing examples, there remain a great many mysteries associated with the present deck.

It consists of 32 cards, as well as a title card, which identifies the title as 'Cartes Recréatives 1819', and an extra card, on which the deck is explained. The Ace and court cards show historical and mythological figures, while the pip cards depict quaint and whimsical scenes from everyday life.

These pip cards are in the "transformation" style popular at the time. Houbigant had previously mocked this new vogue, saying that a man could no longer pick up a pencil without card-makers flocking to him to demand new designs.

Of the known decks, the present example is the only one in colour.

Valet
Financier.

Antiquaires discutant sur un Vase.

Un banc du Luxembourg.

Vieux Soldats.

After Alabama, before Maine

35 NICOLLE, H.

Jeu Geographique et Mythologique.

Publication
[Paris, H. Nicolle, c1819/1820].

Description
32 engraved playing cards with text, fine original hand-colour, marbled pattern to verso.

Dimensions
93 by 63mm (3.75 by 2.5 inches).

References
British Museum Schreiber Sheets French 13; van den Bergh p.65; Yale 2610/FRA310.

The Maker

H. Nicolle (fl. 1805-1840) was a publisher and card-maker who owned a shop at No. 12, Rue de Seine, Paris. In addition to decks of cards, Nicolle published a variety of written works on subjects ranging from poetry to history. Similarly, his playing cards reflect a range of themes, including music, mythology and geography, often accompanied by many lines of explanatory and informative text.

The Cards

The present deck of cards contains a wealth of geographical and mythological information. Each suit represents a continent, namely:

Clubs – Europe
Diamonds – America
Hearts – Africa
Spades – Asia

In the upper left-hand corner is a character relating to a specific region or country, while in the upper right is a mythological figure. Between them is a miniature version of the playing card in the standard French pattern, with the court cards displaying the full length figures of the Kings, Queens and Jacks. Beneath these images is a thorough description in French of the country and myth represented above.

The title of the deck appears on the King of Clubs as 'Jeu Geographique et Mythologique'. On the Queen of Diamonds, the text describes the confederation of America as consisting of 22 states. Alabama was the 22nd state and acceded on 14th December 1819. Maine joined as the 23rd state on the 15th of March 1820, which allows this deck to be dated to some time during this period.

19
LAHIRE
EGYPTE
LA FORTUNE
POPULATION DE L'EGYPTE 3,000,000 D'HABITANS.
L'Egypte est un pays très fertile quoique sablonneux, situé dans la partie orientale et septentrionale de l'Afrique et baigné par la méditerranée et la mer rouge, et arrosé à peu près dans le milieu par le Nil dont les inondations régulières lui apportent chaque année la fécondité. Il ne pleut jamais en Egypte. On la divise en trois parties, la haute, au Sud, la basse au Nord, et celle du milieu. La haute Egypte, l'ancienne Thébaïde était peuplée autrefois par un nombre prodigieux d'Anachorètes ou Solitaires. Sa Cap. était la célèbre Thèbes. La basse Egypte appelée aussi le Delta est située entre les bouches du Nil. Les principales villes de l'Egypte sont le Caire, belle ville Cap. Alexandrie, Damiette, Mansoura, Suez. Ce pays qui appartient au grand Seigneur ou Empereur de Turquie, est gouverné par un Pacha. On voit à trois lieues du Caire sur la rive gauche du Nil, les fameuses Pyramides qui ont passé autrefois pour une des sept merveilles du monde, elles servaient de tombeaux aux anciens rois d'Egypte.
La Fortune présidait au bien et au mal; on la représente sous différentes formes; mais le plus souvent avec un bandeau sur les yeux, une corne d'abondance à la main avec des ailes aux pieds, dont l'un est sur une roue qui tourne sans cesse, symbole de son inconstance.

5
FRANCE
PAN
FAUNE ou SATYRE
POPULATon DE CE ROYAUME 30,500,000 HABIT.
La France est bornée au N. Par la Manche et les Pays-Bas; à l'E. par le Rhin, et les Alpes; qui la séparent de l'Italie, au S. par la Méditerranée, et les Pyrenées qui la séparent de l'Espagne; à l'O. par l'Océan. Avant 1789 on la divisait en 32 Provinces ou Gouvernemens, On la divise maintenant en 86 Dépts dont la plupart prennent le nom de quelque montagne, ou de quelque rivière qui les traverse. Ce royaume, un des plus anciens de l'Europe, et l'un des plus considérables par son commerce et son industrie, est arrosé par plusieurs grandes rivières, savoir: la Seine, la Loire et la Garonne qui se jettent dans l'Océan, et le Rhône qui se jette dans la Méditerranée. le Rhin la sépare de l'Allemagne. Ses principales villes sont: Paris, Cap. sur la Seine, centre des Arts, des Sciences et de l'Industrie. On y compte plus de 700000 habitans. Lyon, Marseille, Bordeaux, Rouen, Nantes, Lille. &c.
Pan Dieu des Campagnes, des troupeaux et des bergers était particulièrement honoré à Rome et en Arcadie. On le représente, une flute à la main, avec des cornes, et la partie inférieure du corps semblable à celle d'un bouc. Les Faunes et les Satyres étaient aussi des divinités Champêtres.

29
AMAZONES
ET PARAGUAY
L'AURORE.
LA POPon DE CES 2 PAYS N'EST PAS BIEN CONNUE
En pénétrant dans l'intérieur des terres, à l'E. du Pérou, on trouve une vaste contrée qu'on appelle Pays des Amazones, parcequ'un aventurier revenant de ce pays a raconté en Europe, qu'il y avait vu une nation de femmes guerrières comme celles de la Mythologie; c'est dans ce pays, comme nous l'avons dit que se trouve la rivière des Amazones, la plus gde de l'univers, et qui parcourt depuis sa source, jusqu'à la mer, un espace de plus de 1500 lieues. En remontant vers le nord, et le long de l'océan atlantique entre l'Orénoque et la rivière des Amazones on trouve la Guyane, pays extrêmement chaud, à cause de sa position vers l'équateur. Ses villes principales sont: St. Thomas; Cayenne, dans l'île de ce nom. Cumana près laquelle est le petit village de Vérine fameux par son tabac. La Guyane se divise en Française, Anglaise et Hollandaise.
Le Paraguai à l'Est du Pérou et au sud du Brésil, est appelé aussi Pays de Rio-de-la-Plata du nom de cette grande rivière qui le traverse. On le divise en sept provinces. Ses villes principales sont Buenos-Ayres à l'embouchure de la Plata, Cap. l'Assomption, Ciudad-Réal. &c.
L'Aurore, qui présidait à la naissance du jour, était fille de Titan et de la Terre. On la représente ordinairement sur un char couvert de rubis et de roses. Avant-courrière du Soleil, elle ouvre les portes de l'Orient. Elle est accompagnée des heures, et voit fuir à son approche la nuit et le sommeil.

10
PALLAS
ITALIE
MINERVE ou PALLAS
POPULATION DE L'ITALIE 19,690,000 HABITANS.
L'Italie pays charmant, est une grande presqu'île entourée par la Méditerranée, et bornée au N. par les Alpes qui la séparent de la France, de la Suisse et de l'Allemagne, elle est arrosée par le Pô, l'Adige, l'Arno et le Tibre. On la divise en plusieurs états savoir, 1o le Royaume de Sardaigne Cap. Turin, 2o le Royaume Lombard Vénitien à l'Autriche Cap. Milan. 3o le Duché de Parme, 4o le Duché de Modène. 5o le grand Duché de Toscane, Cap. Florence, 6o la Principauté de Lucques 7o l'Etat de l'Eglise dont le souverain est le Pape et qui a pour Cap. Rome sur le Tibre. 8o le Royaume de Naples au Sud, ayant une Cap. du même nom. On remarque auprès de cette ville le Mont Vésuve, Volcan ou Montagne qui vomit des flammes. La Sicile, la Corse, la Sardaigne et l'Ile de Malte, sont des Iles dépendant de l'Italie.
Minerve ou Pallas sortit toute armée du cerveau de Jupiter. Comme Déesse de la guerre on la nomme Pallas, comme Déesse des sciences et de la Sagesse, on la nomme Minerve. On la représente avec le Casque sur la tête, tenant une lance à la main, et ayant auprès d'elle un hibou et divers instrumens d'Arts et de Sciences.

One of the smallest transformation decks published during the nineteenth century

36 [ANONYMOUS]

[Classical playing cards].

Publication
[Paris, Mozard, c1820].

Description
32 engraved playing cards with fine original hand-colour, versos blank.

Dimensions
51 by 42mm (2 by 1.75 inches).

References
Van den Bergh pp.162-163.

The Maker
The Mozard firm was located at 43, Rue des Lombards 43 in Paris and seems to have operated between 1811 and 1823. We have been unable to trace any other examples of playing cards produced by Mozard.

The Cards
One of the most notable aspects of the present deck is its size, being one of the smallest transformation decks published during the nineteenth century.

Another interesting feature is the difference in style between the court and Ace cards, and the pip cards. The former show characters from classical mythology, including Zeus, Cupid and Charon, elegantly engraved and uncoloured. The combination of copper engraving and stippling gives these cards a particularly unique impression.

In contrast, the latter are ingrained with humor and satire, and often coloured in gaudy hues. The Eight of Hearts, for instance, shows two rotund men engaged in a fencing contest, while the Nine of Clubs depicts a headstone reading: "Il mourut pour l'honneur et sa dame" ("He died for honour and his lady").

The deck is extremely rare, and I know of only one other complete pack in private ownership (van den Bergh).

L'Ecaillère.
L'Enfant Prodigue.
Le Conseil des Rats.
Les quatre fils Aimon
Pagode Chinoise.
Les Dervîches
Les Innocens.
Philosephe Chinois.
La tentation de St Antoine.
ROI.
Jupiter.

The Bourbon Restoration shows its hand

37 [MIGNERET, Mathieu] [attributed to]

Jeu de la bataille.

Publication
Paris, Mathieu Migneret, 1820.

Description
52 engraved playing cards with fine original hand-colour, versos white, housed within pink paper slipcase with printed title.

Dimensions
70 by 55mm (2.75 by 2.25 inches).

References
Guiard 70; van den Bergh pp.126-27.

The Maker
There is an example of the present deck which has a wrapper bearing the imprint, "Imprimerie de Migneret, rue du Dragon, n° 20". Mathieu Migneret was a Parisian printer and bookseller from 1811 until his death in 1814, upon which his widow, and later his son Nicolas, ran the family firm.

The Cards
Migneret has replaced the traditional French suits with reassuring military alternatives: Cavalerie, Infanterie Légère, Artillerie and Infanterie de Ligne. Likewise, in the place of the Ace, King, Queen and Jack cards are found the Réserve, Maréchal de France, Lieutenant Général and Maréchal de Camp. With Napoleon banished (nearly dead), and the July Revolution of 1830 still to come, the Bourbon Restoration is reflected in this militarily precise deck.

The Ace and Court cards show their respective military leaders, while the pip cards show small scenes depicting soldiers in various modes of action. The number of vignettes on each card corresponds to its value, meaning that the higher value cards are swamped with tiny figures. The action has been depicted as realistically as possible, with the infantrymen shooting smoking guns, for instance.

It is clear that at some point during the painting process, however, the attention of the colourist wavered, as some elements have been forgotten, such as a horse on the Ten of Cavalerie. With the cards comes a booklet titled 'Notice pour le jeu de la Bataille' in which the rules of this new game are explained.

An extremely rare deck. The present deck is possibly the only complete copy in private ownership (van den Bergh).

Maréchal de France
Infanterie de Ligne.
Réserve.

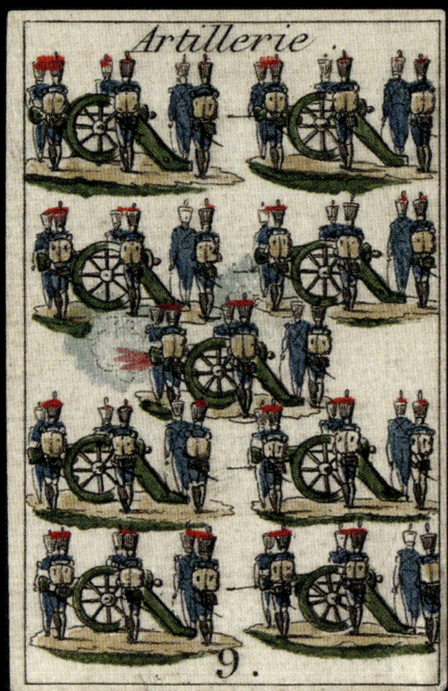
Artillerie
9.

Artillerie.
Réserve.

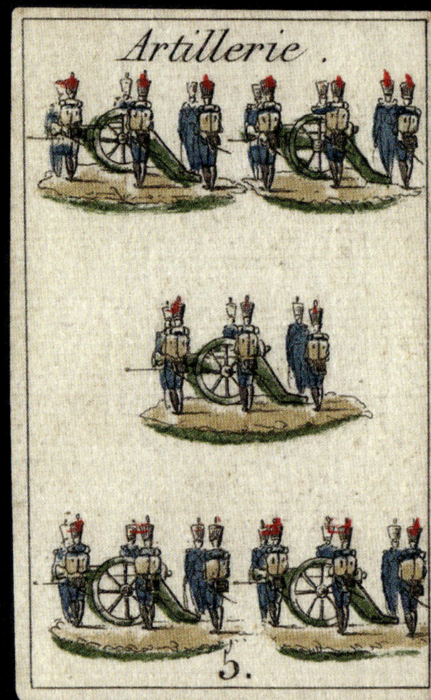
Artillerie.
5.

Lieutenant Général.

Cavalerie.
10.

Cavalerie.
4

Infanterie Légère
8.
Infanterie de Ligne.
Réserve.
Infanterie Légère.
6.
Artillerie.
Réserve.
Infanterie de Ligne.
10.
Maréchal de France.

A Bavarian Royal Flush

38 **FETSCHER, Joseph**

[Aristocratic playing cards].

Publication
[Munich, Joseph Fetscher, c1820].

Description
52 engraved playing cards with fine original hand-colour.

Dimensions
900 by 53mm (35.5 by 2 inches).

References
Van den Bergh p.238; Yale 2948/GER546.

The Maker

On the shield of the Jack of Hearts an imprint reads "Joseph Fetscher B: Karten fabricant in München Burggaße 183". Fetscher, who was granted a privilege to make playing cards in 1792, was part of a many-branched playing card family.

From 1799 he headed his company in the Burggaße in Munich. Following his death around 1824, his widow took over the company and eventually his son would do the same in 1831.

The Cards

Very typical of Fetscher's style, especially the decorative border that frames the image, this deck is invariably creative, carefully printed and delicately coloured. The double-figure court cards show the royal characters magnificently dressed in traditional yet impressive costumes. The suit marks are shown in the upper left- and lower right-hand corners.

The pip and Ace cards are presented simply, with the number of suit marks indicating the value of the card. The original wrapper in which the cards came bears the coat of arms of Bavaria, held up by two lions. The crest is topped with a crown.

Like most of Fetscher's decks of playing cards, the present example is a rare survival.

Joseph
Fetscher
B. Karten
fabricant in
München
Burggaße
183

In solitary?

39 **STEINBERGER, Johann Anton**

[Solitaire playing cards].

Publication
[Frankfurt, Johann Anton Steinberger, c1820].

Description
Two decks of 52 lithograph playing cards with fine original hand-colour, total 104, black dot pattern printed to versos.

Dimensions
55 by 33mm (2.25 by 1.25 inches).

References
Van den Bergh pp.241.

The Maker
On the Jack of Diamonds the name of the maker is printed 'Fabricirt von Joh: Anton Steinberger in Frankfurth am Main'. Steinberger was active as a card-maker and editor in Frankfurt from 1817 to 1860. Following his death the firm was taken over by his widow, who later sold it to Johann Müller in 1872. His cards were copied numerous times, but the replicas were invariably of a lower quality.

The Cards
These solitaire cards are part of a set of two decks. Each one would be stored away in its own slipcase, charmingly modelled on small books. Both cases fit within an accessory box that accompanied the decks.

The cards themselves are pleasantly designed, with the court cards showing full-length figures coloured in bright hues of pink, yellow, green and blue. The suit mark is shown in the upper left corner of the image.

Fabricirt
von
Joh: Anton
Steinberger
in
Frankfurth
am Main

With a comical twist

40 **SUSSE, Nicolas & Victor**

Jeu des Caricatures.

Publication
[Paris, Susse Papetier, c1820].

Description
32 engraved playing cards with fine original hand-colour, plain white versos.

Dimensions
90 by 60mm (3.5 by 2.25 inches).

References
Van den Bergh pp.224-225.

The Maker
A small imprint is found on the little box in which the cards come, reading: "Susse Papetier, Passage des Panoramas N° 7, a Paris". During the nineteenth century, the brothers Nicolas and Victor Susse had a paper business located at the Passage Des Panoramas. Around 1825, they changed their activities from producing paper to making bronze art.

The Cards
The Susse brothers quickly won national success with these popular playing cards, due to the comical images displayed on all of its cards. Each one shows a farcical scene or caricatures with exceptional hand-colour. Some of the figures are taken from the Commedia dell'Arte (see item 4), such as Polichinelle on the Ace of Hearts, La mere Gigogne on the Queen of Hearts, Arlequin on the Jack of Hearts and Paillasse on the Eight of Spades.

There are also characters from literature and popular legend, such as Don Quixote on the King of Diamonds, as well as invented figures such as "Mr Wig" on the Ace of Clubs. Each card identified the name or title of the character shown, and shows a miniature version of the playing card in an upper corner.

Within the literature, the deck is mentioned both as an uncolored uncut sheet and as a deck with individual coloured cards.

LA MÈRE GIGOGNE

Mr TOUPET

Mr DIAFOIRUS

SANCHO-PANÇA

Never alone

41 WÜST, Conrad Ludwig

[Solitaire playing cards].

Publication
[Frankfurt, C. L. Wu üst, c1820].

Description
52 engraved playing cards with fine original hand-colour.

Dimensions
58 by 40mm (2.25 by 1.5 inches).

References
Van den Bergh p.275.

The Maker
Both the Jack of Hearts and the Jack of Spades bear shields with the name of the maker written on them: "Conrad Ludwig Wüst in Frankfurt am Main". In 1811, Conrad Ludwig Wüst (1783-1843) was granted a license to operate as a card-maker, and over the following decades he produced many decks of playing cards with a wide range of themes. Notably, he developed an association with the Frankfurt Theatre by producing cards that featured the faces of prominent actors and actresses. The industrial developments of the nineteenth century catalysed Wüst's production, as cards could be printed by a steam-driven press and his employees could work later hours thanks to the installation of gas lighting. After Wüst's death, his son took over the firm, which remained in the family until 1910.

The Cards
Around 1810, the Industrie Comptoir firm in Leipzig published a solitaire deck which would go on to inspire Frankfurt card-maker Conrad Ludwig Wüst to produce the present deck roughly ten years later. These cards are almost identical to the original deck, with even the border around the edge of each image using the same leaf pattern.

The court cards show full-length figures, with the Kings traditionally dressed in royal finery, the Queens in more relaxed yet nonetheless regal outfits, and the Jacks depicted as soldiers. They each hold the traditional axe, but wear a range of military dress, the Jack of Clubs in a helmet, and the rest in hats.

Later, other playing card makers would also publish decks with a strong resemblance to the present cards. The solitaire cards of Steinberger (see item 39) are one notable, although perhaps not surprising, example, as he had worked for Wu üst as an apprentice.

“Passetemps de soirées”

42 [ANONYMOUS]

Cartes de Visites a Rire.

Publication
[France, ?c1825].

Description
48 of 52 engraved playing cards and two title cards, with fine original hand-colour, plain white versos.

Dimensions
94 by 59mm (3.75 by 2.25 inches).

References
Van den Bergh pp.226-227.

The Maker
Nothing is known about the designer or manufacturer of these cards, since they do not seem to have been published as part of a traditional deck of playing cards.

The Cards
Entitled, ‘Cartes de Visites à Rire’, but apparently not belonging to any traditional deck, these are nonetheless fine examples of nineteenth century playing cards. They do not show any suit marks or card values, but can still be used to play a game. According to the rules, it is meant to be used as a cozy means of passing the evening (“passetemps de soirées”).

The distinguishing feature of this deck is its sharp satirical sense of humour. Each card displays a caricature on the upper half, beneath which are two lines of rhyming verse, often packed with puns. The characters are from a variety of literary, theatrical and folklore sources, including Polichinelle from the Commedia dell’Arte.

Classique immittit habenas
VIRG. Œneid. Lib. VII.
Le Classique quitte les les rênes
VIRG. Œneide. Liv. VII.
LE CLASSIQUE.
Quai de l'Ecole, N° 301.
Le Classique est venu, quoique à l'Extrémité, Rire du Romantique avec Sévérité.
Les trois unités
I. I. I.
ARISTOTELES

Mr. DU FRISSON,
Acteur Tragique.
Quai des Morfondus.
L'Espoir de notre scene, ACHILLE DU FRISSON,
Est venu du Vampire écouter la Leçon.
Perfide tu mourras.
Ainsi j'effacerai Talma Le Kain La Rive.

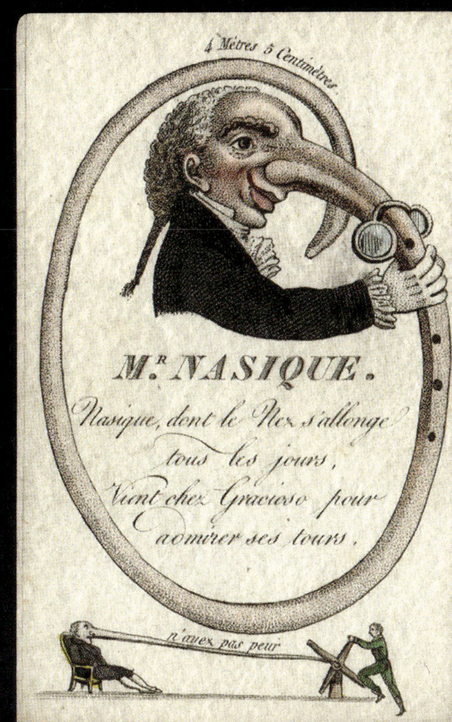

4 Mètres 5 Centimètres
Mr. NASIQUE.
Nasique, dont le Nez s'allonge tous les jours, Vient chez Gracioso pour admirer ses tours.
n'ayez pas peur

LE VAMPIRE
Le Vampire est venu suivi du Vent-coulis Embrasser Barbe-bleue exemple des Maris.
Vent le Vampire l'Age &c

Starring François-Joseph Talma in the role of Nero in 'Britannicus'

43 ?[WÜST, Conrad Ludwig]

?[Jeu de Talma].

Publication
[Frankfurt, C.L. Wüst, c1825].

Description
52 engraved playing card with fine original hand-colour, pink petal pattern to versos.

Dimensions
90 by 61mm (3.5 by 2.5 inches).

References
Giuard 23; van den Bergh pp.214-215.

The Maker
For a description of Conrad Ludwig Wüst, please see item 41.

The Cards
A series of celebrities from the early nineteenth century appear in the present deck, the majority of whom are figures from the stage. The double-figure court cards show these actors, singers and dancers in a range of theatrical costumes, such as François-Joseph Talma, whom the deck is named after, in the role of Nero in the play 'Britannicus'.

Popular French operas such as 'Le barbier de Seville' and 'Le calife de Bagdad' are represented on the Jack of Clubs and the King of Diamonds. The only play that appears twice, on the Jack of Spades and Queen of Clubs, is 'Robin Des Bois' (Robin Hood).

The Ace and pip cards are simply presented, with the number of suit marks corresponding to the value of each card.

The deck is undoubtedly German in origin, but was also published by Antoine Dieudonné, from Grevenmacher in Luxembourg. Dieudonné copied German cards regularly but the quality of his decks were invariably inferior to the original editions.

VALET
POTIER
Rôle de Jacques dans le Conscrit
DAME
Mme VALÈRE
Rôle d'Anna dans Robin des Bois
DAME
Mlle LEVERD
Rôle de Célimène dans le Misanthrope
VALET
LEPEINTRE
Rôle de Birbeth dans Trilby

The most beautiful deck published in the nineteenth century

44 **HODGES, Charles**

[Celestial playing cards].

Publication
London, Stopforth & Son, 1827.

Description
52 engraved playing cards with fine original hand-colour, versos plain.

Dimensions
95 by 63mm (3.75 by 2.5 inches).

References
Hargrave p.179; van den Bergh pp.76-79; Yale 2283/ENG137.

The Maker
Charles Hodges operated as a stationer and bookseller from his shop at 27 Portman Street, London from 1825-1830. He was best known for his two decks of ornately engraved playing cards on the themes of geography and astronomy that appeared in 1827. These were among the last decks of engraved cards published in London, as chromolithography soon took over. They are thought to have been printed for Hodges by the firm of Stopforth & Son, which was also active in London during the early nineteenth century.

The Cards
The present cards are widely considered to form the most beautiful deck published in the nineteenth century. The gold print, detailed images and lively colours create a sense of luxury to match the heavenly subject matter. Each Ace card shows three signs of the zodiac corresponding to a certain season, labelled in Latin above the images. The same signs are also found on the Eight, Nine and Ten pip cards. On the Aces, the sigils surround their respective suit marks, although the Spades symbol is missing. The deck is therefore technically incomplete, meaning that it conveniently avoids being classified as a taxable good.

The court cards depict the divine figures of classical mythology, shown with their associated accoutrements:

King, Queen, Jack:
Club – Apollo, Diana, Bacchus
Diamond – Mars, Minerva, Vulcan
Heart – Jupiter, Juno, Mercury
Spade– Neptune, Venus, Saturn

The pip cards are equally as impressive, with each one displaying a constellation or mythological character. The value of the card corresponds to the number of suit marks shown, and even the symbols themselves are distinctive. Both of Hodges' impressive decks are characterised by their elongated carmine Hearts, green trefoil Clubs, gold Diamonds and blue pike-head Spades.

VER

AUTUMNUS

AESTAS

HIEMS

JUPITER

CASSIOPEIA
CEPHEUS
ANDROMEDA
PERSEUS
CAMELOPARDALIS

SCORPIO
LIBRA
LUPUS

APOLLO

MINERVA

VIRGO
LEO
CORVUS
BOOTES
LIBRA

PISCES
PEGASUS
ARIES
AQUARIUS
CETUS

NEPTUNE

A royal flush of world leaders

45 **HODGES, Charles**

[New royal playing cards].

Publication
London, Stopforth & Son, 1827.

Description
52 engraved playing cards with fine original hand-colour, versos plain.

Dimensions
95 by 63mm (3.75 by 2.5 inches).

References
Hargrave p.179; Van den Bergh pp.80-83; Yale 2253/ENG106.

The Maker
For a description of Charles Hodges, please see item 44.

The Cards
In 1825, Parisian card-maker René Janet published a deck of cards entitled 'Boston de l'Univers ou Jeu des Quatre Parties du Monde' ('Boston [cards] of the Universe, or Game of the Four Parts of the World'). Each suit in this deck represented a continent: Hearts for Europe, Spades for America, Diamonds for Asia and Clubs for Africa. Two years later, Charles Hodges appropriated Janet's concept and produced his 'New Royal Playing Cards, Patronised by His Majesty'.

Hodges' deck far outshone Janet's in both beauty and popularity, and is widely held as the most beautiful set of geographical playing cards ever made. Each Ace shows a general map of the continent represented by that suit, simply but effectively outlined in colour. Similarly, the pip cards show national maps of significant countries in each continent, their value corresponding to the number of suit marks displayed. Even the symbols themselves are attractively designed, with elongated carmine Hearts, green trefoil Clubs, gold Diamonds and blue pike-head Spades.

The court cards each depict a full length figure, representing either a native of their continent or a historical personage closely associated with it:

King, Queen, Jack:
Club – Saladin, Zulema of Algiers, Moroab of Morocco
Diamond – Kien Long, Statire of Persia, Hyder Ali of Mysore
Heart – George IV, Catherine II of Russia, Robespierre
Spade– George Washington, Neala of Canada, Telasco of Mexico

Not all of these figures had appeared on the original deck by Janet, and Hodges' most notable addition is certainly that of Robespierre. In the decades after his ousting from power and ironic execution at the guillotine, the legacy of the French revolutionary fluctuated continually, making it difficult to tell whether his representation as the Jack of Hearts is designed as a celebration or condemnation of his memory.

EUROPE
Spitzbergen
Iceland
Nova Zembla
White Sea
Archangel
BRITISH ISLES
Dublin
London
Paris
FRANCE
SPAIN
Madrid
Lyons
Berlin
Vienna
St. Petersburgh
RUSSIA
Moscow
Smolensk
Warsaw
Kiev
AUSTRIAN STATES
TURKEY
BLACK SEA
Constantinople
AFRICA
ASIA
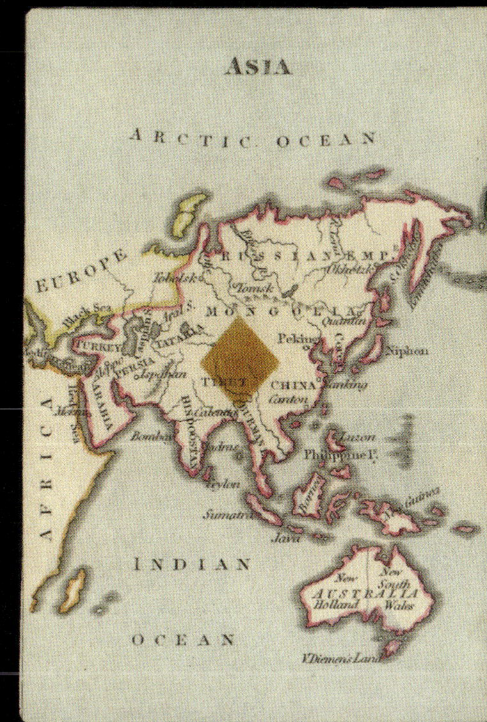
ASIA
ARCTIC OCEAN
EUROPE
RUSSIAN EMP.
Tobolsk
Tomsk
MONGOLIA
TURKEY
PERSIA
ARABIA
TARTARY
TIBET
CHINA
Pekin
Nanking
Canton
Niphon
Bombay
Calcutta
Ceylon
Sumatra
Java
Luzon
Philippine Is.
AFRICA
INDIAN OCEAN
New Holland
New South Wales
AUSTRALIA
V. Diemens Land

AFRICA
EUROPE
ASIA
Gibraltar
BARBARY
Morocco
Mourzuk
Gr. Cairo
EGYPT
NUBIA
Dongola
ARABIA
SAHARA
Timbuctoo
Bornou
Benin
Guinea
C. Palmas
Cape Coast
Loango
NIMEAMAY
Mozambique
C. Negro
S. Helena
Caffraria
Cape Town
Col. Good Hope
Socotra
Madagascar
SOUTHERN OCEAN
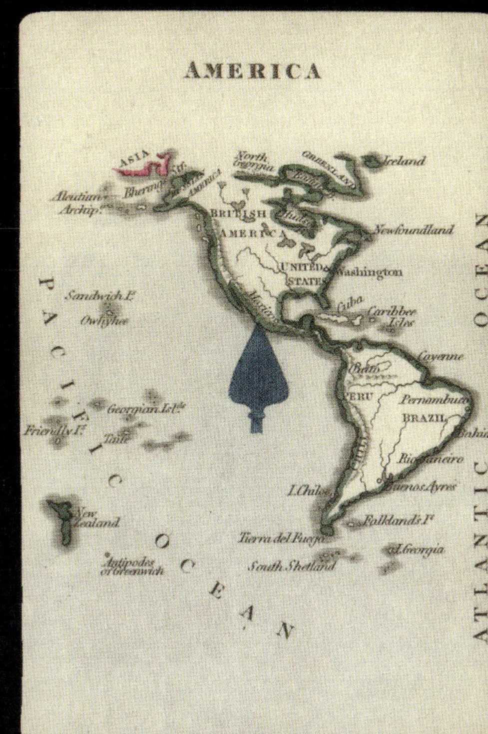
AMERICA
ASIA
Iceland
Aleutian Archip.
BRITISH AMERICA
Newfoundland
UNITED STATES
Washington
Sandwich Is.
Owhyhee
Cuba
Caribbee Isles
PACIFIC OCEAN
PERU
BRAZIL
Pernambuco
Bahia
Buenos Ayres
I. Chiloe
Falkland Is.
S. Georgia
Tierra del Fuego
South Shetland
New Zealand
Friendly Is.
Georgian Is.
ATLANTIC OCEAN

BRITISH ISLES
ATLANTIC
OCEAN
NORTH
SEA
SCOTLAND
Edinburgh
Dublin
LONDON
English Channel
FRANCE

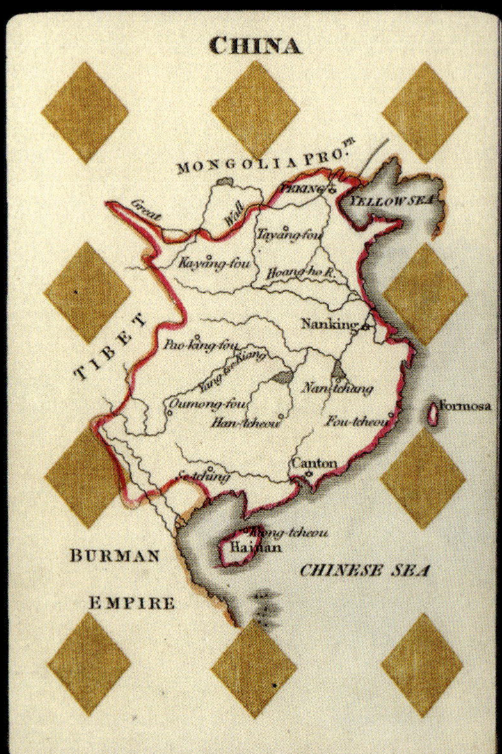
CHINA
MONGOLIA PRO.
YELLOW SEA
TIBET
Nanking
Canton
Formosa
BURMAN
EMPIRE
CHINESE SEA

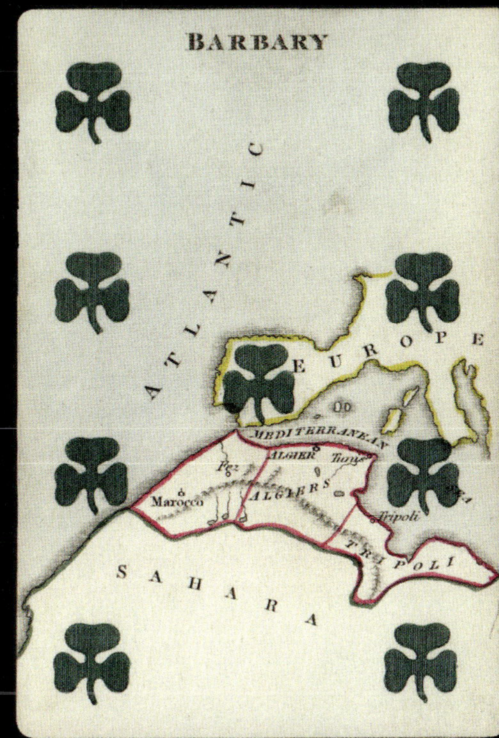
BARBARY
ATLANTIC
EUROPE
MEDITERRANEAN
Marocco
ALGIERS
Tripoli
TRIPOLI
SAHARA

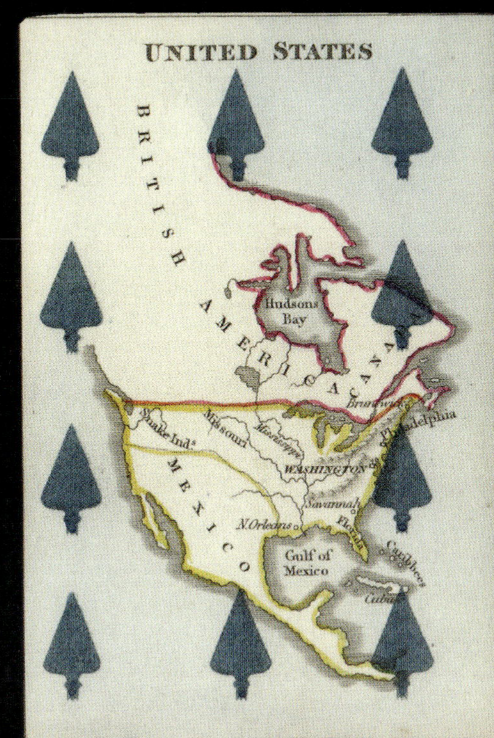
UNITED STATES
BRITISH AMERICA
Hudsons Bay
Philadelphia
WASHINGTON
MEXICO
N.Orleans
Savannah
Gulf of Mexico

Seasonal suits

46 [ANONYMOUS]

[Four Seasons playing cards].

Publication
[Germany, c1830].

Description
52 engraved playing cards with fine original hand-colour, blue printed pattern to versos.

Dimensions
86 by 600mm (3.5 by 23.5 inches).

References
Van den Bergh p.240.

The Maker
We have been unable to trace any information about the maker or origins of this deck. Although it has been attributed to Wüst, there is little solid evidence for this speculation.

The Cards
A typical deck from Germany in the early-mid nineteenth century.

An interesting feature is that the clothing of the four double-figure Queens reflect the four seasons, with the Queen of Clubs representing summer, Diamonds autumn, Hearts winter and Spades spring.

By contrast, the garment worn by the Kings and Jacks do not appear to follow any particular pattern, and the pip cards are regular.

Keeping their cards close to their chests

47 [ANONYMOUS]

Jeu Grotesque.

Publication
[France, c1830].

Description
32 engraved playing cards with fine original hand-colour.

Dimensions
100 by 63mm (4 by 2.5 inches).

References
Van den Bergh pp.222-223.

The Maker
Nothing is known about the maker of this extraordinary deck of cards.

The Cards
Without a doubt one of the finest examples of all the extraordinary playing cards in circulation during the nineteenth century. It features a series of "grotesque" figures with playing cards for their chests.

The concept of the "grotesque" emerged in eighteenth century art and literature as a forerunner of the gothic; it involves distorted, mysterious or incongruous forms and ideas. The characters shown on the present cards can be categorised as "grotesque" due to their inhuman bodies and often the strange situations they are shown in, with the Seven of Hearts standing by a decapitated head, for instance.

The figures on the King and Queen cards are labelled with the names of Roman and Greek gods, while some of the pip and Ace cards are captioned as characters from literature and folklore, such as Doctor Diafoirus, Gargantua, Don Quichotte and Sancho.

Only a few copies of this deck are known, and it is remarkable that they are all different. The decks in the Schreiber collection, the Cary collection and in D'Allemagne, bear a strong resemblance to the cards that are displayed here. The deck in the collection Verame differs greatly, and is only printed in red, yellow and blue.

Junon
Perruquier Bichon

Perruquier Bichon.

Vulcain

Amphitrite.

Le Joueur de flutte.

Diafoirus.

Le Chinois.

Le Magicien Rotomago

Sancho

One of the earliest card games played in Europe

48 BACKOFEN, Johann Gottfried

[Playing cards].

Publication
[Nuremberg, J.G. Backofen, c1830].

Description
40 engraved playing cards with original colour, blue dot and asterisk pattern to versos.

Dimensions
92 by 57mm (3.5 by 2.25 inches).

References
Van den Bergh p.266, Yale 2062/GER131.

The Maker
The name of the maker is found on the upper shield on the Jack of Hearts, "Joh: Gottfried Backofen", while his address, "in Gostenhof an Nürnberg N° 104" is found on the lower shield. Johann Gottfried Backofen (1773-1851) originally went to Nuremberg to study music, but later became a card-maker, producing numerous decks over the course of his career, which stretched from 1809 to 1849.

The Cards
These are a typical example of the copper-engraved cards produced during the nineteenth century, which were then coloured using templates. The court cards feature a wealth of colour, including blue yellow, green, red and pink. Another interesting feature of the court cards is that many of the figures adopt the poses more commonly associated with others, such as the King of Spades, who is shown with the orb and sword in the style typically shown on the King of Hearts, while the Jack of Spades takes on the Jack of Diamond's right profile.

The deck was designed to be used for the four-person card game known as 'L'Hombre'. It was one of the earliest games played in Europe and became most popular during the sixteenth century, although the production of these cards suggests that it persisted three centuries later. 'L'Hombre' is played with 40 cards, with the Eights, Nines and Tens of all suits excluded. Although typically associated with the Spanish suit system, the present cards use the French.

Napoleon deals death across Europe

49 WÜST, Conrad Lugwig

[Napoleon European Victories playing cards].

Publication
Frankfurt, C. L. Wüst, c1830.

Description
52 engraved playing cards with fine original hand-colour, blue printed pattern to versos.

Dimensions
81 by 51mm (3.25 by 2 inches).

References
Guiard 13; van den Bergh p.94; Yale 2068/ GER137.

The Maker
For a description of Conrad Ludwig Wüst, please see item 41.

The Cards
Celebrating the battles won by Napoleon between 1796 and 1812, as the French leader charged a seemingly unstoppable path across the continent, these cards were produced in Frankfurt, one of the major European cities taken over by the Napoleonic regime, nearly two decades earlier.

Each Ace depicts two battle-scenes showing the victorious French army. Napoleon himself appears in all but one of these, often sat astride his distinctive white horse:

Club – Passage du Pont d'Arcole (15 Novemb. 1796) / Bataille de Wagram (16 Juillet 1809)
Diamond – Bataille des Piramides (22 Juillet 1798) / Bataille de Marengo (14 Juin 1800)
Heart – Bataille de Jena (14 Octobre 1806) / Bataille de Lutzen (2 Mai 1812)
Spade – Passage du Mont St Bernard (15 Mai 1800) / Bataille d'Austerlitz (2 Decembre 1805)

The double-figure court cards show the royal characters in standard poses, with the suit marks displayed in the upper left and lower right corners. The value of the pip cards is simply indicated by the number of suit marks shown.

The present deck was one of Wüst's most successful and ran to numerous editions, but in spite of its popularity is now among his rarest.

Bataille des Pyramides 22 Juill
1798.

Passage du Pont d'Arcole 15 Novemb, 1796.

Passage du Mont St Bernard 15 Mai
1800.

Bataille de Jéna 14 Octobre 1806.

"Veillons au salut de l'empire,
Veillons au maintien de nos droits"

50 **MASSARD, Leopold**

[Jeu de barricades].

Publication
Paris, Grimaud, 1831.

Description
32 engraved playing cards with fine original hand-colour, versos plain, with booklet.

Dimensions
94 by 63mm (3.75 by 2.5 inches).

References
Guiard 142; van den Bergh pp.108-109.

The Maker

The booklet that accompanies the present deck states that it was designed by French engraver Leopold Massard (1812-1889). It also gives the initials J.-B.G., suggesting that it was published by Grimaud. In 1848, Baptiste-Paul Grimaud founded a small playing card factory in Paris, producing decks on a range of themes and subjects. The firm continued to prosper throughout the subsequent century, and in 1962 was bought by a larger company, Ducale-France Cartes. It continues today as part of the Cartamundi Group.

The Cards

The heroes of the July Revolution feature prominently on the present deck of cards. The revolution lasted from 27 to 29 July 1830, and saw King Charles X ousted from power. Shockwaves were felt across Europe, most significantly resulting in the partition of Belgium and the foundation of the Netherlands as an independent state. The accompanying booklet explains that each suit represents a specific aspect of the revolution:

Clubs – legislation and political institutions
Diamonds – the barricades and conflict
Hearts – national interest and the army
Spades – suffering and death

Each card features a detailed image illustrating the key players and events of the revolution, captioned with a title and accompanied by several lines of French verse. Louis Philippe, for instance, is shown as the King of Hearts with the caption 'Roi Citoyen' ('First Citizen') and the lines:

> "Veillons au salut de l'empire,
> Veillons au maintien de nos droits"
> ("Let us ensure the salvation of the empire,
> Let us ensure that our rights are maintained")

In the upper left-hand corner a miniature version of the playing card is shown, identifying its suit and value, and the entire card is bordered by a continuous olive branch.

ROI CITOYEN.
Veillons au salut de l'Empire,
Veillons au maintien de nos droits....

LA VICTOIRE.
La Victoire en chantant nous ouvre
la Barrière......

TOMBES DE JUILLET.
Mourir pour sa Patrie!
C'est le sort le plus beau, le plus
digne d'envie.

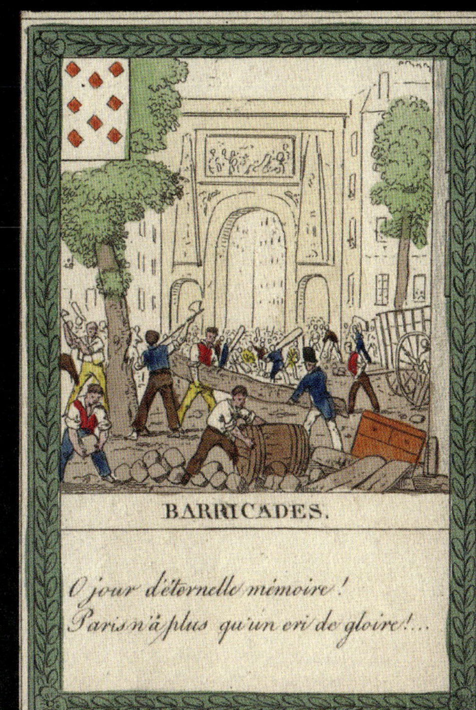
BARRICADES.
O jour d'éternelle mémoire!
Paris n'a plus qu'un cri de gloire!...

An Exotic suit...

51 **ACKERMANN, Rudolph**

Pictorial Playing Cards.

Publication
New York, Caleb Bartlett, 1833.

Description
52 chromolithograph playing cards, versos green.

Dimensions
92 by 65mm (3.5 by 2.5 inches).

References
Van den Bergh pp.172-173; Yale 462/ USA271.

The Maker

The present cards were originally designed by Rudolf Ackermann and published by Caleb Bartlett in 1833. Ackerman was a Ango-German bookseller, publisher and lithographer known for his popular long-running monthly periodical 'Repository of Arts, Literature, Fashions' from 1809 to 1829, His shop by the same name on the Strand in London offered prints, illustrated books, paper, art supplies and other decorative items.

Bartlett was an early American card-maker based in New York, who operated between 1830 and 1850. He is not to be confused with Charles Bartlet, the pseudonym of Philadelphia card-maker Samuel Hart. Bartlett seems to have mainly sourced his designs from earlier European decks rather than making his own cards.

The Cards

Rudolf Ackermann originally released these cards in 1817, and he subsequently reissued the deck in 1818 in London in the 'Repository of Arts', in Vienna by Heinrich Friedrich Müller (see item 23) and in Paris by Gide Fils. 15 years later, in 1833, Caleb Bartlett came out with this version in New York, entitled 'Pictorial Playing Cards'.

The four versions are easily distinguishable. The court cards of Gide and Müller have no background, and the cards by Ackermann and Gide are printed more clearly than those of Müller and Bartlett. Besides, Müller was the only one who printed his name on one of the cards, the King of Hearts, which reads 'Zu finden in Wien bey H.F. Müller Kunsthandler'.

The American edition, as here, is almost an exact copy of Ackermann's original deck, except that the colouring is far heavier and brighter, no doubt the result of technological progression in chromolithography in the early decades of the nineteenth century.

The cards are themed around the exotic, with the Ace and court cards showing eastern figures and icons, such as the Persian emperor smoking a long pipe on the Ace of Spades and an ominous Egyptian idol on the Ace of Diamonds. The suit marks are shown in the upper right-hand corner or centre, merging into the background as is typical on transformation cards.

The pip cards show scenes of passion, humour or drama, again with the suit marks set within the central image. A half-naked youth reclines on a club symbol on the Five of Clubs, while a heart hovers in the air above an embracing couple on the Four of Hearts.

S·P·Q·R

“Liberdade”

52 [ANONYMOUS]

[Portuguese Civil War playing cards].

Publication
[?Portugal, post-1834].

Description
52 engraved cards with fine original hand-colour, red pattern to versos.

Dimensions
87 by 55mm (3.5 by 2.25 inches).

References
Van den Bergh pp.110-111.

The Maker
None of the cards in the present deck has an imprint, nor are there any features that allow the maker to be identified. The text is in Portuguese, however, and the subject matter naturally points towards a Portuguese manufacturer. It is possible that the deck may have been published by the Impressão Régia (Royal Press), which was known to have produced other decks of playing cards.

The Cards
From 1832 to 1834, a civil war unfolded in Portugal between Emperor Peter IV (also reigning as Peter I of Brazil) and the self-proclaimed King Michael I. Determined to keep control of the country while ruling across the Atlantic, Peter had declared his daughter Queen Maria II of Portugal, promising that she would come to marry Michael. The marriage failed to materialise, however, leading Michael to challenge Peter directly for the throne. Their followers fought for three years until Peter emerged victorious and Michael and his family fled to Austria.

The present deck of cards commemorates this war, with two of its memorable events depicted on each Ace. The double-figured court cards show the Portuguese monarchs and military leaders involved in the conflict, with the suit marks appearing in the upper left- and lower right-hand corners. The swords of the Jacks identify the causes that were being fought for, “Maria II” or “Liberdade”, for instance.

Entrada do Ex.to Libert.or na Cidade do Porto
Entrada do Ex.te Libertador em Lisboa

Dispelling the myth that there were no card-makers active in Basel during the nineteenth century

53 BOURCARD, Joseph

Cartes à jouer fines.

Publication
[Basel, Joseph Bourcard, c1835].

Description
32 engraved cards with fine original hand-colour, blue and black dotted pattern to verso.

Dimensions
90 by 60mm (3.5 by 2.25 inches).

References
Guiard 226; van den Bergh p.64.

The Maker
Originally issued in a wrapper with the imprint, 'Cartes à jouer fines de Joseph Bourcard à Basle en Suisse' ('Fine playing cards by Joseph Bourcard in Basle, Switzerland'). This dispelled the widespread misconception that there were no card-makers active in Basel during the nineteenth century, and by coincidence, two decks by Joseph Bourcard were discovered in quick succession during the twentieth century. Guiard lists the maker's name as Joseph Burckhardt.

The Cards
In keeping with the format generally used for souvenir playing cards, the Aces display two scenic views of Swiss towns or landscapes, with the suit mark in the central circle:

Club – Porte de St Paul à Bale/Pierre pertuis
Diamond – La chûte du Rhin pres Schaffhausen/Pont de Lauffenbourg
Heart – Tellen Platte/Chapelle de Guillaume Tell à Burglen
Spade – Chateau de Zwingen Rigi Kulm

The double-figure court cards show different styles of native Swiss dress, with the suit mark found in the upper left and lower right corners.

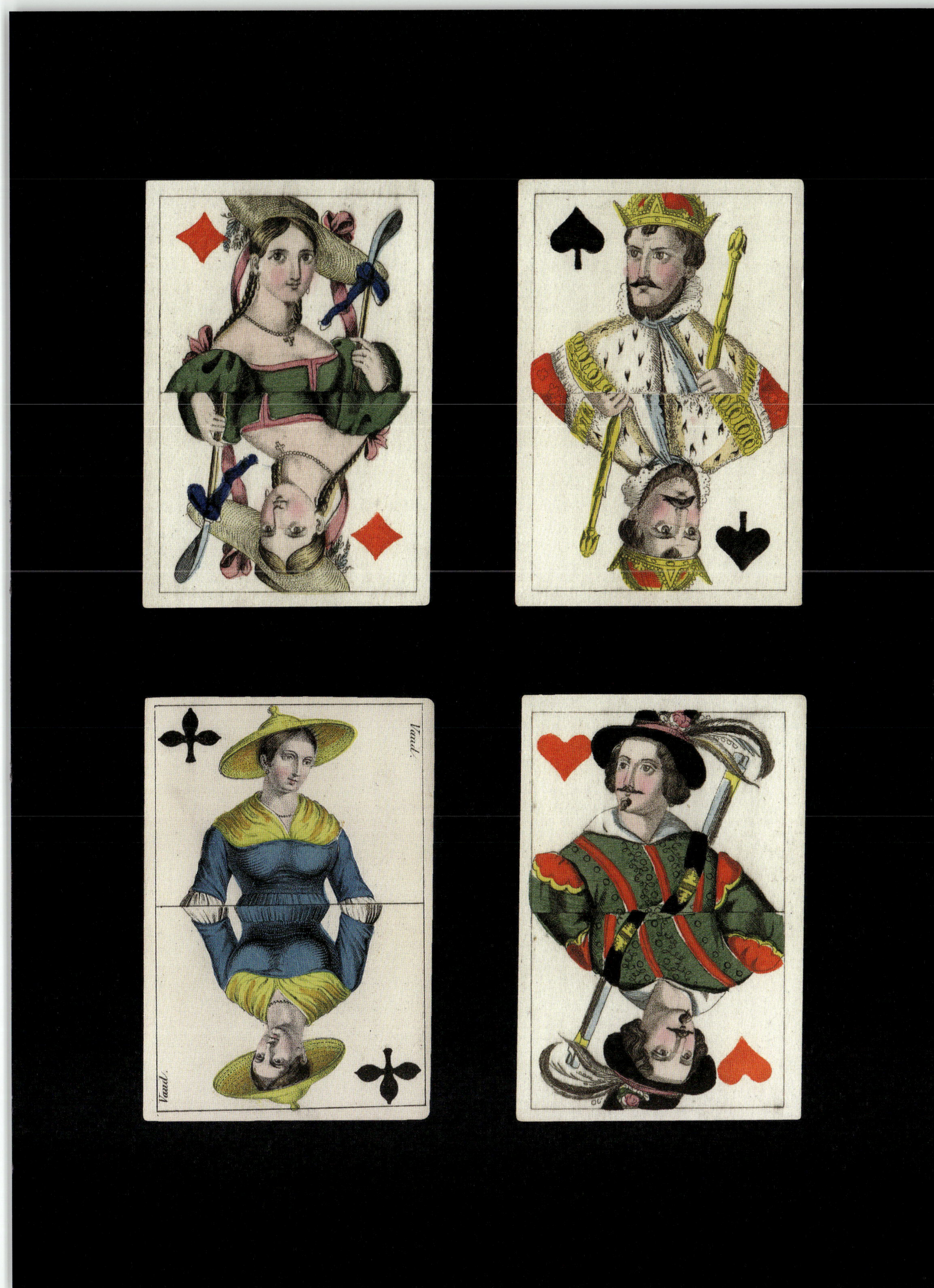
Vaud.
Vaud.

Fiendishly rare

54 **NANTEUIL, Célestin**

[Hellish playing cards].

Publication
Paris, Montoux, 1838.

Description
32 lithograph playing cards with fine original hand-colour, orange and blue floral pattern to versos.

Dimensions
83 by 54mm (3.25 by 2.25 inches).

References
BnF FRBNF40918551; Van den Bergh pp.260-261, Yale 2683/FRA383.

The Maker

Designed by French painter, engraver and illustrator Célestin Nanteuil (1813-1873), who studied under the legendary artist Dominique Ingres, and later became Director of Académie des Beaux-arts. His work embodies the French Romantic movement.

This is the only deck of cards designed by Nanteuil; their publication is attributed to a firm named Montoux. We have been unable to trace any further evidence of this manufacturer, and only the present deck is thought to have been made by them.

The Cards

The present deck of cards is extraordinary in a number of ways. Each suit has its own theme, with clubs dedicated to trade and justice, diamonds to soldiers, hearts to women and, notably, spades to the devil.

The court cards show full-length figures in keeping with these themes, the most striking being the King of Spades, which depicts the devil, complete with horns, hoofs and wings. The Queen of Spades is masked and dressed in black, while the Jack has ominously pointed ears and feline facial features. The rest of the court cards present more familiar royal characters, dressed in rich robes in bold colours.

The Ace cards show a cameo portrait within a cartouche of flames or leaves. The value of the pip cards are not given as numbers, nor do they correspond to the amount of suit marks shown; instead they are indicated by the number of different portraits present on each card.

Extremely rare. Most copies of this deck of 32 cards are incomplete, including the copy in the Yale collection and the Bibliothèque national de France. Two copies are known to be privately owned, the deck that is shown here and a copy in the collection Verame. In 2011, a complete deck was offered for sale but the exact whereabouts of the deck is not known.

Time to change the rules of the game

55 **HODGES, Charles**

[Court game of Geography].

Publication
London, Willian & Henry Rock, 1839.

Description
52 engraved playing cards, suits in hand-colour, with booklet, contained within black morocco slipcase.

Dimensions
95 by 64mm (3.75 by 2.5 inches).

References
Met 59.654.16(30); van den Bergh pp.84-85.

The Makers
William Frederick Rock (1801-1890) was a British publisher who ran a successful firm with his brother Henry, specialising in topographical prints, maps, luxurious stationery and playing cards. Having come from a humble background, William Rock used his wealth and influence as a self-made business man to fund a number of philanthropic ventures in his hometown of Barnstaple. For a description of Charles Hodges, see item 44.

The Cards
After Charles Hodges stopped publishing in 1830, his plates appear to have been acquired by the Rock brothers, as they later published a new edition of his geographical playing cards.

Under the new title of 'Court Game of Geography', the deck showed the same design but was not nearly as luxurious as the original edition, being neither fully coloured nor embellished with gold. It did, however, come with an additional booklet, which contained a set of rules for a new game invented by the publishers.

EUROPE
Spitzbergen
Iceland
Nova Zembla
NORWAY
White Sea
Archangel
BRITISH ISLES
Dublin
London
DENMK
St. Petersburgh
RUSSIA
Moscow
Smolensk
Paris
FRANCE
Berlin
Warsaw
Kiev
Vienna
AUSTRIAN STATES
Lyons
SPAIN
Madrid
Naples
TURKEY
BLACK SEA
Constantinople
AFRICA
ASIA

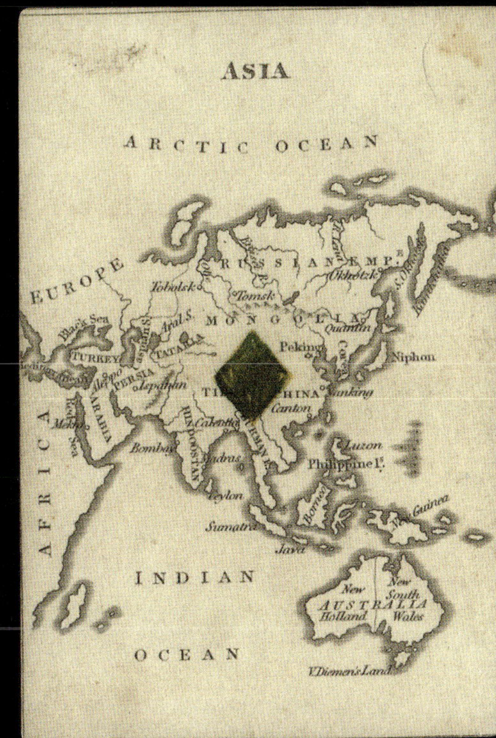
ASIA
ARCTIC OCEAN
EUROPE
RUSSIAN EMP.
Tobolsk
Tomsk
MONGOLIA
Peking
Niphon
PERSIA
ARABIA
CHINA
Nanking
Canton
Calcutta
Bombay
Luzon
Philippine I.
Ceylon
Sumatra
Java
AFRICA
INDIAN OCEAN
New Holland
AUSTRALIA
New South Wales
V.Diemen's Land

AFRICA
EUROPE
ASIA
Gibraltar
Algier
Fez
Morocco
BARBARY
Canary I.
Gr. Cairo
EGYPT
NUBIA
Dongola
SAHARA
Tombuctoo
C.Blanco
S.Louis
C.Verd
Bornou
C.Palmas
Cape Coast
Benin
Guinea
Loango
ARABIA
Socatra
NIMEAMAY
Mozambique
Mahé I.
St. Helena
C.Negro
Madagascar
Bourbon
Caffraria
Cape Town
C. of Good Hope
INDIAN OCEAN
SOUTHERN OCEAN

AMERICA
ASIA
Iceland
Aleutian Archip.
BRITISH AMERICA
Newfoundland
UNITED STATES
Washington
Sandwich I.
Owhyhee
Cuba
Caribbee Isles
PACIFIC OCEAN
Cayenne
PERU
Pernambuco
BRAZIL
Bahia
Rio Janeiro
Buenos Ayres
Georgian Isl.
Friendly I.
Taite
New Zealand
Falkland I.
Terra del Fuego
South Shetland
S.Georgia
ATLANTIC OCEAN

Love among the flowers

56 [ANONYMOUS]

[Valentine playing cards].

Publication
[Germany, c1840].

Description
52 engraved playing cards with fine original hand-colour, printed purple pattern to verso.

Dimensions
88 by 62mm (3.5 by 2.5 inches).

References
Van den Bergh p.252.

The Maker
Nothing is known for certain about the maker or origins of the present deck, although the cards appear to be from Germany.

The Cards
Overflowing with Romantic imagery, in a style reminiscent of the trends of the 1840s, each Ace card shows a single suit mark wreathed with an elaborate frame of either clouds or flowers. Atop the clouds sits a naked putti, while the flowers are surmounted by a letter-bearing dove. Symbols of harmony and idyllic romanticism are found below, such as a cornucopia or a handshake. The background pattern on each Ace is designed to reflect its respective suit, and all cards are cornered with a delicate design.

The double-figure court cards present the royal characters in traditional poses, with the suit marks shown in the upper left and lower right corners. It is noticeable that, in contrast to the Kings and Jacks, all the Queens are set against a horticultural background.

Do-mino, Ré-chaud, Mi-mi, Fa-got, Sol-dat, La-pin and Si-flet

57 BOBOEUF, Pierre Alexis Francis

Cartes Musical.

Publication
[Paris, Bobœuf, c1840].

Description
32 chromolithograph playing cards with fine original hand-colour, versos white.

Dimensions
84 by 58mm (3.25 by 2.25 inches).

References
Van den Bergh p.220; Yale 2553/FRA253.

The Maker

The Parisian card-maker Pierre Alexis Francis Bobœuf operated from No. 23 Rue Cadet during the 1840s. Three strikingly ornate decks are attributed to him from this time, dedicated to the educational themes of music, mathematics and the alphabet. His imprint appears at the bottom of several of the cards in this deck.

The Cards

Representing a creative approach to musical education, with the Seven of Clubs reading:

"Jeu de CARTES MUSICAL approuvé par M. H. BERTON membre de l'institut Profes de hauts Composition au conservatoire, pour apprendre la Musique aux Enfants en Jouant à la BATAILLE"

("Game of MUSICAL CARDS approved by Mr. H.BERTON, member of the professional institute of composition at the Conservatoire, to teach music to children through a playing a CONTEST").

Each of the court cards explains a different note from the octave, captioned with the words: Do-mino, Ré-chaud, Mi-mi, Fa-got, Sol-dat, La-pin and Si-flet. The pip and Ace cards then show three small staves with one or two notes on each; by combining these, the user could produce melodies of various degrees of difficulty.

At the top of each card, a miniature version of the playing card is shown, so that they could still be used as a functional playing deck. In addition to being helpful educational tools, the present cards are also intricately designed, with whimsical floral motifs and other elaborate patterns adorning each one.

Do.
Do-do
1° La Musique s'écrit sur cinq lignes horizontales &
dont la réunion s'appelle portée
2° La première ligne commence en bas
Les caractères que l'on met dessus ou entre les lignes
servent à représenter des sons et s'appellent Notes
Il y a sept notes: Do ou Ut, Ré, Mi, Fa, Sol, La, Si,
la 8me n'est que la répétition de la 1re

Ré.
Ré-chaud
1° La Musique s'écrit sur cinq lignes horizontales &
dont la réunion s'appelle portée
2° La première ligne commence en bas
Les caractères que l'on met dessus ou entre les lignes
servent à représenter des sons et s'appellent Notes
Il y a sept notes: Do ou Ut, Ré, Mi, Fa, Sol, La, Si,
la 8me n'est que la répétition de la 1re

La.
La-pin
1° La Musique s'écrit sur cinq lignes horizontales &
dont la réunion s'appelle portée
2° La première ligne commence en bas
Les caractères que l'on met dessus ou entre les lignes
servent à représenter des sons et s'appellent Notes
Il y a sept notes: Do ou Ut, Ré, Mi, Fa, Sol, La, Si,
la 8me n'est que la répétition de la 1re

Fa.
Fa-got
1° La Musique s'écrit sur cinq lignes horizontales &
dont la réunion s'appelle portée
2° La première ligne commence en bas
Les caractères que l'on met dessus ou entre les lignes
servent à représenter des sons et s'appellent Notes
Il y a sept notes: Do ou Ut, Ré, Mi, Fa, Sol, La, Si,
la 8me n'est que la répétition de la 1re

Look ahead

58 BOHME, F. A.

[Luxury playing cards].

Publication
[Dresden, F.A. Böhme, c1840].

Description
52 engraved playing cards with fine original hand colour, stamp to one, red floral pattern to versos.

Dimensions
89 by 56mm (3.5 by 2.25 inches).

References
Van den Bergh p.246, Yale 2901/GER499.

The Maker
The name of the maker, "F A Böhme in Dresden", is printed on the Jack of Spades. Friedrich August Böhme, born in 1772, took over his father's card factory in Dresden in 1798, and published playing cards and postcards. The making of playing cards continued as the family business when his son, Friedrich Albert Böhme, took over his father's production responsibilities in 1856.

The Cards
Following a standard design from the mid-nineteenth century, this deck contains double-figure court cards with their suit marks in the upper left and lower right corners. It is interesting that some of the figures, namely the King and Queen of Clubs and Jack of Spades, are looking directly out of the image, rather than in the more common three-quarter pose that characterises the others.

The pip and Ace cards convey their value by the number of suit marks shown on each card in its respective colour.

F. A. Böhme
in Dresden.

With the elusive Ace of Diamonds

59 **STEINBERGER, Johann Anton**

[Romantic playing cards].

Publication
[Frankfurt, Johann Anton Steinberger, c1840].

Description
52 engraved playing cards with fine original hand-colour, blue dot pattern to versos.

Dimensions
56 by 38mm (2.25 by 1.5 inches).

References
Van den Bergh pp.228-229; Yale 2985/GER582.

The Maker
The shield of the Jack of Diamonds bears the name of the maker: "Fabriqué par Jean Antoine Steinberger à Frankfort a/M". For a description of Steinberger, see item 39.

The Cards
A remarkable deck, for the fact that, for once, it is the pip cards that are the centre of attention. The court cards show a series of fairly traditional full-length royal characters, while the pip and Ace cards depict romantic and lightly erotic scenes.

On the Ace of Diamonds is the mythological story of Leda and the swan, in which the supreme god Zeus turns himself into a swan in order to sleep with the beautiful Leda. One of the children begotten by this union was Helen, whose face would famously launch a thousand ships. The story of Leda and the swan resurfaces in many works by artists, including Michelangelo and Leonardo da Vinci.

With still only 51 cards, the current deck was acquired from the Kenter collection; Kenter had spent more than 20 years looking for the missing Ace of Diamonds. Only two months after the sale, the missing card was found by chance and the deck was completed. There are, most likely, only two complete copies in private ownership (van den Bergh).

Willem Tell's tale

60 **WÜST, Conrad Ludwig**

[William Tell playing cards].

Publication
[Frankfurt, C.L. Wüst, c1840].

Description
32 engraved playing cards with fine original hand-colour, blue line and dot pattern and later ink stamp to versos.

Dimensions
90 by 61mm (3.5 by 2.5 inches).

References
Van den Bergh pp.210-211.

The Maker
For a description of Conrad Ludwig Wüst, please see item 41.

The Cards
Telling the tale of William Tell through boldly coloured illustrations, two scenes appear on each Ace, with the suit mark shown in the centre of this deck. Dating back to the early fourteenth century, the story of Tell tells of how the hero assassinated an evil tyrant using his crossbow. Tell became a symbol of restoration and resistance, re-emerging during the 1848 revolutions against the House of Habsburg. The double-figure court cards show elaborately dressed royal characters, although the Queen of Diamonds seems to be suffering from something of a fashion faux pas.

Provenance:
1. The verso of each card bears the oval ink-stamp of the "Schreiber Collection". Lady Charlotte Schreiber (1812 – 1895) amassed great collections of porcelain, fans and playing cards, which she donated to the British Museum upon her death. The "BM" initials are found in the centre of the stamp, and below them the year "1895".
2. The private collection of Sylvia Mann. Mann was a founding member and the first president of the International Playing-Card Society; she published several books and catalogues on playing cards, and is considered an authority on the subject.

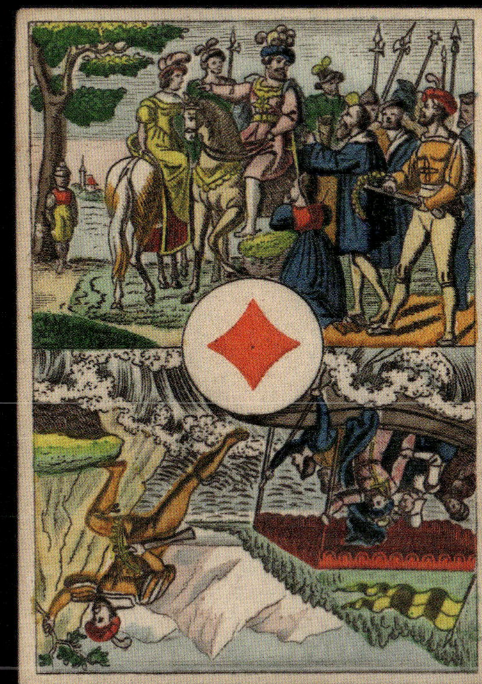

DAME

ROI

A straight run: from Lombards to Holy Roman Emperors

61 GUMPPENBERG, Ferdinando

[History of the German-Italian kings playing cards].

Publication
Milan, Gumppenberg, 1843.

Description
52 engraved playing cards, court cards in full colour, stamp to one, blue printed pattern to versos.

Dimensions
91 by 54mm (3.5 by 2.25 inches).

References
Van den Bergh pp.118-119.

The Maker

The imprint "Fabbrica Gumppenberg Milano invento" is found on the shield of the Jack of Diamonds. Ferdinand Gumppenberg was a German card designer and manufacturer who moved to Milan in 1809, where he set up a small factory. Introducing technical innovations from his native country, his cards soon became highly successful and were copied by a number of other manufacturers.

The Cards

The leaders of two of the most important early European powers, Lombardy and the Holy Roman Empire, are celebrated in the present deck. The double-figure court cards show the portraits of the historically significant Kings and Queens, and depict images of contemporary soldiers on the Jack cards:

Clubs – Charles V, Eleonora, soldier with gun
Diamonds – Louis the Bavarian, Margherita, soldier with dagger
Hearts – Agilulf, Teodolinda, soldier with axe
Spades – Charlemagne, Emengarda, soldier with sword

The reigns of these historical figures span from the sixth to the sixteenth century, from the Lombards, a Bavarian tribe who ruled Italy from the sixth to the eighth centuries, to the Holy Roman Emperors, joint kings of Italy and Germany from the eighth to the eighteenth centuries. The value of the remaining cards is simply indicated by the number of suit marks shown on each card.

The Kings' rules

62 DAVELUY, Édouard Alexis

[Flemish playing cards].

Publication
[Bruges, Daveluy, c1847].

Description
52 chromolithographic playing cards, blue printed pattern to versos.

Dimensions
88 by 59mm (3.5 by 2.25 inches).

References
Van den Bergh p.276.

The Makers

The imprint on the King of Hearts reads "Daveluy Bruges Déposé". Daveluy was a playing card maker active in Bruges between 1840 and 1890. Many of his decks show a distinctive fantastical style reminiscent of medieval cards, but improved with modern chromolithographic technology, which set him apart from his contemporaries. He exhibited in Paris at the Universal Exhibitions of 1855, 1867 and 1878, before passing the business on to his eldest son.

The Cards

Depicting famous kings from across history was a particular penchant of Daveluy's, and several of the leaders shown in this deck also appear on the cards of other decks he published.

The Kings are represented by the double-figure images of Charles V, Charlemagne, Richard Lionheart and Pepin the Short, each one identified by name in French. Remarkably, the anonymous Queens are shown sitting, with various accessories from flowers to birds. Each Jack has a different shield emblazoned on his chest, showing the coats-of-arms of various Belgian regions. The upper Jack of Spades, for instance, bears the Flemish crest, while his lower reflection wears that of West-Flanders.

The Ace cards are ornately presented, with the central suit mark surrounded by a decorative and brightly coloured floral wreath.

CHARLES QUINT.
DAVELUY, BRUGES
Déposé
CHARLES QUINT.

One of the earliest printers to use chromolithograph

63 LANGE, Victor

[Celestial playing cards].

Publication
[Paris, Victor Lange and Victor Arouy, 1848].

Description
32 chromolithograph playing cards, pink versos.

Dimensions
82 by 55mm (3.25 by 2.25 inches).

References
Van den Bergh p.67; cf. Verame p.76.

The Maker
Victor Lange, whose firm was located at 67, Rue St. Honoré in Paris, was one of the earliest printers to use chromolithograph to produce playing cards. Victor Arouy, who operated from the same address as Lange, was responsible for the design of the present deck, and both Lange and Arouy's names are found at the base of the Jack and Ace of Clubs.

The Cards
This celestial deck of cards focuses on the stories and creatures of classical mythology which star in the constellations of western astrology. Each one is intricately illustrated and identified with French text. On the Ace cards, two small vignettes show scenes from various myths, such as the voyage of the Argo. The court cards show full-length figures of classical gods and goddesses, with the suit marks in the upper left-hand corner:

Clubs – Neptune
Diamonds – Mars
Hearts – Jupiter
Spades – Pluto

On the pip cards there are two small cartouches containing images of various mythological creatures, including centaurs and satyrs, which also appear in the heavens. The value of each card is indicated by the corresponding number of suit marks.

LÉDA.
VULCAIN.

CENTAURE
SATYRES

CERBÈRE
CHIMÈRE

Guerre de Troie.
ARGO, Vaisseau ayant pour mât un Chêne, prédisant l'avenir.

Pink backs from the Veuve Sonet-Morin

64 SONET-MORIN, Veuve

[Landmarks of Paris playing cards].

Publication
[Paris, Veuve Sonet-Morin, c1849-1856].

Description
52 engraved playing cards with fine original hand-colour, versos pink.

Dimensions
87 by 57mm (3.5 by 2.25 inches).

References
Guiard 158; van den Bergh p.66.

The Maker

The maker of the present deck, known only as the widow Sonet-Morin, had a small card factory in a passage connecting Rue Genetat and Rue Saint-Denis in Paris. It is not clear whether she took over this workshop after the death of her husband or established it independently, since there is no evidence of any publications by Monsieur Sonet-Morin. In addition to this deck, the widow Sonet-Morin appears to have produced cards with a variety of themes, including fashion and history. Many of her cards are characterised by their distinctive pink backs, suggesting that they were designed for the parlours of Paris' most genteel ladies.

The Cards

A true celebration of Paris, which was the epicentre of Napoleon III's empire at the time. The Second French Empire spanned the 1850s and 1860s, and during this period the population of Paris doubled in size, with its cultural, industrial and commercial output increasing proportionately. Each of the Ace cards proudly displays two of the city's most iconic, famous or beautiful views, and several feature a fluttering tricolore:

Clubs – Palais Royal Palais du Luxembourg
Diamonds – Château de Versailles Cascade de St Cloud
Hearts – Château des Tuileries Place de la Concorde
Spades – Hôtel des Invalides Pont des Arts

The double-figure court cards show the royal characters sumptuously dressed in furs and capes. The suit marks appear in the upper left- and lower-hand right corners, and in the centre of the Aces.

The widow Sonet-Morin, whose name appears on the Jack of Clubs, was active in Paris between 1849 and 1856, allowing the present deck to be dated within this seven year period.

Château des Tuileries.
Place de la Concorde

Vve SONET-MORIN, à Paris.
Vve SONET-MORIN, à Paris.

Palais du Luxembourg.
Palais Royal

Colour me blue… or pink

65 **[?WÜST, Conrad Ludwig]**

[Luxury playing cards].

Publication
[?Frankfurt, C.L. Wüst, c1850].

Description
52 engraved playing cards with fine original hand-colour, with gilt edges, plain white versos.

Dimensions
87 by 55mm (3.5 by 2.25 inches).

References
Van den Bergh p.269.

The Maker
The origins of the present deck of playing cards are not known for certain. Based on the court figures, some have attributed them to Reuter in Darmstadt, but Sylvia Mann has confidently attributed a very similar deck to Wüst. For a description of Conrad Ludwig Wüst, please see item 41.

The Cards
The most impressive feature of these cards is undoubtedly the fine, fresh colours used to embellish the court cards. The double-figure images show characters not only reversed in perspective but also in colours, with the upper Queen of Spades wearing a blue gown, and her lower reflection wearing a pink one. As usual, the suit marks are shown in the upper left and lower right corners of each court card.

The gilt edging and bright colours make the present deck particularly distinctive.

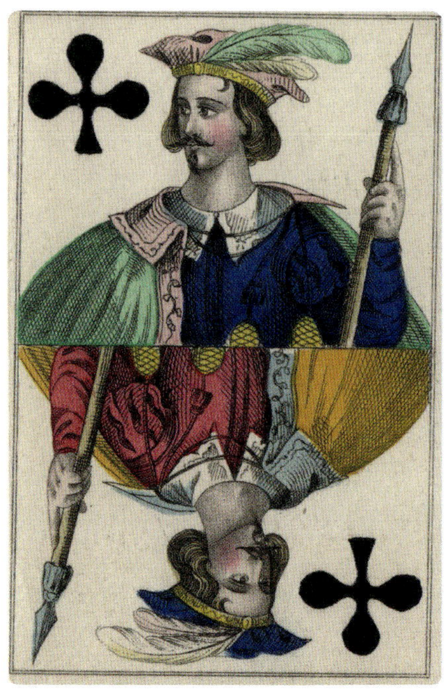

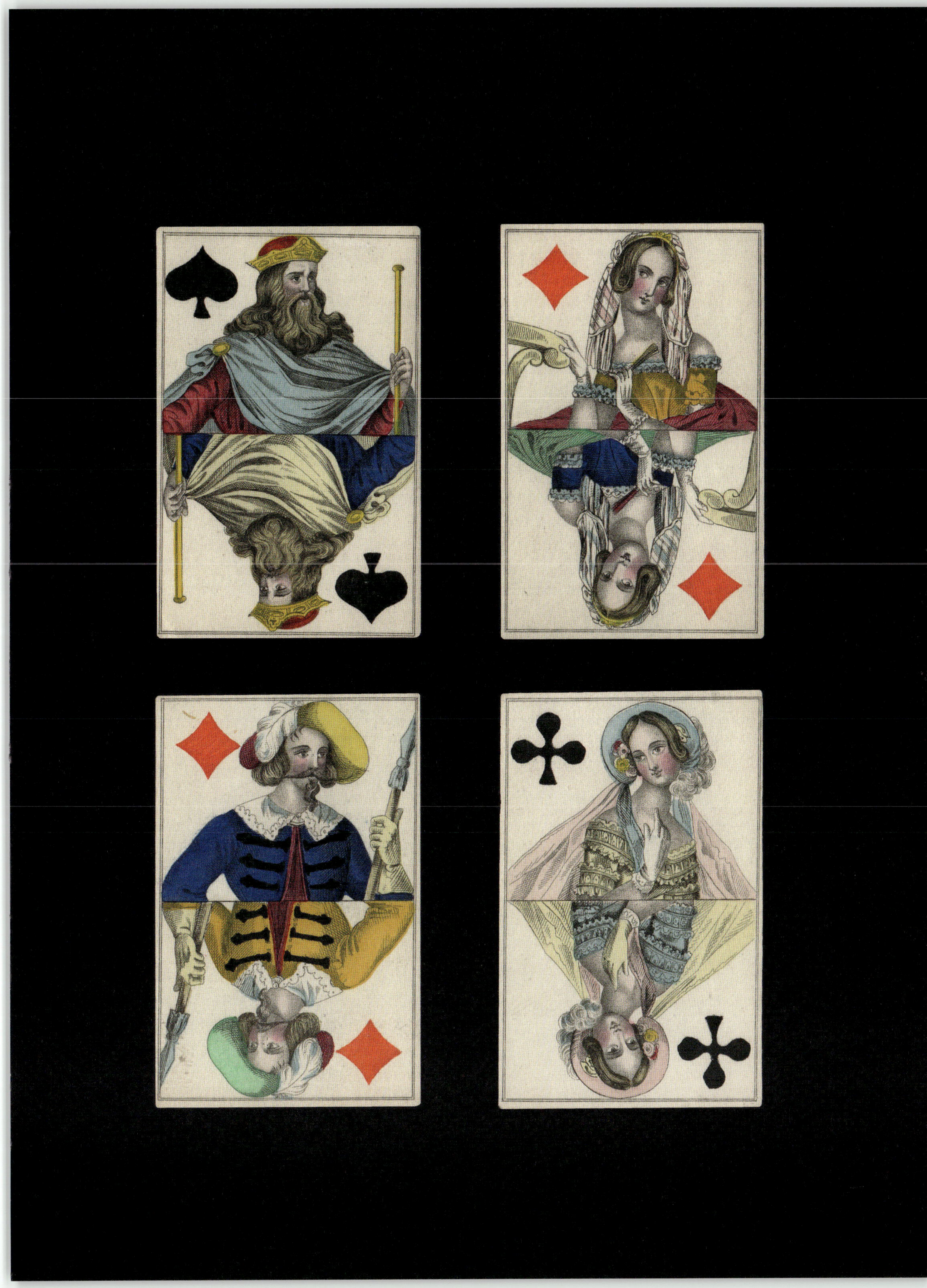

The thrill of the chase

66 [STEINBERGER, Johann Anton] [attributed to].

[Hunting playing cards].

Publication
[Frankfurt, Johann Anton Steinberger, c1850].

Description
32 engraved playing cards with fine original hand-colour, blue printed pattern to versos.

Dimensions
89 by 61mm (3.5 by 2.5 inches).

References
Van den Bergh pp.250-251.

The Maker

The deck is a classic example of a deck of cards that has yet to be attributed to a certain source. J.A. Steinberger and C.L.Wüst are often mentioned as the possible maker, but also J.C. Jegel and even G.H. Dieudonné from Grevenmacher in Luxembourg. The latter seems unlikely, considering the beautiful quality and images of the cards. Usually, cards by Dieudonné are of lesser quality than those of his German colleagues.

Overall, Steinberger seems the most likely candidate, due to the quality and style of the cards. For a description of Steinberger, please see item 39.

The Cards

The hunt is the central theme of this deck of cards. Each Ace shows two hunting scenes, generally consisting of a group of nobles on horseback chasing a deer, fox or hares. The court cards fall into an interesting position: the Kings, Queens and Jacks are carrying all the accoutrements of the hunt, such as a rifle, horn and arrow, but they do not appear to be dressed in hunting clothes, instead maintaining their traditional court finery.

William Tell aces the apple test; while Dürer deals with Maximilian

67 POMMER, Georg

[Deutsche Gesichtskarte].

Publication
Nuremberg, Johann Conrad Jegel, 1850.

Description
36 engraved playing cards with fine original hand-colour, contemporary stamp to one, red cross and dot pattern to versos.

Dimensions
103 by 62mm (4 by 2.5 inches).

References
Guiard 5; van den Bergh p.95; Yale 2814/GER411.

The Makers

As stated on the Knave of Leaves and Eight of Bells, the present deck was designed and engraved by Georg Pommer, and published by Johann Conrad Jegel. Jegel established his firm in Nuremberg in the early nineteenth century, and which his widow continued to run after his death. In 1857, it was taken over by Johann Wilhelm Sass, who continued to produce playing cards.

The Cards

German history is celebrated on the present deck, with its depiction of iconic national characters and events. The 36 cards form a standard German deck, with the suits represented as Acorns, Bells, Hearts and Leaves. The three major German rivers of the Weser, Rhine and Donau appear on the Ace of Bells, Hearts and Leaves respectively, while a female figure on the Ace of Acorns personifies Germania herself.

The court cards show German figures from history and folklore, such as the legendary Wilhelm Tell as the Knave of Bells. (see item 60). Each pip card also depicts a significant historical event, such as Empress Maria Theresa rousing the Hungarian troops to fight for her against Prussia, the Battle of Leipzig and Albrecht Dürer meeting with Maximilian I.

1176. Friedrich Rothbart vor Papst Alexander III.
in Mailand.

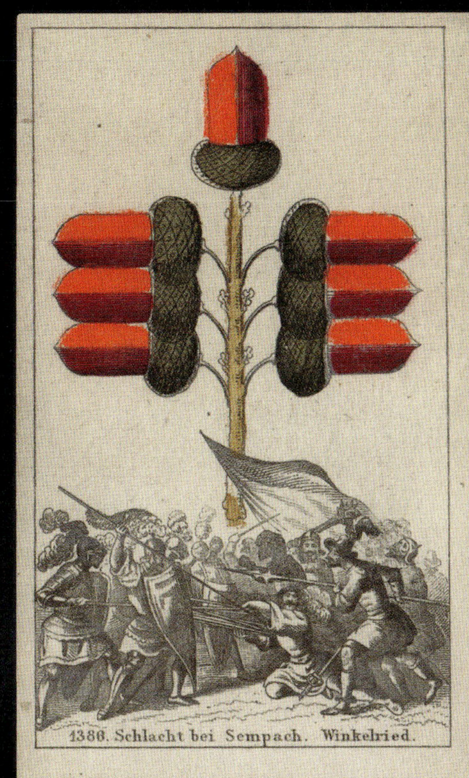
1386. Schlacht bei Sempach. Winkelried.

Off with his head!

68 **TELLIER, E. Le**

Jeanne l'Hachette.

Publication
Paris, B. P. Grimaud et Cie., c1850.

Description
52 chromolithograph playing cards, versos plain.

Dimensions
104 by 70mm (4 by 2.75 inches).

References
Guiard 220, 221; van den Bergh pp.156-157.

The Maker
Text on the King of Hearts gives the name of the artist as 'E. Le Tellier', and the lithographer as 'Belin', but we have been unable to trace any other evidence of these two artists. The cards were published by the Grimaud firm, as written on the Jack of Hearts. For a description of Baptiste-Paul Grimaud, please see item 50.

The Cards
Published under the title 'Jeanne l'Hachette', the present deck of cards is loosely centred around the siege of Beauvais, which occurred in 1472. The daughter of a peasant, nicknamed after her weapon of choice, Jeanne l' Hachette defended her city from the troops of Charles the Bold, Duke of Burgundy. Jeanne herself is shown on the Queen of Spades, axe in hand. The other court cards show a range of single-figure characters, some from the story and some quite unrelated.

The pip cards are examples of the transformation style that was growing in popularity during the nineteenth century. They are more simplistic than earlier examples, with the suit marks incorporated into the image while still retaining their characteristic shapes. The light-hearted illustrations, which often include a dose of humor, show a stark contrast with the more stiff and formal German cards of the time.

Grrrand
SPECTACLE

The game's afoot...

69 WÜST, Conrad Ludwig

[Hunting playing cards].

Publication
[Frankfurt, C.L. Wüst, c1850].

Description
32 engraved playing cards with fine original hand-colour, blue printed pattern to versos.

Dimensions
87 by 60mm (3.5 by 2.25 inches).

References
Van den Bergh pp.248-249.

The Maker
For a description of Conrad Ludwig Wüst, please see item 41.

The Cards
Centred around the hunt, each Ace shows two scenes depicting various types of hunting, such as bird shooting on the Ace of Clubs and deer hunting on the Ace of Spades and Hearts. The only form of hunting that was not practiced by nobles is whaling, which is portrayed on the lower half of the Ace of Clubs.

The court cards also revolve around this theme, with the double-figure Kings, Queens and Jacks pictured with all the accoutrements of the hunt, such as bow and arrow, a fishing rod, a spear and a hunting horn.

Dressed for dinner

70 **GILBERT, O.**

Cartes Parisiennes.

Publication
[Paris, O. Gilbert, c1853].

Description
52 engraved playing cards with fine original hand-colour, pink versos.

Dimensions
86 by 56mm (3.5 by 2.25 inches).

References
Van den Bergh pp.244-245.

The Maker
The name of the maker is printed on the Jack of Diamonds, 'Gilbert à Paris'. Parisian card-maker O. Gilbert, whose company was located on the Rue des Signes 3, became known for the production of cards with characters in beautiful costumes.

The Cards
This is Gilbert's second "costume deck", with full-length figures of French nobles in an array of fine costumes shown on the court cards. While the Queen of Diamonds wears an immense Rococo gown, the Queen of Spades appears to be dressed fit for a medieval banquet. On the Kings and Queens, the name of the noble is mentioned at the bottom of the card, while the Jacks are presented as nicely-dressed esquires.

Clubs – Cinq-mars, Marion Delorme
Diamonds – Chev-er D'Eon, C-tesse de Rochefort
Hearts – Bussy D'Amboise, Dame de Monsoreau
Spades – C-te de Brissac, Diane de Poitiers

The pip cards are presented simply with the number of suit marks shown corresponding to the value of each card. The Aces also have their single pip at the centre, but it is enclosed within decorative framework.

DIANE DE POITIERS.

C^TESSE DE ROCHEFORT.

CINQ-MARS.

"Aurea Libertas": the endgame of the Eighty Years War

71 LENSSEN, Gustav

Nationale Speelkaarten.

Publication
[Netherlands, Gustav Lenssen, c1855].

Description
52 engraved playing cards with fine original hand-colour, blue printed pattern to verso.

Dimensions
95 by 65mm (3.75 by 2.5 inches).

References
Van den Bergh p59; for similar see British Museum Schreiber Sheets Dutch 4.

The Maker
Gustav Lenssen (fl 1838-1859) was a card-maker who allegedly ran a playing card 'factory' based in Maastricht, although there is only one scarce deck attributed to him today. Advertisements in Dutch newspapers from 1838 give Lenssen's first name as 'Gusaaf', but he appears to have used the French equivalent on the majority of his publications. His son Oscar followed in his footsteps, founding a separate card company in 1860 with a factory in Zevenaar and sales offices in Dusseldorf. Oscar Lenssen & Co. eventually took over Gustav's business.

The Cards
Celebrating the history and architecture of the Netherlands, two Dutch cities are depicted on each of the Ace cards, with the suit mark in the centre:

Clubs – Amsterdam and Zaandam
Diamonds – Rotterdam and Dordrecht
Hearts – Leeuwarden and Middelburg
Spades – Scheveningen and The Hague

The court cards present portraits in the double-figure format that had become popular during the early nineteenth century. The Queens and Jacks wear regional clothing and are labelled with their respective place of origin, while the King cards show important figures from the Eighty Years War, namely:

Clubs – Prince Frederik Henrik
Diamonds – Prince Willem I
Hearts – Prince Maurits
Spades – Prince Willem III

A banner of the King of Diamonds reads 'Aurea Libertas' ('Golden Liberty'). The same motto is found on the tomb of William I and refers to a political system in which the king was elected by the nobles. William I was the Stadtholder of Friesland who led the Dutch Revolt against the Spanish Empire in 1568, resulting in the independence of the United Provinces 80 years later. Prince Maurits was his son, who became Stadtholder after his father, followed by his half-brother Frederik Henrik in 1625. Prince Willem III inherited the Stadthold in 1672, and was later crowned King William III of England, Scotland and Ireland.

Zuid Holland.
Zuid Holland.
AMSTERDAM.
ZAANDAM.
ROTTERDAM.
DORDRECHT.
Prins Willem III.
Prins Willem III.

From Austria's ace producer of games

72 PIATNIK, Ferdinand

[European city playing cards].

Publication
[Vienna, Ferdinand Piatnik vormals Anton Moser, c1855].

Description
52 engraved playing cards with fine original hand-colour.

Dimensions
83 by 54mm (3.25 by 2.25 inches).

References
Van den Bergh p.68.

The Maker
Born in Hungary, Ferdinand Piatnik bought the card company of Anton Moser in 1843, transforming it into one of the most successful manufacturers in the world. Between 1843 and 1882, the firm operated under the name 'Ferdinand Piatnik vormals ['formerly'] Anton Moser', and from 1882 onwards became 'Ferdinand Piatnik & Söhne'. The company continues today as Austria's largest producer of games.

The Cards
The present deck of cards celebrates the cities of central Europe, one of which is shown on each Ace card:

Clubs – Budapest
Diamonds – Prague
Hearts – Vienna
Spades – Milan

The two vignettes on the Ace of Clubs are labelled 'Pest' and 'Ofen', the latter being the German name for Buda, where Piatnik himself was born. The lower image shows the chain bridge constructed in the city in 1849, providing an *ante post quem* for the deck.

The double-figure court cards show the royal characters sumptuously dressed, with the suit marks in the upper left- and lower right-hand corners.

PEST
PRAG

A souvenir of the World Expo 1855

73 THOMAS, A.

[Exposition Universelle playing cards].

Publication
[France, c1855].

Description
52 engraved cards with fine original hand-colour, pink verso.

Dimensions
89 by 57mm (3.5 by 2.25 inches).

References
Van den Bergh p.70.

The Maker
The imprint 'A. Thomas Ft. Paris Déposé' is found on the Jack of Clubs, but we have been unable to trace any further evidence of a card-maker operating in the city under this name during the nineteenth century.

The Cards
A souvenir of the Exposition Universelle of 1855, an international exhibition held on Paris' iconic Champs-Élysées. Emperor Napoleon III was determined to secure the city's position as the cultural capital of Europe by hosting an exhibition that would surpass that held at London's Crystal Palace four years earlier. Each Ace bears two images of Paris' most and iconic buildings, specifically:

Clubs – Colonne Vendôme & Arc de Triomphe
Diamonds – Hotel de Ville & Chateau de Versailles
Hearts – Place de la Concorde & Palais de l'Industrie
Spades – Palais du Louvre & Palais des Tuileries

As part of the preparation, the emperor had commissioned the construction of the Palais de l'Industrie, an immense structure almost 300 metres in length and over 100 in width. Despite its vast scale, the building was still not large enough to house the thousands of exhibitors at the show. 43 years later, the Palais de l'Industrie was demolished and replaced by the Grand Palais, which would go on to become the central building at the Exposition Universelle of 1900.

The double-figure court cards shown the sumptuously dressed royal characters, with the suit marks in the upper left- and lower right-hand corners.

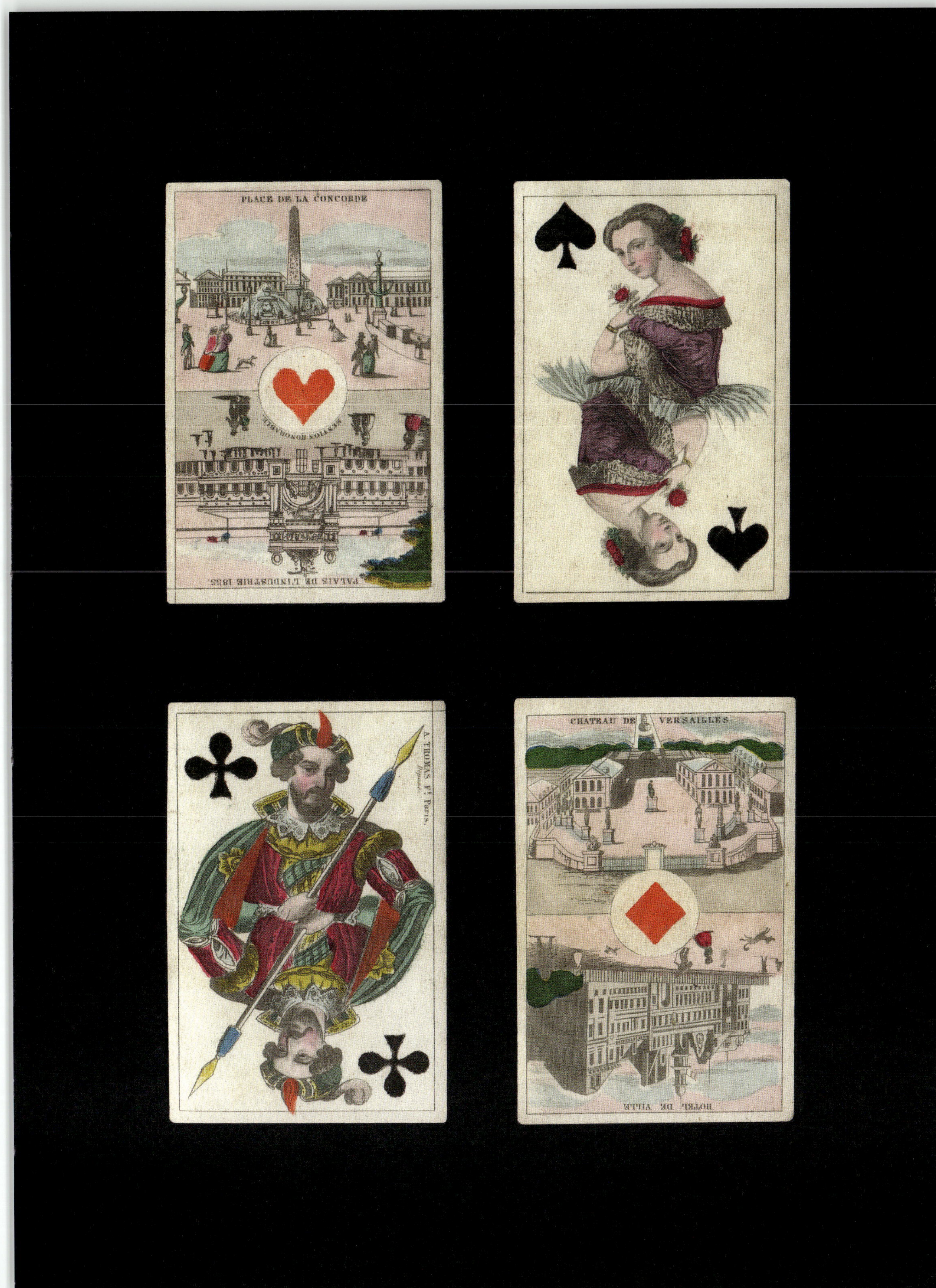
PLACE DE LA CONCORDE
MENTION HONORABLE
PALAIS DE L'INDUSTRIE 1855.
A. THOMAS Fr Paris.
CHATEAU DE VERSAILLES
HOTEL DE VILLE

“Into the valley of death…”

74 **JEGEL, Conrad Johann**

[Crimean War playing cards].

Publication
[Frankfurt, C. L. Wüst, post-1856].

Description
52 engraved playing cards with fine original hand-colour, two stamps to one, blue printed haxagonal pattern to versos.

Dimensions
87 by 60mm (3.5 by 2.25 inches).

References
Guiard 14; van den Bergh pp.112-113.

The Maker
Although his imprint is not found on any of the cards, the present deck is thought to be the work of Conrad Johann Jegel. For a description of Jegel, please see item 67.

The Cards
Just like the Napoleonic battles, the Crimean War inspired many nineteenth century card makers to publish decks commemorating the conflict. The war broke out in October 1853 when Russisa attempted to expand into the Turkish-controlled Danube region. Over the course of the following three years, an alliance of the Ottoman, British, Sardinian, French and Austrian Empires fought against the Russian Empire, supported by Greece, eventually winning a victory in March 1856. The present cards form the most successful deck produced in the aftermath of the conflict.

Each Ace card depicts two battle-scenes on land and at sea, the most famous of which is undoubtedly the Battle of Balaklava, shown on the Ace of Hearts. This conflict was immortalised by Alfred Lord Tennyson in his poem ‘The Charge of the Light Brigade’. The double-figured court cards represent the monarchs and military leaders from the warring empires:

King, Queen, Jack:
Clubs – Russia: Tsar Alexander II/Tsar Nicolas I, Alexandrovna, Marechal St Arnaud/Prince Gortschakoff
Diamonds – England and Sardinia: Victor Emanuel of Sardinia, Queen Victoria, Lord Raglan/Admiral Sir E. Lyons
Hearts – France: Napoleon III, Eugenie, imperatrice des Francais, Marechal Pelissier/Marechal Canrobert
Spades – Turkey: Sultan Abdul Medschid, the Sultana, Schamil/Omer Pascha

NAPOLÉON III empereur.
NAPOLÉON III, empereur.
ALEXANDROVA, impératrice de Russie.
ALEXANDROVA, impératrice de Russie.
le Bombardement de Bomarsund 21 Juin 1854.
Bataille navale de Sinope 18 Novembre 1853
Prise du Malakoff 8 Septembre 1855
Défense de Silistrie 14 Juin 1854.

Haute couture

75 **GILBERT, O.**

Cartes Parisiennes.

Publication
Paris, O. Gilbert, 1857.

Description
52 engraved playing cards with fine original hand-colour, pink versos.

Dimensions
84 by 55mm (3.25 by 2.25 inches).

References
Van den Bergh pp.242-243.

The Maker
The Jack of Clubs bears an imprint showing the maker's name. For a description of O. Gilbert, see item 70.

The Cards
Gilbert sold a number of decks under the title 'Cartes Parisiennes', with several different editions made, among them a more exlusive deck with gold print. These cards have come to be known as "costume decks" for the obvious reason of their characters' wonderful clothing.

Here, the Jack and King of Hearts are dressed ready for the hunt, with dogs in tow, while the other male court figures are all in clothing typical of the aristocratic upper classes from the nineteenth century. The Queens are dressed in huge dresses, and the Queens of Hearts and Clubs look ready to take a stroll.

The pip cards are presented simply with the number of suit marks shown corresponding to the value of each card, while the Ace cards have their pip surrounded by elaborate framework.

Viennese Rummy...

76 **GLANZ, Joseph**

Theater-Whist.

Publication
Vienna, Joseph Glanz, 1857.

Description
52 engraved playing cards with fine original hand-colour, blue and red lattice pattern to versos.

Dimensions
90 by 55mm (3.5 by 2.25 inches).

References
Van den Bergh p.213; Yale 1591/AUS149.

The Maker
On the Jack of Clubs the name of the maker is identified as "Joseph Glanz", whose address is listed as "Nierderlage in Wien Kohlmarkt 279". The present deck was initially published by Max Uffenheimer under the title 'Theater-Whist', and when Uffenheimer sold his company to Joseph Glanz, the latter continued production.

Glanz was a carpenter, medalist and printer, who is considered a founding figure of Vienna's artistic heritage. During his career, he produced numerous decks of cards, with a wide range of themes and styles.

The Cards
These cards depict the kaleidescope that is the Viennese arts and the theatre-scene: a host of splendid theatres were built in Vienna during the eighteenth and nineteenth centuries, and its world-famous opera house would open 12 years after this deck was published. The double-figure court cards show characters from drama and literature, as well as historical personages and mythological figures:

Clubs – Saladin, Brunhilde, Lancelot
Diamonds – Macbeth, Maria von Burgund, Hans Sachs
Hearts – Ingurd, Maria Stuart, Fridolin
Spades – King Lear, Elisabeth, Troubadour

The Ace and pip cards are simply identified by the number of suit marks shown on each card.

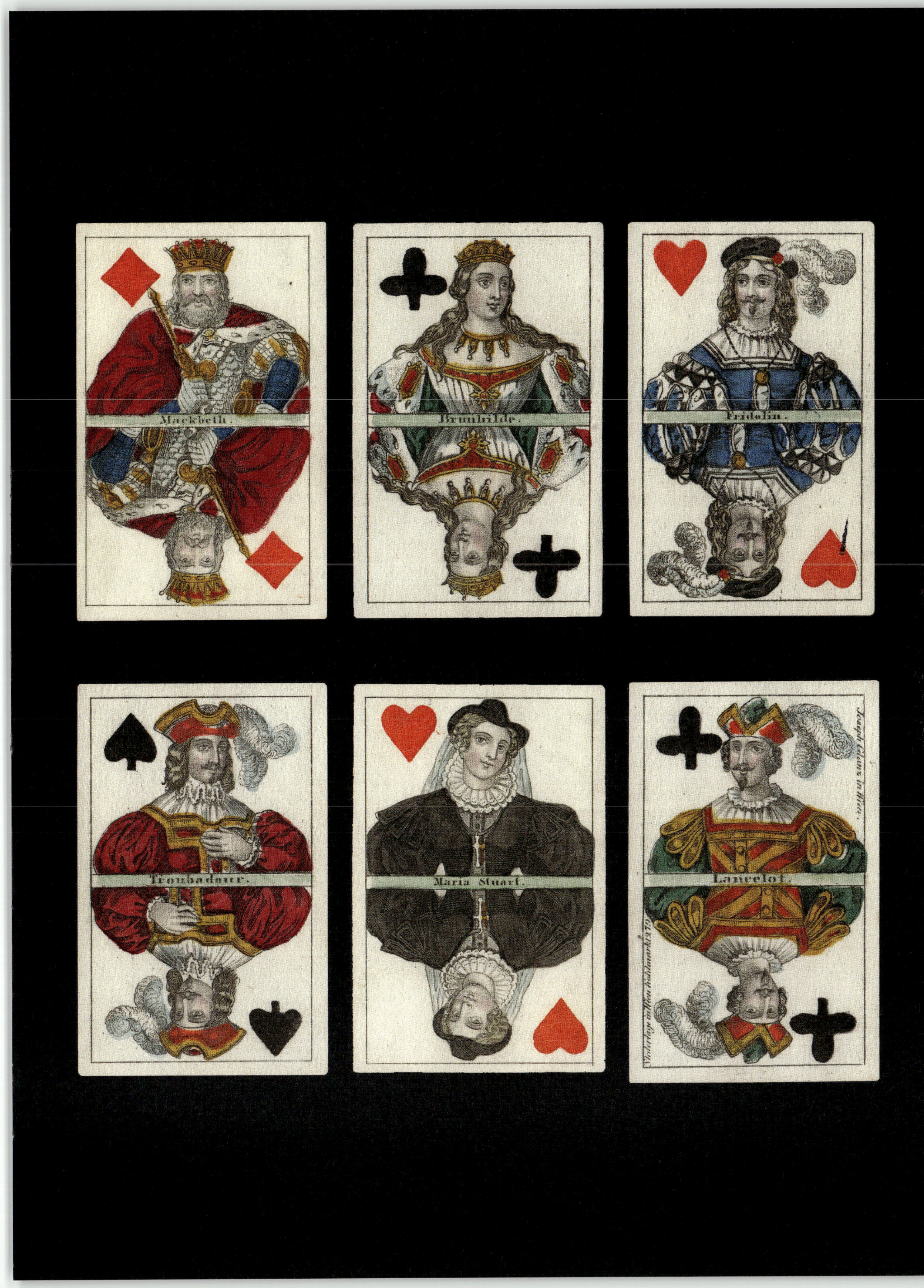
Mackbeth.
Brunhilde.
Fridolin.
Troubadour.
Maria Stuart.
Lancelot.

The founders of western civilisation

77 AROUY

Cartes Heroïques.

Publication
Paris, W. Gripon & Cie, 1858.

Description
32 chromolithographic playing cards, blue printed pattern to versos.

Dimensions
81 by 52mm (3.25 by 2 inches).

References
Van den Bergh p.268.

The Maker
According to the information on the box that came with the cards, the present deck was published by Gripon and sold under the title 'Cartes Héroïques' at all "Papetiers et Bureaux de Tabac". Gripon was a printer active in Paris in the mid-nineteenth century, with premises at 24 Rue Rambuteau. The lithographer's name is identified on the Ace of Spades as Arouy.

The Cards
A wide range of themes are illustrated on the present cards, which together can be said to outline and depict the foundations of western civilisation.

Each Ace card shows two scenes from biblical stories, such as the murder of Abel by his brother Cain, while the Kings represent great leaders, heroes and inventors, such as Julius Caesar and Charlemagne. The Queens show female warriors, and the Jacks warlords from across history.

The value of the pip cards is shown not by the number of suit marks, but by the number of portraits of great men. Among them are composers, painters, statesmen and scientists, such as William Shakespeare, Isaac Newton and George Washington.

The lithography is done in black and gold, and hand colour has then been applied in red and blue, giving the present cards a particularly distinctive look.

DESCARTES 1596
PASCAL 1623
WASHINGTON 1733
CROMWELL 1590
BACON 1561
LINNE 1707
BOSSUET 1627
PIERRE-LE-GRAND 1672
LAPEROUSE 1741
PAPIN 1647

HEROS
CAPITU-
LAIRES
ECOLES
CHARLEMAGNE 762.814

CHRISTOPHE COLOMB 1492
1506. AMERIQUE.

CAÏN. ET ABEL 4760 AV.J.C.
LITH. AROUY.

Game of Thrones

78 **GRIMAUD, B[aptiste]-P[aul]**

Jeu Impérial.

Publication
Paris, Grimaud, 1858.

Description
52 engraved playing cards with fine original hand-colour, versos plain.

Dimensions
85 by 55mm (3.25 by 2.25 inches).

References
Guiard 154; van den Bergh pp.102-103; Yale 2587/FRA287.

The Maker
The Jack of Clubs shows the maker's name to be "B. P. Grimaud". For a description of Baptiste-Paul Grimaud, see item 50.

The Cards
Grimaud published the present deck under the title 'Jeu Impérial', since it is dedicated to the four most important superpowers of the age, each one of which is represented by a suit. The Aces show the coats-of-arms of the respective country and identify it by name, while the King and Queen cards represent the monarchs, naturally dressed in sumptuous furs and fabrics:

Clubs – France, Emperor Napoleon III & Eugenie
Diamonds – Austria, Emperor Frans Joseph & Elisabeth
Hearts – England, Prince Albert & Queen Victoria
Spades – Russia, Tsar Alexander II and Maria Alexandrovna

AUTRICHE.
B. P. GRIMAUD ET Cie PARIS. FRANCE
RUSSIE.

A souvenir of Frankfurt

79 [ANONYMOUS]

[Landmakers of Frankfurt playing cards].

Publication
[Germany, c1860].

Description
52 engraved playing cards with fine original hand-colour, blue printed pattern to verso.

Dimensions
86 by 59mm (3.5 by 2.25 inches).

References
Van den Bergh p.61.

The Maker
We have not been able to identify any details about the maker of this deck.

The Cards
Crafted during the years of the nineteenth century when Frankfurt was a fully sovereign city state, in between its domination by the Napoleonic Empire and its annexation to Prussia in 1866, these cards celebrate the city's architecture, with each Ace card depicting two cityscapes showing Frankfurt's famous buildings and monuments:

Club – Romerberg and Fahrthor
Diamond – Zeil and Rossmarkt
Heart – St Katharinen and Kirche Eschenheimr Thurm
Spade – Ariadne and Bibliothek

The court cards, painted in bold colours, are in the double-figure format that had become prominent during the early nineteenth century. The suit marks appear in the upper left and lower right corner on the court cards, and in the centre of the Aces.

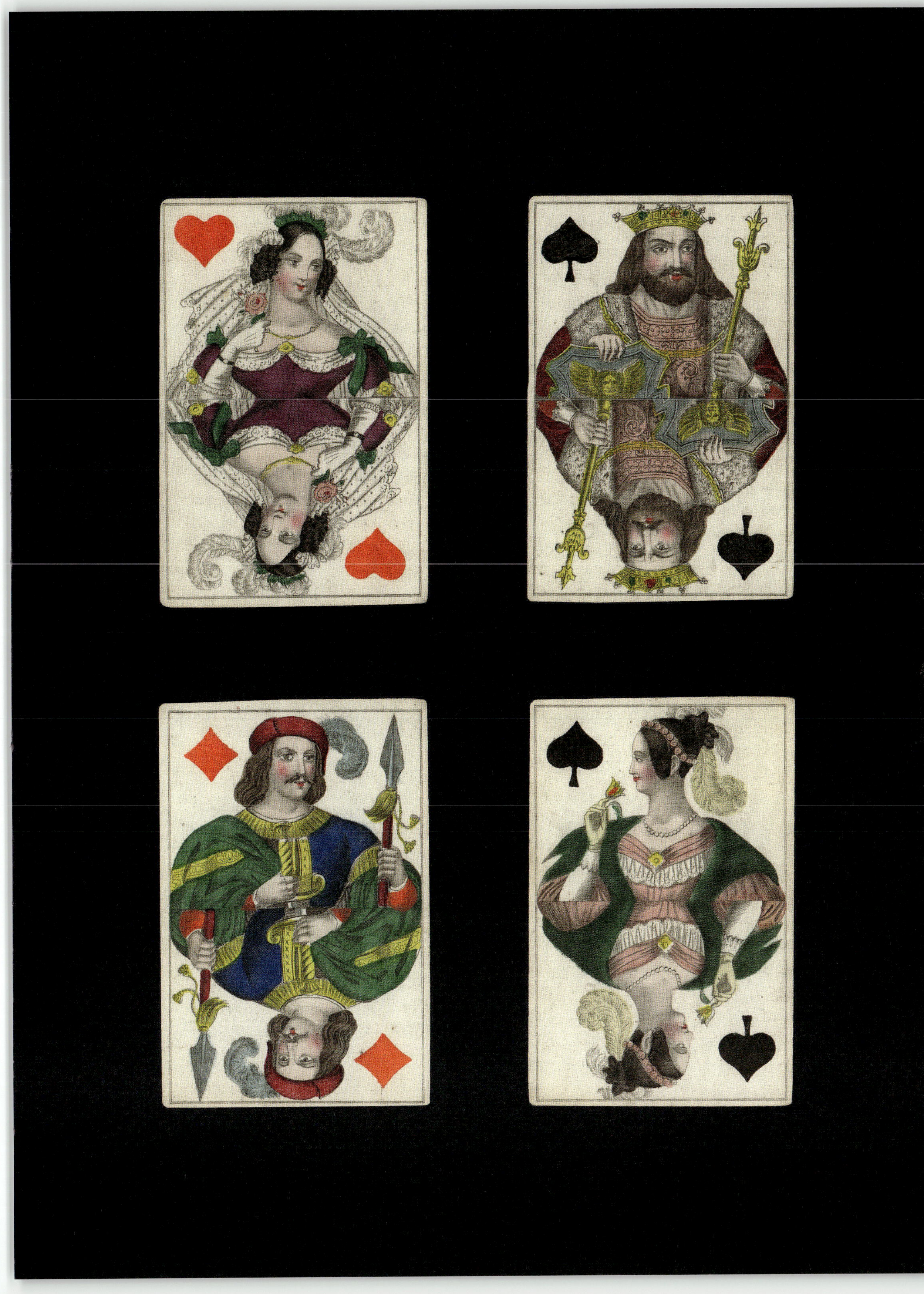

Patience in miniature

80 **B. DONDORF G.M.B.H.**

No 25 Patience-Karten.

Publication
Frankfurt am Main, c1860.

Description
52 chromolithograph miniature playing cards, red printed ornithological scene printed to versos, contained within red printed paper box labelled "Whist a 52 Blatt.".

Dimensions
55 by 37mm (2.25 by 1.5 inches).

The Maker
Bernard J. Dondorf was born in Frankfurt on 19 March, 1809, the son of Jewish immigrants. After serving his apprenticeship at C. Naumann printers, he opened a lithographic printing business in 1833. Playing cards were first mentioned in advertisements in 1839, with the first packs produced in the 1840s by steel engraving and stencil-coloured lithography. In 1853 he purchased a steam engine and gradually increased his output of playing cards under the name "B. Dondorf, Frankfurt a. M." In 1871 Dondorf opened a new factory in Bockenheimer Landstrasse. In 1872 he retired leaving the business in the hands of his sons who continued to expand the business and build new factories.

The Cards
The Aces are decorated with cherubim, with the picture cards decorated with twee rosy-cheeked figures bearing various accoutrements.

B. DONDORF GmbH
FRANCFORT s/M.

Wild cards

81 **DONDORF, Bernhard**

Cartes Comiques.

Publication
[Frankfurt, Bernhard Dondorf, c1860].

Description
52 chromolithograph playing cards, purple and gold vignette to versos.

Dimensions
93 by 64mm (3.75 by 2.5 inches).

References
Van den Bergh pp.216-217; Yale 2913/GER511.

The Maker
For a description of Bernhard Dondorf, please see item 80.

The Cards
This deck is probably the earliest known deck by the German firm of Dondorf, two versions of which exist. The present cards form the more risqué version: on the Ace of Spades, for instance, the woman's dress is far more low-cut, and on the King of Clubs there is a urinating dog.

Another remarkable feature is that the royal characters on the court cards are represened by animals, with the King of Spades a cow and the Queen of Hearts a swan. To distinguish them, crowns are found above the suit symbol on the Kings, slippers on the Queens and axes on the Jack. This allowed them to remain viable as a deck of playing cards.

All the pip cards show a romantic or comical scene in shades of either red or green. The number of suit marks on top of these background images indicates the suit and value of each card.

L'AMOUREUX
B. Dondorf
Francfort s/M.
Non plus ultra
FORCE et BÊTISE
SOIF D'ARGENT

A chalky likeness

82 GASSMAN, François

Cartes Neuves.

Publication
[Geneva, F. Gassman, c1860].

Description
32 chalk-lithographic playing cards with fine original hand-colour., pink versos.

Dimensions
79 by 53mm (3 by 2 inches).

References
Van den Bergh p.254.

The Maker
The imprint of "Gassman à Genève" is found across the Jacks of Spades and Clubs. François Gassmann was a card-maker who produced a number of successful tarot decks, along with several decks of playing cards.

He also experimented with the novel printing technique of chalk lithography, which left less than desirable results, as exhibited on the present deck. For his other decks, Gassman returned to standard lithography.

The Cards
Showing a standard arrangement of the French suit system: the double-figure court cards present the familiar royal characters in typical poses, with the Jacks carrying axes and Kings and Queens bearing sceptres or swords. The suit marks are shown in the upper left and lower right corners, with some showing inept handling by the colourist: one of the symbols on the King of Spades, for instance, overlaps with the border.

The Ace and pip cards are stylistically straightforward, with the number of suit marks corresponding to the value of each card. The present deck demonstrates why the technique of chalk lithography never took off, as it left rather faint impressions with a lack of clear detail.

GASSMANN
A GENEVE.

I went to Switzerland and all I got was this deck of cards

83 LANG, Rudolf

[Landmarks of Switzerland playing cards].

Publication
[Switzerland, Rudolf Lang, c1860].

Description
36 engraved playing cards with fine original hand-colour, printed red floral pattern to versos.

Dimensions
87 by 60mm (3.5 by 2.25 inches).

References
Van den Bergh p.58.

The Maker
We have been unable to find any record of a card-maker operating under the name Rudolf Lang.

The Cards
The technological progress and cultural developments of the nineteenth century gave rise to a tourism boom across Europe. Switzerland's central location between France, Germany, Austria and Italy meant that the country experienced a huge surge in the number of tourists travelling within its borders. Enterprising printers and card-makers responded to the increasing number of visitors by producing souvenir decks, which showed iconic Swiss landmarks, buildings and figures.

The present deck is an early example of these mementos. The court cards show the double-figured Kings, Queens and Jacks wearing native Swiss dress. The costumes of the Queens and Jacks are labelled with a specific place of origin, which extend to include locations outside of Switzerland, such as the Alsace, the Black Forrest and Tyrol. The Ace cards show scenic depictions of famous places across Switzerland, namely:

Clubs – Hospie de St Bernhard/Château de Chillon
Hearts – Chapelle de Guillaume Tell/Righi Koulm
Spades – Monument à Lucerne/Chûte du Rhin
Diamonds – Bains de Loueche/La Jungfrau

The suit marks are shown in the centre of the Aces, and in both the upper left and lower right corners of the other cards.

We have only been able to trace one other complete example of this deck; that of the collection Verame.

Zoug.
Zoug.
Monument à Lucerne
Chûte du Rhin
Chapelle de Guillaume Tell
Righi Kulm

Kenter's opening gambit

84 **PIATNIK, Ferdinand**

[Luxury playing cards].

Publication
[Vienna, F. Piatnik, c1860].

Description
52 engraved playing cards with fine original hand-colour, maroon printed foliate design to versos.

Dimensions
90 by 58mm (3.5 by 2.25 inches).

References
Van den Bergh p.262.

The Maker

On the sash of the Jack of Hearts reads the name of the maker, "Ferdinand Piatnik", and around the edge of the same card are the notices "Eigenthum des Verlegers" ("owner of the publishers") and "Mit Vorbehalt des Nachdrucks" ("reprinting reserved"). For a description of Piatnik, please see item 72.

The Cards

The most notable feature of these cards is the rich colour found on the court cards. The traditional double-figure images of the royal characters are embellished in green, blue, purple, red and yellow with a luxurious effect. The Ace and pip cards are typical in their design, with the value of each card conveyed by the number of suit marks shown.

One of the first decks acquired by Harry Kenter, forming the foundation of what would become one of the world's largest playing card collections. Today, the majority of the collection can be found in museums across the Netherlands and Belgium, while a few decks remain in private ownership. The emotional connection that Kenter had with the present deck, as the first of his collection, meant that he decided to sell it last of all.

Eigenthum des Verlegers
Mit Vorbehalt des Nachdruckes

Hamburger cards

85 **WÜST, Conrad Ludwig**

Hamburger Spielkarten.

Publication
[Frankfurt, H. Rübcke, c1860].

Description
52 engraved playing cards with fine original hand-colour, with one manuscript inscription, blue printed pattern to verso.

Dimensions
89 by 58mm (3.5 by 2.25 inches).

References
British Museum Schreiber Sheets German 44; van den Berg p.63.

The Maker
For a description of Conrad Ludwig Wüst, see item 41.

The Cards
Issued as an homage to the city of Hamburg, which at the time of publication was still undergoing major restoration and renovation after the great fire of 1848. The fire blazed continuously for four days and left 20,000 Hamburgers homeless. These cards celebrate the city's most impressive and iconic buildings, monuments and views, which are displayed on the Aces and the pip cards. The double-figure court cards show a range of historical personages, famous statues and German men and women in native dress. The suit marks appear in the upper left- and lower right-hand corners, and in the centre of the Aces. The unusually slender Spade symbols are characteristic of Wüst's cards.

The coat-of-arms of Hamburg appears on the Ace of Hearts, surrounded by a banner which reads 'Hamburger Spielkarten bei der Verlag H. Rübcke' ('Hamburg playing cards from the publishing house of H. Rübcke'). It was previously believed that Rübcke was entirely responsible for the deck, but recent research has concluded that the cards were in fact made by Wüst.

Verlag der Hamburger Spielkarten bei G. Kübcke.
das alte Bank-Gebäude.

Holste: Buttermädchen.
Tatenbergerin.

Helgoländerin.
Blankeneserin.

Bürgermeister.
Rathsherr.

Shuffling the heads of nineteenth century Europe

86 [JEGEL, Conrad Johann] [attributed to]

[European monarchs].

Publication
[?Nuremberg, post-1861].

Description
52 engraved playing cards with fine original hand-colour, stamp to one, blue printed hexagonal pattern to versos.

Dimensions
89 by 60mm (3.5 by 2.25 inches).

References
Van den Bergh pp.114-115.

The Maker
Although his imprint is not found on any of the cards, the present deck is thought to be the work of Conrad Johann Jegel. For a description of Jegel, please see item 67.

The Cards
Although the text appears in French, the present deck of cards is thought to have been made in Germany. It shows the most important European monarchs and their palaces. Some of these appear countless times on playing cards of the nineteenth century, such as Queen Victoria and Tsar Alexander II, but it also includes a few rulers who are less well-represented, such as the Turkish Sultan Abdul-Aziz and Queen Amalie of Greece.

Each Ace card shows two of the impressive palaces or residences of the Kings and Queens across Europe. Interestingly, only France receives two vignettes dedicated to its buildings:

Clubs – Kremlin, Moscow & Buckingham Palace, London
Diamonds – Tuileries Palace, Paris & Fontainebleu Palace, Paris
Hearts – Royal Palace, Madrid & Saray, Constantinople
Spades – Schönbrunn Palace, Vienna & Royal Palace, Athens

The court cards show a range of internationally notable figures, the Kings and Queens represented by monarchs, and the Jack cards showing renowned military leaders:

Clubs – Sultan Abdul-Aziz, Isabella of Spain, Admiral d'Autriche/ Archduke Ferdinand Max
Diamonds – Napoleon III/Victor Emanuel, Eugenie of France, Marshall Pellissier/Garibaldi
Hearts – Alexander II, Victoria, Omar Pasha
Spades – Franz-Joseph I, Amelie of Greece, Field-Marshall Count Orloff

The cards can be dated based on the monarchs shown. Both Victor Emanuel of Italy and Abdul-Aziz of Turkey ascended to their thrones in 1861, providing an *ante post quem* for the deck. The inclusion two most eastern rulers in the deck, Abdul-Aziz, and Queen Amelie of Greece, is interesting, as they had both recently been "in the news". Abdul-Aziz was the first Ottoman Sultan to travel extensively in Western Europe; while Queen Amelie and her husband, the King of Greece, were expelled from their country in 1862, living out the rest their days in Bavaria.

Palais royal de Madrid.
Serail de Constantinople.

Gloriette de Schönbrunn.
Palais royal d'Athènes.

Kremlin à Moscou.
Palais de Buckingham à Londres.

Palais des tuileries.
Fontainebleau.

Alexandre II.
Empereur de Russie.

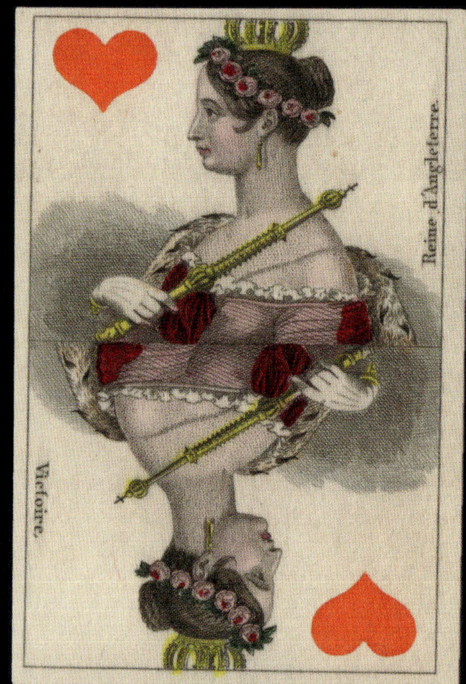
Reine d'Angleterre.
Victoire.

Isabelle.
Reine d'Espagne.

Empereur turc.
Abdul-Aziz.

Reine de Grèce
Amalie
Feld-maréchal de Russie
Comte Orloff
Impératrice de France
Eugénie
Napoléon III Empereur de France
Victor Emanuel Roi d'Italie

One of the earliest for the Kingdom of Italy

87 **DOTTI, Edoardo**

[Luxury playing cards].

Publication
Milan, Edoardo Dotti, 1862.

Description
52 engraved playing cards with fine original hand colour, printed red square pattern to versos.

Dimensions
93 by 54mm (3.75 by 2.25 inches).

References
Van den Bergh pp.264-265.

The Maker
Above the suit mark on the Ace of Hearts is found the imprint of "Edoardo Dotti, Milan". Dotti produced a number of decks of cards during the mid-nineteenth century. He used both the French and the Italian suit systems, and published tarot and playing cards from his workshop in Milan.

Along with the imprint is a taxation stamp which shows that the deck was published in 1862. The rest of the text on the stamp reads 'REGNO D'ITALIA LEGGE 21 Sett. 1862 Gen 30'; the cards were published in the early years of the Kingdom of Italy.

The Cards
A standard set of playing cards using the French suit system, with the double-figure court cards show the royal characters dressed in magnificent costumes. The King and Jack of Diamonds appear set for battle, both wearing ornate armour, while the Jack of Spades is shown wildly brandishing his sword. The figures representing the suit of Hearts are all in eastern costume, with both the men and the woman wearing turbans and the Jack holding a curved sword. The suit marks are shown in the upper left and lower right corner, as usual.

The Ace and pip cards are simple, with the number of suit marks corresponding to the value of each card. On the King of Spades text reads "deposta alla R. Biblioteca" ('placed in R. Library'), although it is not clear to which particular institution this note refers.

Marked down for the 'Erste Deutsches Bundesschiessen'

88 FROMMANN, Maximilian Joseph

Frankfurter Schutzenkarte.

Publication
Darmstadt, M. Frommann, 1862.

Description
32 chromolithograph playing cards, pink pattern to versos.

Dimensions
93 by 62mm (3.75 by 2.5 inches).

References
Guiard 2, Van den Bergh pp.256-257.

The Maker

Maximilian Joseph Frommann (1813-1866) was an illustrator and cardmaker based in Darmstadt, Germany. After his death, his daughter Anna started a publishing business with her husband Georg Bünte, under the name Frommann & Bünte, while his son Friedrich formed his own firm with Friedrich Morian, named Frommann & Morian. From 1866 to 1872, the siblings worked together to manage their late father's affairs, and later both went on to publish their own decks of playing cards.

The Cards

The 'Frankfurter Schützenkarte' were published in honor of the 'Erste Deutsches Bundesschiessen' ('First German federal shooting competition'), called Schützenfest at that time. This event, with 8000 sharp-shooters from 9 countries, took place from 13 to 21 July, 1862. The Bornheimer Heide, located just outside of Frankfurt, was chosen as festival site; the entrance gate and the party hall are shown on the Aces of Diamonds and Spades.

The court cards are interesting for a variety of reasons. The Schützenfest is again reflected on the Kings of Clubs, Hearts and Spades, which depict competitive marksmen, while the Jacks of Hearts and Diamonds present characters from the Commedia dell'Arte.

The nationalistic spirit is shown on the King of Diamonds and Queen of Clubs, both of which show huge German flags. The sense of patriotism is reinforced by the Queens of Hearts and Diamonds, representing personifications of Germania and Francofurtia.

By contrast, the Jack of Clubs depicts the French king Napoleon III standing beside a boundary marker with clenched fists. Similarly, John Bull, the personification of England, is shown on the Jack of Spades carefully studying the German fleet with binoculars.

The pip cards are more straightforward, with the number of suit marks shown corresponding to the value of each card.

Germania

With cup in one hand and gun in the other...

89 HOFER, R.

Schützenkarte.

Publication
Frankfurt, C.L. Wüst, 1862.

Description
32 chromolithographic playing cards, blue hexagonal and dotted pattern to versos.

Dimensions
95 by 65mm (3.75 by 2.5 inches).

References
Van den Bergh pp.258-259, Yale 2846/ GER444.

The Maker
The imprint of the designer is found on the King of Clubs, reading "R. Hofer in Vervey". We have been unable to trace any further record of any Swiss artist from this time named Hofer.

Published by Conrad Ludwig Wüst, who was based in Frankfurt where the festival was held. For a description of Wüst, please see item 41.

The Cards
Among the cards published to commemorate the Schützenfest of 1862 is the present deck by Wüst.

The pictorial Ace cards each show a scene from the tournament with a small heading in German, while the court cards represent the countries and provinces that sent marksmen to compete in the shooting contest.

Clubs – Switzerland
Diamonds – Tyrol
Hearts – Frankfurt
Spades – Bremen

The Kings are depicted as individual competitors holding their guns in one hand and a cup in the other – a worrying combination, perhaps. The Queens of Diamonds and Hearts show personifications of Frankfurt and Germany respectively, while the other Queens show women wearing impressive gowns and presenting ornate urns. The Jack of each suit shows a character dressed in the typical clothing associated with the regions represented.

The pip cards simply convey their value through the number of suit marks shown on each one.

Francofurtia

Schweizer Schütz

Bremer Schütz

Frankfurter Turner Trommler

Charles VI's card-maker

90 [ANONYMOUS]

Jacquemin Gringonneur.

Publication
[?Paris, Mlle Hautot et M. Paris, 1864].

Description
52 chromolithograph playing cards, pink pattern to versos.

Dimensions
99 by 64mm (4 by 2.5 inches).

References
Giuard 152, Van den Bergh p.253.

The Maker
We have been unable to discover who designed the present playing cards, but on September 12, 1863, a deed with the title 'Fabrication de cartes à jouer dites historiques' was drawn up for the production of this deck, which was published the following year, entitled 'Jacquemin Gringonneur', after a fourteenth century card-maker who had produced three decks of cards for Charles VI.

After the first edition published by Hautot and Paris, this deck was also published by other French playing card makers, amongst which was Avril (see item 91). Little information can be found about Mademoiselle Hautot and M. Paris, and there are no other decks attributed to them.

The Cards
Among the most notable features of this deck are its beautiful suit marks: with the interesting exception of the Spades, the symbols are exquisitely filled with flowers (clubs), birds (hearts) and fruit (diamonds). Furthermore, gold print was used to give the cards an additional sense of luxury.

The full-length court cards show a range of royal or noble figures from across mythology and history, from Hector of Troy as the King of Diamonds and Alexander the Great as the King of Spades to the biblical women such as Judith and Rachel, dressed in quite ridiculously anachronistic gowns. The value of the Ace and pip cards is indicated by the number of ornate suit marks shown.

Alexandre
Judith
Hector

Ready for your close-up?

91 **AVRIL, Stanislas-Desire**

[Photographic playing cards].

Publication
[Paris, Avril & Cie, c1864].

Description
52 photographic playing cards, with suits in hand-colour, plain white versos.

Dimensions
98 by 65mm (3.75 by 2.5 inches).

References
Van den Bergh p.221.

The Maker
Card-maker Stanislas-Desire Avril was active in Paris from 1862 until his bankruptcy in 1868. His firm produced engraved and lithographed cards, and then in 1864 he received a patent to make photographic playing cards. His imprint appears on all the court cards.

The Cards
Probably the first example of the photographic printing technique being used on playing cards. It is only used, however, on the court cards, with the Kings, Queens and Jacks all shown with full-length lifelike images. The characters are portrayed by actors and actresses posing in elaborate theatrical costumes. The suit mark appears in the upper left corner, and opposite them the name of the actor or actress is found.

By contrast, the Ace and pip cards shown standard designs, with the value of each card represented by the number of suit marks shown.

M. BELVAL
Avril et Ce Paris, France
Mme CHARTON-DEMEUR
Avril et Ce Paris, France
M. BRESSANT
Mlle CICO
Avril et Ce Paris, France

Three's a crown

92 **GRIMAUD, Baptiste-Paul**

[French Court playing cards].

Publication
Paris, Grimaud, 1864.

Description
52 engraved playing cards, court cards with fine original hand-colour, plain white verso.

Dimensions
85 by 55mm (3.25 by 2.25 inches).

References
Van den Bergh pp.106-107, Yale 2808/ GER405.

The Maker
The imprint on the Jack of Clubs identifies the maker of the present deck as Baptiste-Paul Grimaud. For a description of Grimaud, please see item 50.

The Cards
First designed and published in 1856, the present deck takes a tongue-in-cheek approach to the traditional court cards. The Kings are represented by four important French rulers, but rather than being accompanied by their wives, the Queen cards each show one of their mistresses:

Clubs – Francois I, Anne de Pisseleu, Duchess of Etampes
Diamonds – Henri IV, Gabrielle d'Estrée
Hearts – Louis XIV, Duchess of La Vallière
Spades – Charles VI, Odette de Champdivers

In their own times and in popular memory, the Royal Mistresses were the subject of scandal, gossip and rumour. Their stories were undoubtedly exaggerated and embellished over the centuries that followed, turning them into near-legendary figures. Each of the relationships, with the exception of Francois I and Anne de Pisseleu, resulted in at least one child, which served to secure the paramours' position in the history of the French monarchy.

Typical court squires appear on the Jack cards, preparing to attend upon their masters with refreshments, entertainment or military equipment. The Ace cards simply show the suit mark surrounded by a delicate floral wreath.

The deck appears to have been very popular. It was published numerous times throughout the late nineteenth century, perhaps demonstrating the pleasure that the French continued to take in deriding the monarchs of the Ancien Regime.

Louis XIV
Dsse de La Vallière
François Ier
Grimaud — Paris
France
Dsse d'Etampes

CHARLES VI
ODETTE
HENRI IV.
GABRIELLE D'ESTRÉE

"Nothing but a pack of cards!"

93 [ANONYMOUS]

[Cartes Fantastiques].

Publication
[France, c1865].

Description
52 engraved playing cards with fine original hand-colour, pink versos.

Dimensions
87 by 57mm (3.5 by 2.25 inches).

References
Van den Bergh pp.164-165.

The Maker
The present deck undoubtedly originated in France, but nothing is known about its maker or date of publication.

The Cards
An extremely rare deck entitled 'Cartes Fantastiques' in which each card shows a scene from a fable, folklore or fairy tales. These range from the bizarre, to the macabre, to the romantic, with princesses, demons and animals alike. The images are intricately detailed, and the value of each card is indicated by the number of suit marks shown.

Van den Bergh suggests that, if the Queen of Clubs is meant to represent the evil queen from 'Alice in Wonderland', the deck has been made after 1865, when Lewis Carroll wrote his world-famous book. On the box, the title is shown "Cartes Fantastiques".

A chronicle of nineteenth century Nuremberg skyline

94 [JEGEL, Johann Conrad] [attributed to]

[Landmarks of Nuremberg playing cards].

Publication
[Nuremberg, Johann Wilhelm Sass, ?c1865].

Description
52 engraved playing cards with fine original hand-colour, printed red dot pattern to verso.

Dimensions
56 by 41mm (2.25 by 1.5 inches).

References
Van den Bergh p.60.

The Maker
Probably first published by Johann Conrad Jegel (1791-1837), for a description of whom, see item 67.

The Cards
The technological developments of the nineteenth century saw the industrial city of Nuremberg grow to become one of Germany's most prosperous cities, and these cards, made during this period, celebrate its architecture and monuments. Each Ace card displays two of Nuremberg's impressive buildings, including:

Clubs – Alt Nürnberg Kirche
Diamonds – Keizerburcht
Hearts – Sebalduskirche
Spades – Delsenbach bridge over the river Pegnitz

The court cards, painted in bold colours, are in the double-figure format that had become prominent during the early nineteenth century. The suit marks appear in the upper left- and lower right-hand corner on the court cards, and in the centre of the Aces.

Top trumps of Prussia

95 **BENEDICT, J.**

[Landmarks of Prussia playing cards].

Publication
[Goslar, Friedrich Adolf Lattmann, c1865].

Description
52 engraved playing cards with fine original hand colour, stamp to one, red line and dot pattern to versos.

Dimensions
91 by 61mm (3.5 by 2.5 inches).

References
Van den Bergh pp.104-105, Yale 2808/GER405.

The Maker

The name of the designer of the present deck, J. Benedict, appears (though hardly noticeable) on the sceptre held by the Jack of Spades. Benedict was a well-known card designer from Vienna whose work was generally published by Friedrich Adolf Lattmann, whose name appears more visibly on the Jack of Clubs.

In 1794, Ernst Wilhelm Gottlieb Kircher had transformed his family printing business into a playing card factory. Political upheaval in the following decades meant that the factory was closed, but after its reopening some years later, it was taken over by Friedrich Adolf Lattmann, under whom the company prospered. Lattman produced English, French and German decks centred around a range of themes and subjects. The firm continued to operate until 1929.

The Cards

The prestigious and wealthy state of Prussia is displayed in all its glory on the present cards. At the time of publication, Prussia was one of the most powerful countries in the still-divided Germany thanks to its modern army. Each Ace card shows two of its magnificent palaces and public buildings:

Clubs – Babelsberg / Kronprintzl. Palais in Berlin
Diamonds – Breslauer Schloss / Konigl. Palais in Berlin
Hearts – Konigl. Schloss in Berlin / Sanssouci
Spades – Konigsberger Schloss / Schloss Nikolsburg

Likewise, the double-figure court cards display portraits of important Prussian figures, the Kings and Queens showing the aristocracy and the Jacks as decorated military servicemen:

Clubs – Friedrich Wilhelm I/Friedrich d. Grosse, Grosherzogin Alexandrine/Furstin Liegnitz, Graf v. Bismarck/v. Roon
Diamonds – Friedrich Wilhelm III/Friedrich Wilhelm II, Prinzss Friedr. Carl/Prinzessin Carl, Horwarth von Bittenfeld/von Steinmetz
Hearts – Friedrich Wilhelm IV/Konig v. Preussen, Kronprinzss. V. Preussen/Konigin v. Preussen, Fried. Wilh. Kronpr. v. Preuss/Fried. Carl Prinz v. Preuss
Spades – Grosse Kurfurst/Friedrich I, Konigin Louise/Konigin Wwe v. Preussen, Vogel von Falkenstein/von Moltke

Vogel v. Falkenstein
v. Moltke
Kronprinzeß v. Preußen
Königin v. Preußen
Friedrich Wilh. III
Friedrich Wilh. II.
Großherzogin Alexandrine
Fürstin Liegnitz

Musical magic cards which can be played without difficulty

96 [?FROMMANN, Maximilian Joseph]

Musicalische Zauberkarte 100.000 Tänze für das Piano.

Publication
[?Darmstadt, ?M. Frommann, c1869].

Description
32 lithograph playing cards with fine original hand-colour, red hexagon and dot pattern to versos.

Dimensions
93 by 63mm (3.75 by 2.5 inches).

References
Van den Bergh pp.206-207.

The Maker
There remains little clarity regarding the origin of the present deck. The German version was most likely produced by Maximilian Frommann from Darmstadt and was published under the title 'Musicalische Zauberkarte 100.000 Tänze für das Piano' ('Musical Magic Cards. 100,000 dances for the piano'). For a description of Frommann, please see item 88.

The deck can be roughly dated to 1869 because of a review in 'Polybiblion: Universal Bibliographic Review' from that year.

The Cards
Besides being used as playing cards, the present deck can also be used as "musical magic cards" to generate a multitude of melodies. Each card has a musical stave, accompanied by an illustration of figures playing various instruments. Instructions accompanying a later facsimile read:

"Select indiscriminately and place on the musicdesk, in the middle a 1, on the left-hand extremity a picture-card, and on the right a seven. Fill each of the two intervening spaces by any three cards taken also indiscriminately... It will then be found that the nine cards placed together form two pieces of dance-music which can be played without difficulty."

The cards proved popular enough to warrant reproduction and translation into several languages, including French and Italian. The Laemmert firm in Rio de Janeiro was responsible for English and Portuguese versions too.

Walzer
Paukenschlag Polka

Walzer
Polka

Amazonen Walzer
Polka

Walzer
Polka

With ten new playing cards

97 **FROMMANN, Maximilian Joseph**

[Transformation playing cards].

Publication
[Darmstadt, Frommann & Bünte, c1870].

Description
52 chromolithograph playing cards, red printed pattern to versos.

Dimensions
89 by 65mm (3.5 by 2.5 inches).

References
Van den Bergh pp.158-159.

The Maker
For a description of Maximilian Joseph Frommann, see item 88.

The Cards
Maximilian Frommann had designed ten new cards shortly before his death, which were later incorporated into the present deck, along with 19 cards copied from an 1852 deck published by German firm Braun & Schneider, and 23 taken from Grimaud's 1850 deck (see item 68).

Frommann's new designs are shown on the pip cards, and fall into the category of "transformation card". The suit marks are incorporated into the main image in a simple yet clear way. A club symbol, for example, forms part of the design on a knight's breastplate, while a spade serves as a spearhead.

There were in total three editions of this deck, of which the present example is the second, distinguished by the letters "M" and "F" found on the Eight of Diamonds, referring to Maximilian.

A run of continents

98 HAUSMANN, Friedrich Karl

Vier continenten.

Publication
Frankfurt, Bernhard Dondorf, 1870.

Description
52 chromolithograph playing cards, pattern printed to versos in blue, black and yellow.

Dimensions
93 by 65mm (3.75 by 2.5 inches).

References
Van den Bergh pp.74-75; for similar see Guiard 4.

The Maker
German painter and director of the Hanau Drawing Academy, Friedrich Karl Hausmann (1825-1886) was responsible for the design of the cards. His name is prominently displayed on the folding sheet that can be found in the appendix, which describes all the cards and their topics. Throughout his career, Hausmann worked closely with the lithographic institution of Bernhard Dondorf, who published his illustrations and thus provided a stable income. The Dondorf firm was highly successful, printing not only playing cards, but also banknotes, postage stamps and decorative prints. Its name appears on all the Ace cards.

The Cards
Designed with geography in mind, with each suit is represented by one of the four continents, their Ace cards depicting scenes symbolising the respective cultures:

Club – America; the sailing of Columbus
Diamond – Europe; a personification of justice
Heart – Asia; an elephant carrying a howdah
Spade – Africa; camels in front of a mosque

The court cards show the royal figures as three-quarter portraits, subtly distinguished by their symbolic elements on their costumes. The pip cards display Dondorf's original approach of printing them all in a uniform colour, here sepia, as he had earlier done on his famous 'Cartes Comiques'. The continent deck proved extremely popular and ran into numerous editions, of which the present example is the first.

B·DONDORF
FRANCFORT

B·DONDORF
FRANCFORT

B·DONDORF
FRANCFORT

B·DONDORF
FRANCFORT

B. DONDORF, FRANCFORT s/M

Gilded luxury

99 **HOLMBLAD, Lauritz Peter**

[Danish playing cards].

Publication
[Copenhagen, L. P. Holmblads Fabrik, c1870].

Description
52 chromolithograph playing cards, with gilt edges, red printed papter pattern to versos.

Dimensions
94 by 59mm (3.75 by 2.25 inches).

References
Van den Bergh p.255.

The Maker

The name of the maker "L.P. Holmblads Fabrik i Kjobenhavn" is found on the Jack of Clubs. While playing cards were made in Denmark before 1820, the production really took off when Jacob Holmblad received a royal license to make playing cards in 1820.

After his death in 1837, his son Lauritz Peter Holmblad expanded the firm, using new techniques and commissioning new designs for his cards. Over his career he produced a range of decks for playing different games, including Danish Tarok, a three-player game using 78 cards.

The Cards

These new cards were made by Lauritz Peter Holmblad to keep abreast with the nineteenth century's increasing competition in the Danish market. The double-figure court cards depict the familiar royal characters, but they are shown in slightly more subtle and naturalistic poses, with the King of Spades sulkily folding his arms, while the Queen of Hearts gazes coyly over her shoulder.

They are beautifully coloured in rich, harmonious hues, and gilt edges add an extra touch of luxury. The suit marks are shown, as standard, in the upper left and lower right corners. The Ace and pip cards are simple, with the number of suit marks shown corresponding to the value of each card.

L. P. Holmblads Fabrik i Kjøbenhavn

Italy follows suit

100 [JEGEL, Conrad Johann] [attributed to]

[Unification of Italy playing cards].

Publication
[?Nuremberg, c1871].

Description
52 engraved playing cards, with fine original hand colour, stamp to one, blue printed pattern to versos.

Dimensions
92 by 61mm (3.5 by 2.5 inches).

References
Van den Bergh pp.116-117.

The Maker
Although his imprint is not found on any of the cards, the present deck is thought to be the work of Conrad Johann Jegel. For a description of Jegel, please see item 67.

The Cards
The unification of Italy in 1871 inspired the present deck of cards. The Risorgimento unfolded across the nineteenth century as the Italian states became increasingly concerned about their defences against the powerful Austria-Hungarian Empire. After decades of negotiations, conflicts and alliances, Italy was finally unified in 1871, when Rome was made its capital and Victor Emanuel its first king.

Each Ace card shows two scenic views of notable cities and regions across Italy, with the suit mark in between:

Clubs – Rome & Genoa
Diamonds – Naples & Caprera
Hearts – Palermo & Turin
Spades – Messina & Gaeta

The double-figure court cards show various important people connected to the unification:

Clubs – Victor Emanuel, Queen Victoria, Bixio, Cialdini
Diamonds – Garibaldi, personification of Italia, Camillo Benso di Cavour
Hearts – Franz II, Marie, Persano/Bosco
Spades – Louis Napoleon III, Eugene, Lamarmora, Fanti

Cathédrale in Palermo.
Parlamentsgebäude in Turin

EUGENIE.
EUGENIE.

TÜRR.
CAVOUR.

Rom.
Genua

A cheeky inverted-heart-cum-bottom!

101 [ANONYMOUS]

[Animal playing cards].

Publication
[?Germany, ?1873].

Description
32 engraved playing cards with fine original hand-colour.

Dimensions
92 by 62mm (3.5 by 2.5 inches).

References
Van den Bergh pp.182-183.

The Maker

The original deck of cards published with the present design was the work of Braun & Schneider, a printing company that operated from Munich during the latter half of the nineteenth century. Along with its playing cards, the firm was well-known for the series of plates it published from 1861 to 1890 in its magazine, illustrating historic and contemporary fashions.

The maker of this pirated edition is not identified on the cards, and we have been unable to trace any other information about him.

The Cards

In 1852, Braun & Schneider published a deck with transformation cards which proved so popular that a number of other card-makers appropriated the design, among them Frommann & Bunte (see item 97). Likewise, the present example includes pip and court cards taken from Braun & Schneider's legendary deck, including the cheeky inverted-heart-cum-bottom!

A remarkable change occurs, however, on the court cards of the diamond and heart suits: the heads of the royal characters have been replaced by those of animals. The Queen of Hearts, for instance, has become a pigeon and the King of Diamonds a lion. It is not at all clear why the maker has chosen to modify the cards in such a bizarre way, but it certainly does help to distinguish the deck from other facsimiles of Braun & Schneider's.

While the maker of this deck remains unknown, there is much speculation around the subject, with Daveluy from Belgium and Wüst from Germany being mentioned as possible candidates. Similarly, there is no definite proof of its origin, and the frequently cited year of publication, 1873, has yet to be soundly substantiated.

Dame.
Valet
Roi.
1.

A souvenir of Thomas Cook's Switzerland

102 WÜST, Conrad Ludwig

[Landmarks of Switzerland playing cards].

Publication
[Frankfurt, C.L. Wüst, c1875].

Description
52 engraved playing cards with fine original hand-colour, blue printed hexagon and dot pattern to versos.

Dimensions
89 by 60mm (3.5 by 2.25 inches).

References
Guiard 16; van den Bergh p.71.

The Maker
For a description of C.L. Wüst, please see item number 41.

The Cards
A souvenir for travellers in Switzerland, to which Thomas Cook & Co., had recently started offering guided holidays. The country's iconic and idyllic landscapes are captured on the Ace cards, each of which shows two scenic views, specifically:

Club – Berne/Chapelle de Guillaume Tell
Diamond – Rigi Staffel/Neuchatel
Heart – Lausanne/Interlaken
Spade – Thoune/Vevey

The double-figured court cards show natives from the various regions of Switzerland wearing typical dress. In the upper right corner above them the crest and name of the region appears, and in the opposite corner is the suit mark. Kings are distinguished from Jacks by the crowns surmounting the suit marks. It is interesting that the deck uses the French pattern rather than the Swiss, which perhaps made the cards more appealing to foreign travellers.

Berne.
Thurgovie.
Lucerne.
Soleure.
Argovie.
Bâle.
Saint-Gall.
Zurich.

The Raphael of Cats

103 **FLINZER, Fedor**

Ovale Salon-spielkarten.

Publication
[Leipzig, A.Twietmeyer, c1877].

Description
32 oval-shaped chromolithograph playing cards, stamp to one, maroon hexagonal pattern to versos, contained withn decorative printed paper oval case.

Dimensions
104 by 69mm (4 by 2.75 inches).

References
Van den Bergh p.235; Yale 2986/GER583.

The Maker
The cards were printed at the Leipziger Spielkarten-Fabrik Friedrich Günthel and published by A.Twietmeyer in Leipzig, whose name is printed on the Jack of Spades.

The images on the cards are designed by Fedor Flinzer (1832-1911). Flinzer was a German author, educator and illustrator, who was most famous for his paintings of felines, which earned him the nickname "The Raphael of Cats".

The Cards
A remarkable deck, although not unique, for the oval shape of its cards. It is, however, an extremely early example. The Wüst firm in Frankfurt made several decks with oval cards around 1900, and during the 1970s; the Japanese playing card manufacturer, and now electronic game-maker, Nintendo even made multiple decks with completely circular cards.

Apart from its size, the deck maintains the standard suits and values found on traditional cards. Each suit takes on its own theme, with the court cards of Clubs representing agriculture, Diamonds trade, Hearts education and Spades the military.

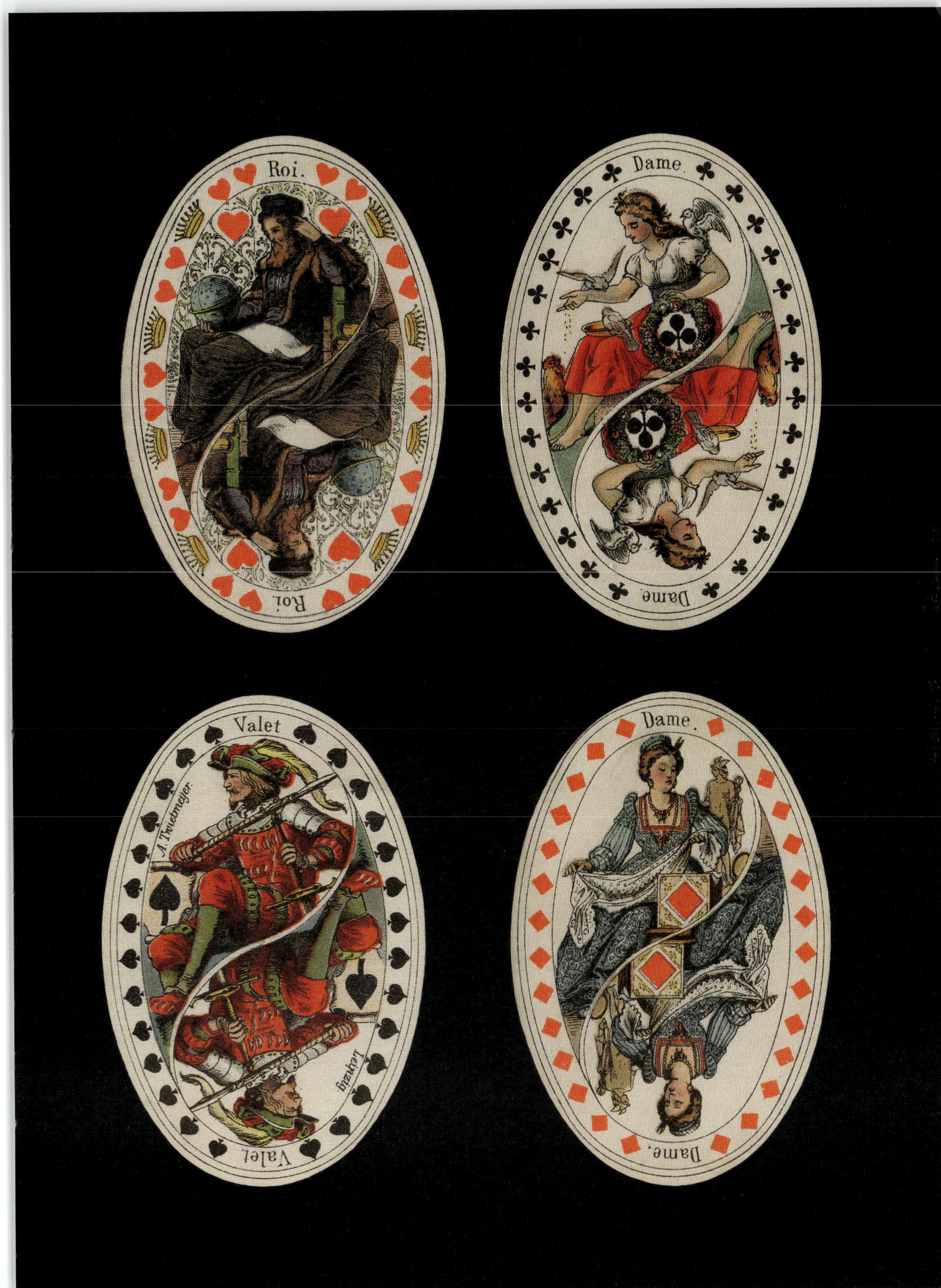
Roi.
Roi.
Dame
Dame.
Valet
A. Twietmeyer.
Leipzig
Valet.
Dame.
Dame.

"One for his nob!"

104 **CHAPMAN, T. S.**

[Whimsical character playing cards].

Publication
London, Reynolds & Sons, 1878.

Description
52 engraved playing cards with fine original hand-colour, versos green.

Dimensions
93 by 64mm (3.75 by 2.5 inches).

References
Van den Bergh pp.170-171; Yale 2295/ENG149.

The Maker

The name of the designer, T. S. Chapman, is found on all the pip cards, while the publisher's imprint is found on the Ace of Spades. Reynolds & Sons were, along with several other English card-making firms, responsible for the modernisation of the traditional court card designs.

As well as standard decks, Reynolds & Sons produced a variety of new cards, including fortune-telling packs and the transformation cards designed by T. S. Chapman and Crowquill, the pseudonym of writer and illustrator Alfred Henry Forrester. Shortly after the present deck was published, Charles Goodall & Son acquired the firm.

The Cards

The court cards, which are an early example of the design that would later become standard for playing cards worldwide, are significant. The double-figure cards show stylised images of the royal characters, with the suit marks shown in the upper right and lower left corners.

The Aces and pip cards are different from other transformation decks in that no effort has been made to assign a certain theme to each suit. Instead, each card displays a seemingly random whimsical image, with the suit marks incorporated into the design. Among the most charming of these is "a Christmas card" showing a robin whose red breast is made up by the heart symbol, while one of the most tongue-in-cheek depicts an aristocratic gentleman holding a large cane, labelled "one for his nob"!

One for his Nob.
REGISTERED
T.S.Chapman.

REGISTERED
A Strong Hand
T.S.Chapman.

Before the Joker, there was 'the Best Card'

105 DOUGHERTY, Andrew

[Advertising playing cards].

Publication
[New York, 1883].

Description
52 engraved playing cards and one extra card, court cards in full-colour, number cards with suits in hand-colour.

Dimensions
88 by 62mm (3.5 by 2.5 inches).

References
Van den Bergh pp.174-175.

The Maker
Andrew Dougherty is a key figure in the history of the American playing card industry, operating from 78 Cliff Street, New York between 1849 and 1858. He can be credited with several innovations to playing cards, such as his stylised double-figure court cards, which were reminiscent of the old woodblock prints but subsequently came back into fashion among his contemporaries.

The Cards
One of the earliest examples of an advertising deck: the text and images on each card refer to the products of the Murphy Varnish Company. The Murphy Varnish Company had been established in 1865 by the former Governor of New Jersey, Franklin Murphy. By the time the present deck was published, it had branches in New York, St. Louis and Cleveland, and the firm was clearly looking to expand its audience.

The cards show caricatures of varnish salesman, customers worshipping cans of the product and illustrations of the many uses of Murphy Varnish. A banner across the King of Diamonds, for instance, boldly declares that "Murphy is the King of Varnish Makers".

The pip cards inject an extra layer of humour with their cheeky illustrations, which incorporate the suit marks into the image in the typical transformation style. The diamond symbol is used as a hat, clubs and spades as comic exaggerations of the human form, and an inverted heart even serves as the backside of a man who has fallen through the ceiling! An extra card was added to the deck with the title 'the Best Card', which can be considered the forerunner of the joker.

The Murphy Varnish playing cards were highly successful, but it is extremely rare to find a complete surviving deck.

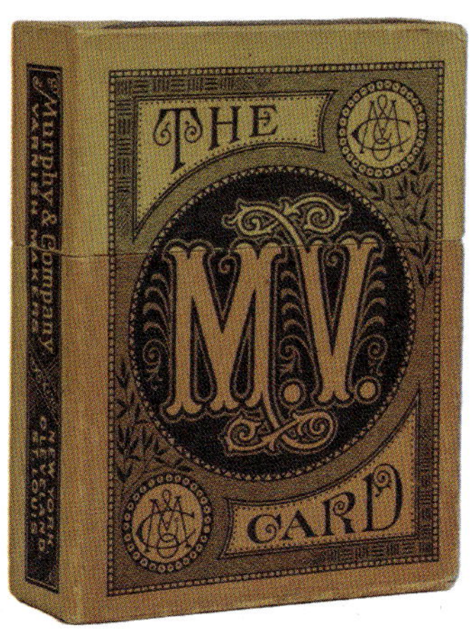

8
VARNISH SALESMEN EN ROUTE
M.V.
8

Q
PERFECTION OF QUALITY!
Q

3
To get rid of "DEVILTRIES" use the MURPHY VARNISH!
MURPHY VARNISH.
MURPHY'S A.B.C. SYSTEM
3

K
M.V.
MURPHY IS THE KING
OF
VARNISH
MAKERS
TRY OUR A.B.C. SYSTEM
K

3
CLUB SKATERS.
DANGER!
TO BE WITHOUT THE MURPHY VARNISH.
3

Acorns, leaves, radishes and sunflowers

106 **HIRSCH, Jacob**

Neue Deutsche Spielkarte.

Publication
Leipzig, J. G. Fritzsche, 1883.

Description
32 chromolithograph playing cards.

Dimensions
109 by 66mm (4.25 by 2.5 inches).

References
Van den Bergh p.277; Yale 2800/GER397.

The Maker

On the Ace of Leaves is printed the name of the publisher, J.G. Fritzsche, who was active in Leipzig in the 1880s, while on the Eight and Nine of Sunflowers are the initials of Timon Schroeter and Jacob Hirsch. The concept behind the present deck, with its new allegorical suits, is attributed to Dr Schroeter, while Hirsch was the artist behind the designs.

The Cards

Originally, this deck was published in the form of a book, but must have proved popular enough to encourage the publisher to produce the cards as a separate deck. Schroeter has done away with the traditional German suits and replaced them with acorns, leaves, radishes and sunflowers. Each suit is supposed to represent the four most important characteristics, given its own distinctive colour, and illustrated by historical figures thought to epitomise them:

Acorns – force, brown, Charlemagne
Leaves – loyalty, green, Frederick Barbarossa
Radishes – diligence, red, Maximilian I
Sunflowers – wisdom, yellow, Rudolf of Habsburg

The Knaves and under-Knaves depict the kings' attendants and footmen, while the Ace cards present their heraldic crests, all labelled in German. The pip cards are equally as ornate: their value is indicated not only by the numbers shown in all four corners, but also by the number of suit marks shown, with acorns, leaves, radishes and sunflowers growing out of the ground. Furthermore, each card has a small illustration at the bottom presenting allegorical objects representing industry, craft, wealth and other virtues.

Multiple editions of this unique and novel deck were published, of which the present example is the first, distinguished by the decorative framework and value markers found in the four corners.

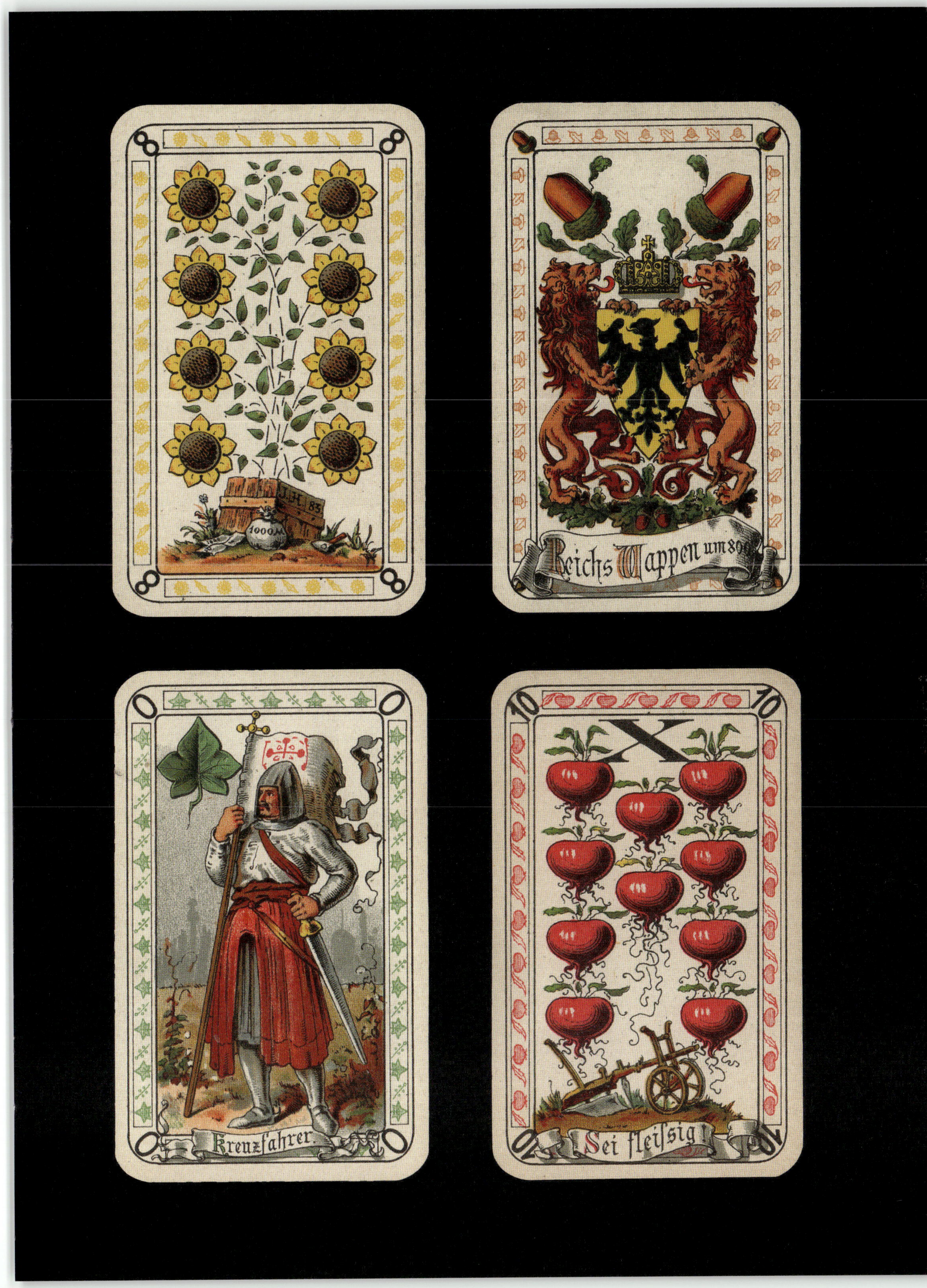

Reichs Wappen um 800
Kreuzfahrer
Sei fleiſsig!

When Queens become horsemen, ...

107 PIATNIK, Ferdinand

[Trappola playing cards].

Publication
[Austria, Ferd. Piatnik & Sohne, c1885].

Description
36 chromolithograph playing cards, black and orange dramatic print to versos.

Dimensions
105 by 56mm (4.25 by 2.25 inches).

References
Van den Bergh pp.270-271.

The Maker

During the nineteenth century, the game of trappola, the first mention of which is found in written records dating back as far as 1530, was played mostly in central Europe. It is therefore no coincidence that the card-makers who produced the most successful trappola decks were based in this region, in cities such as Prague and Vienna.

The name of Ferdinand Piatnik is found on the Ace of Batons. Piatnik is known to have produced multiple trappola decks, of which the present is among the finest examples. For a description of Piatnik, please see item 72.

The Cards

In contrast to the standard deck, trappola is played with 36 cards using the Italian suits of batons, beakers, coins and swords. The Queen cards are replaced with Horsemen and the pip cards from Three to Six are omitted.

The reflected characters on the double-figure court cards merge together more seamlessly than other contemporary designs, and their outfits and accoutrements are shown in great detail. The Ace cards are amongst the most intricate in the deck, consisting of a single suit symbol highly embellished and surrounded by elaborate ornamentation.

The pip cards equally as ornate, with their value indicated both by two Roman numerals, and also by the number of symbols are shown. These often interweave or overlap to create wonderful patterns and displays.

Since 1944, no decks of trappola cards have been published, making the present example an important memento of a bygone era in playing cards.

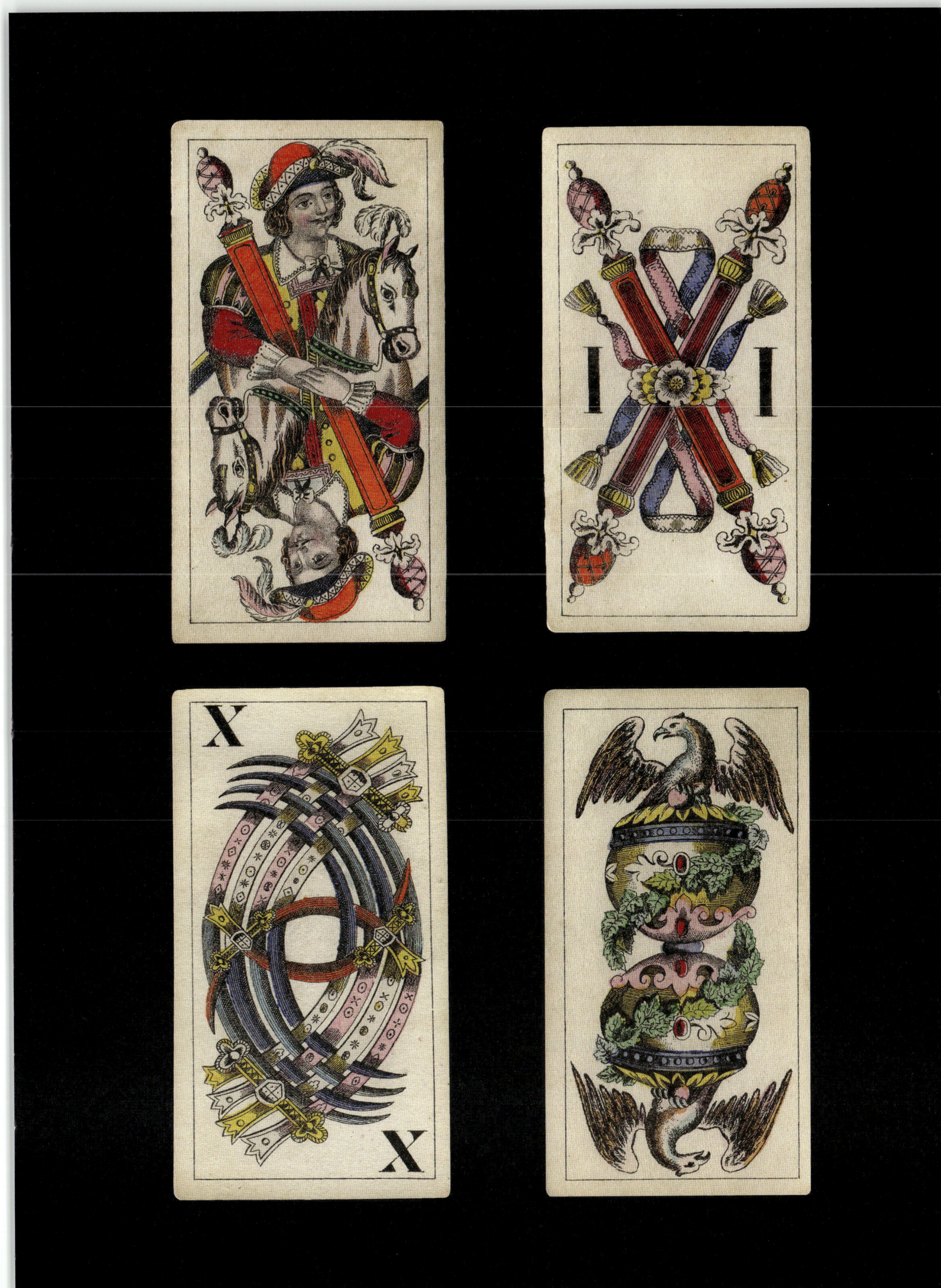

"Smoke and Chew, Kids Plug Cut tobacco"

108 GRAVELY & MILLER TOBACCO CO

[Fancy Playing Cards].

Publication
Danville, Gravely & Miller, c1887.

Description
52 chromolithograph playing cards with one joker and one extra card, blue advertisement to versos.

Dimensions
98 by 57mm (3.75 by 2.25 inches).

]References
Van den Bergh pp.186-187.

The Maker
During the 1870s, the town of Danville in Virginia had become a thriving economic centre due to the establishment of several tobacco factories. Among these was that of Gravely & Miller, a company that started up producing "plug-and-twist" chewing tobacco, but by 1885 had branched out into regular smoking tobacco. The firm never seems to have expanded beyond regional supply, and was fairly short-lived.

The Cards
To obtained a complimentary deck of cards in nineteenth century Virginia, the eager smoker simply had to send back 50 packages of Gravely & Miller's Tobacco Company products to the manufacturer. "Return 50 tin tags taken from any brand of Gravely & Miller's tobacco to Gravely & Miller Danville, VA, by mail And they will send you in Exchange for same a complete Deck of these Fancy Playing Cards". The scarcity of the deck today could be taken to indicate the failure of this innovative marketing technique.

In total the deck shows 14 different images, with the cards of equal value sharing the same picture, and the joker presenting one more. They show women in a variety of different poses, often in low-cut clothing that would have been considered quite scandalous during the late nineteenth century. Similarly remarkable is the fact that the advertisements on the back of each card shows two young children, with the slogan "Smoke and Chew, Kids Plug Cut tobacco".

J
KIDS
Plug Cut.

K
KIDS
Plug Cut.

6
KIDS
Plug Cut.

7
Kids
Plug Cut.

"for distribution to the lady guests of the Master and Wardens of the Worshipful Company of Makers of Playing Cards"

109 WORSHIPFUL COMPANY OF MAKERS OF PLAYING CARDS

[Jeu des Reynes Renommées].

Publication
London, Worshipful Company of Makers of Playing Cards, 1887.

Description
52 engraved playing cards, with booklet.

Dimensions
88 by 54mm (3.5 by 2.25 inches).

References
Hargrave pp.181-182; van den Bergh p.125.

The Maker

The Worshipful Company of Makers of Playing Cards was founded by Royal Charter in 1628, to stem the flow of foreign playing cards that was putting London card-makers at risk. In exchange for a complete ban on all imported cards, a tax was levied at a rate of one farthing per pack. In 1882, at a feast held to mark the inauguration of the Company's new officials, each liveryman was given a commemorative deck of cards, a tradition that has been continued ever since.

The Cards

The present deck is a reproduction of a deck that was published around 1644 by Jean Desmarests, with engravings by the famous Stefano della Bella. The deck was published in book form together with three other decks: 'Jeu des Roys de France', 'Jeu de la Geographie' and 'Jeu des Fables'.

The edition produced over two centuries later by the card-makers guild was very limited, made only "for distribution to the lady guests of the Master and Wardens of the Worshipful Company of Makers of Playing Cards at the summer meeting of the Court of the Company, July 2, 1887". Accordingly, examples are exceedingly rare.

Desmarests' deck was chosen for reproduction because of its title, 'Jeu des reynes renommées' ('The game of famous Queens') which was thought by the Company to fit nicely with the golden jubilee of Queen Victoria.

Each card shows an engragved depiction of a female ruler, ancient and modern, mythological and historical, accompanied by several lines of French text briefly explaining her rule. The suit mark and value of the card is shown in one of the upper corners.

D
Semiramis
Reyne des Assyriens.
Elle regna apres la mort de Ninus son mary, et par sa valeur estendit son Empire de tous costez. elle enuironna la grande Babylone d'vn mur merueilleux.
Vaillante
VA
Penthesilee
Reyne des Amazones. Elle vint au secours des Troyens contre les Grecs, et rendit de grandes preuues de sa vaillance. Elle fut tuée par Achille.
R
Saincte
Anne d'Austriche
Reyne de France, Saincte, Sage, d'vne bonté merueilleuse, et d'vne modestie pareille a sa grandeur. Petite fille d'Empereurs, fille et sœur de deux grands Roys, femme d'vn plus grand encore et tousjours victorieux, et mere d'vn Roy donné du Ciel a ses vœux, qui surpassera tous les Roys du monde.
4
habile
Catherine de Medicis
Femme de Henry 2. Roy de France, et mere de trois Roys de France, François 2, Charles 9, et Henry 3. Princesse judicieuse, accorte et elo= quente. Pendant le regne de ses 3 fils elle se maintint tousjours puissante, en balançant le party des Princes du sang auec celuy des Princes de Lorraine
5
golante
Cleopatre
Reyne d'Egypte. Elle gagna les bonnes graces de Cesar, entrant de nuit dans sa chambre par la fenestre. et il luy confirma le Royaume. Depuis elle se rendit maistresse de l'esprit d'Antoine, qui se perdit auec elle dans les deli= ces, et en perdit l'Empire et la vie. Elle se fit mourir apres luy.
1
heureuse
Ester
Estant simple fille Juiue, elle espousa Assuerus Roy d'Egypte, et par sa pri= ere sauua tout le peuple hebreu dont la totale destruction auoit esté reso= lüe.

Super-size me

110 **PASTOR, Edouard**

[El Barco].

Publication
Valencia, Vidua de Ismael Haase, c1888.

Description
48 chromolithograph playing cards, printed blue advertisement to chocolate factory to verso).

Dimensions
110- by 77mm (4.25 by 3 inches).

References
Van den Bergh p.200-201.

The Makers

The El Barco chocolatier led Valencia's chocolate industry in the late nineteenth century, and was particularly well known for its ornate tin boxes and collectable stickers and playing cards with which its products came. These were printed by a variety of lithographers, including Simeon Durá, J. Esteller and the widow of Ismael Haase. The name of the later is found on many of the present cards, but the Nine of Clubs also identifies J. Esteller as the lithographer.

The cards were designed by illustrator and artist Edouard Pastor, whose name also appears on the Nine of Clubs. Pastor was also responsible for another deck of cards during the previous decade, which were produced by Durá.

The Cards

One of the most notable features of the present deck is its size, with the cards all being considerably larger than average. This allows for highly detailed images, with each whimsical scene integrating the four traditional Spanish suits of coins, cups, clubs and swords. The Twelve of Coins, for instance, shows a cigar-smoking man with a comically large and round head, while the Six of Cups shows a medieval feast at which the participants are all raising their cups in a toast.

With the exception of the Aces, each card features a miniature version of the standard playing card, which is itself sometimes incorporated into the scene. The value of each card is also written in text along the lower edge.

12 FÁBRICA DE CHOCOLATES "EL BARCO" VALENCIA
REY DE OROS.
Lit Vda de Ismael Haase. Colon, 7 y 9 Valencia.

1 FÁBRICA DE CHOCOLATES "EL BARCO" VALENCIA
AS DE BASTOS.
Lit Vda de Ismael Haase. Colon, 7 y 9 Valencia.

1 FÁBRICA DE CHOCOLATES "EL BARCO" VALENCIA
AS DE ESPADAS.
Lit Vda de Ismael Haase. Colon, 7 y 9 Valencia.

8 FÁBRICA DE CHOCOLATES "EL BARCO" VALENCIA
OCHO DE OROS.
Lit Vda de Ismael Haase. Colon, 7 y 9 Valencia.

Sweet Caporal cigarette cards

111 KINNEY BROTHERS

[Harlequin Cards].

Publication
New York, Kinney Tobacco Co., 1889.

Description
52 chromolithograph playing cards and one joker.

Dimensions
88 by 63mm (3.5 by 2.5 inches).

References
Hargrave p.365; van den Bergh pp.176-177; Yale 460/USA269.

The Maker
The Kinney Tobacco Company was one of America's leading cigarette manufacturers during the nineteenth century, merging into the American Tobacco Company in 1890. It was responsible for the creation of the 'Sweet Caporal' cigarette brand, and became particularly famous due to its innovative advertising method. During the 1880s, it created and issued a wide range of playing and trading cards featuring everything from horses to actresses, military paraphernalia to butterflies.

The Cards
Most successful among the Kinney Tobacco Company's marketing cards were the Harlequin Cards; to receive a complimentary deck, one simply had to collect and send in 100 wrappers from Kinney's various tobacco products. The deal was hugely popular, and the cards were in great demand, no doubt due to their comical nature.

The court cards show the traditional full-length royal characters engaged in unconventional activities: the Queen of Hearts plays the banjo, while the King of Diamonds counts his money. The Queen of Clubs is shown taking a swig from a flask, while the Queen of Diamonds examines a diamond-shaped jewel. Each suit follows a theme, with Clubs associated with alcohol, Diamonds with wealth, Hearts with music and Spades, rather more virtuously, with gardening.

The pip cards show all manner of bizarre and humorous scenes, with the suit marks forming key parts of the main image. Some centre around puns, such as the Five of Hearts, which shows chefs with heart-shaped faces busy cooking, labelled 'A Hearty Dinner', and the Two of Hearts, which shows a cock-fight between chickens with heart-shaped bodies, entitled 'Two Brave Hearts'.

Despite their popularity, the present cards are very rare.

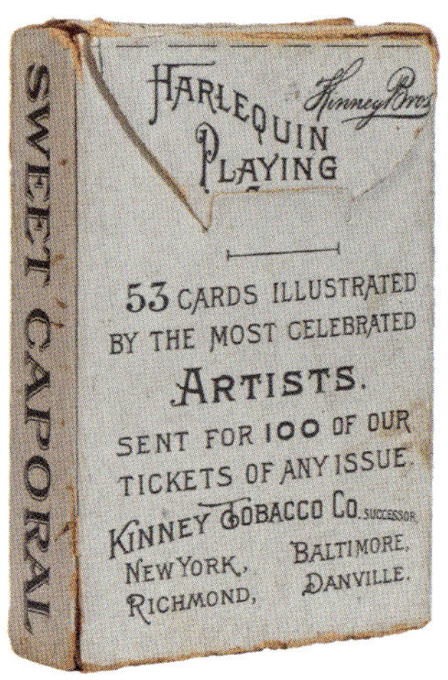

A HEARTY DINNER

EGYPTIAN- CAVALRY

VATER- -LAND.
LAGER

Claude Monet as the Queen of Hearts

112 [ANONYMOUS]

[French caricature playing cards].

Publication
[Paris, Palmier, ?c1890].

Description
32 engraved playing cards with fine original hand-colour, versos plain.

Dimensions
83 by 51mm (3.25 by 2 inches).

References
Van den Bergh p.212.

The Maker
Text on both the Ace of Hearts and Ace of Clubs identifies the maker of the present deck as "Palmier, Paris". While there is evidence of other documents printed by Palmier, there are no other decks of cards attributed to this firm.

The Cards
Each card displays one of a selection of caricatures, often with their heads enlarged to ridiculous proportions. The figures are sourced from everyday French life, with common characters such as the soldier and the policeman making an appearance. The bodies of some are ridiculously exaggerated, while others evoke humour in more bizarre ways, such as the "chasseur à cheval" who has a wooden horse on the King of Diamonds. All card are coloured in gaudy shades of yellow, red and blue.

One interesting card is the Queen of Hearts, which shows "l'artiste". The character shown could perhaps be intended to represent Claude Monet, who started his own artistic career as a caricaturist. The figure certainly bears a strong resemblance to the famous painter. In the upper left corner of each card, there is a miniature version of the playing card.

The simplicity of the deck, with its sketch-like quality, can be attributed to the use of inferior-quality grey paper. This is likely also the reason that the present deck is so rare, and the publishing company of Palmier so little-known.

PALMIER
PARIS
POMPIER de NANTERRE
L'ARTISTE
PALMIER
PARIS
AU MARCHÉ
A L'OPÉRA
LE COLONEL RAMOLLOT
CHASSEUR A CHEVAL

Sleeping Beauty meets Puss in Boots

113 **LEQUART & MIGNOT**

[Fairytale playing cards].

Publication
[Paris, Lequart & Mignot, c1890].

Description
32 engraved playing cards with fine original hand-colour, versos plain.

Dimensions
85 by 53mm (3.25 by 2 inches).

References
British Museum Schreiber French 48; Van den Bergh p.209.

The Maker
The name of the maker "Lequart & Mignot" appears on the Ace of Clubs. The firm operated in Paris from 1878 until 1891, before it was bought by B. P. Grimaud in 1891.

The Cards
A mixture of caricatured figures from everyday life and scenes from popular fairy tales and folklore adorn these cards. The Nine of Diamonds, for instance, depicts Sleeping Beauty and the Ten of Spades Puss in Boots, while a policeman is shown on the Ace of Clubs, and a judge on the Ace of Spades.

Each card has a miniature version of the full playing card dominating the upper left-hand corner, so that they form a fully functional deck as well as an interesting reflection on popular culture. The deck bears a strong resemblance to another deck published around the same time by Courbière in St. Étienne.

DON QUICHOTTE
DANSEUSE
LEQUART & MIGNOT
PARIS
Depose
GENERAL
LA BELLE AU BOIS DORMANT
LE CHAT BOTTÉ
ESPAGNOL

Hard-A-Port Cut Plug, Wake Up Cut Plug and Trumps Long Cut

114 MOORE & CALVI TOBACCO CO.

[Advertising playing cards].

Publication
[New York, Lindner, Eddy & Claus, c1890].

Description
52 chromolithograph playing cards with one joker.

Dimensions
99 by 57mm (4 by 2.25 inches).

References
Van den Bergh pp.188; Yale 290/USA120.

The Maker
Moore & Calvi was a New York-based tobacco manufacturer that is best remembered not for its smoking products but for the playing cards it produced to advertise its various brands of tobacco, including Hard-A-Port Cut Plug, Wake Up Cut Plug and Trumps Long Cut. All three brands had their own separate playing cards with images of graceful ladies.

One of New York's largest lithography companies during the late nineteenth century, Lindner, Eddy & Claus was responsible for the manufacture and publication of Moore & Calvi's cards. They also worked with other tobacco companies, such as Allen & Ginter, on a range of promotional material.

The Cards
The present deck represents one of the most successful ventures into commercial advertising through the medium of playing cards. During the late nineteenth century, Moore & Calvi issued six decks of playing cards to advertise their various products, with the present example promoting their Hard-A-Port Cut Plug tobacco.

The cards' success might be attributed to the risqué poses and outfits worn by the female figures, dressed up for the pantomime or dance hall. The figures on the court cards are distinguished by their crowns, tiaras and various other headwear, and each card bears the name of the product. A story surrounding the deck would have it that the women shown were models from New York, who agreed to pose as models for the designer, although whether this is true has not been confirmed.

Complete decks are extremely rare and still much in demand, so much so that there is still a buzzing trade in individual Moore & Calvi playing cards.

J
HARD-A-PORT
CUT PLUG.

Q
HARD A PORT
CUT PLUG.

K
HARD A PORT
CUT PLUG.

4
HARD A PORT
CUT PLUG.

Queen Wilhelmina of The Netherlands takes the throne

115 **WÜST, Conrad Ludwig**

[Dutch Empire playing cards].

Publication
Frankfurt, Conrad Ludwig Wüst, 1890.

Description
52 lithograph playing cards, blue printed floral pattern to versos.

Dimensions
92 by 62mm (3.5 by 2.5 inches).

References
Van den Bergh p.124.

The Maker
For a description of Conrad Ludwig Wüst, please see item 41.

The Cards
In 1890, Wüst published the present deck to celebrate the ascension of the young Queen Wilhelmina to the Netherlandish throne. As Wilhelmina was only ten years of age, her mother would rule as regent for a period of eight years before she was inaugurated as the new queen in the New Church in Amsterdam on 6 September, 1898.

The case in which the cards were originally issued showed two pictures of Wilhelmina, as a child and then as a young woman. Each Ace card depicts two important Dutch cities, while the Kings show earlier monarchs. The Queen cards show women in traditional Dutch dress, with the Queen of Hearts a personification of the Netherlands: the Dutch Virgin. Interestingly, the Queen of Spades shows a Javanese woman, a reference to the Dutch empire and its history in southeast Asia.

The present deck was reissued once again in 1898 to mark Wilhelmina's inauguration, and a further edition appeared in 1905, with some of the colonial imagery exchanged for typical Dutch images.

AMSTERDAM · HOOGESLUIS.
AMSTERDAM · DE DAM.
Z.M. WILLEM II. KONING DER NEDERLANDEN·1840-1849.
ZEEUWSCHE VROUW
PALEIS VAN DEN GOUVERNEUR · OOST INDIE.
GEZICHT OP CURAÇAO-WEST INDIE.

A souvenir of the World's Fair, 1893

116 CLARK, G. W.

[World's Columbian Exposition playing cards].

Publication
[Chicago, Columbian Souvenir Playing Card Company, 1893].

Description
52 chromolithograph playing cards, with one wild card and extra card, illustrations to versos.

Dimensions
88 by 63mm (3.5 by 2.5 inches).

References
British Museum Schreiber American 3; van den Bergh p.69; Yale 433/USA242.

The Maker
Each card in the deck bears the imprint "Copyrighted 1893 by G.W. Clark". There appears to be only one other deck attributed to G.W. Clark, published in North Carolina in 1936. It shows verses by the Persian poet Omar Khayyam, whose work was experiencing something of a revival in fin de siècle America.

The Cards
A souvenir of the Chicago World Fair in 1893, which celebrated the 400th anniversary of Columbus' arrival in the Americas, lasted six months, attracted 27 million visitors, and took place within 200 newly-constructed temporary buildings across 600 acres. Each of the cards depicts a different building from the fair, with the Ace of Diamonds showing the Palace of Fine Arts, which survives today as the Museum of Science and Industry.

The suit marks are shown in the upper right- and lower left-hand corners, while on the opposite sides appear a miniature version of the playing card. Bold text at the top and bottom of each card identifies its value. On the back of the cards is an illustration of Columbus and his crew disembarking from their boats on the American shore. The wild card shows medallions of the explorer's royal patrons, Ferdinand and Isabella of Spain.

FIVE
NEW JERSEY BL'D'G
COPYRIGHTED 1893 BY G.W. CLARK
KING
TRANSPORTATION BL'DG
COPYRIGHTED 1893 BY G.W. CLARK
QUEEN
AGRICULTURAL BL'DG.
COPYRIGHTED 1893 BY G.W. CLARK
ACE
ART PALACE
COPYRIGHTED 1893 BY G.W. CLARK

The last of the nineteenth century transformation decks

117 UNITED STATES PLAYING CARD COMPANY

Vanity Fair: No 42.

Publication
Cincinnati, United States Playing Card Company, 1895.

Description
52 chromolithograph playing cards and one joker, blue pattern with four clown heads to versos.

Dimensions
88 by 63mm (3.5 by 2.5 inches).

References
Van den Bergh pp.178-179; Yale 401/ USA210.

The Maker

The United States Playing Card Company was established in 1867 as a large manufacturer and distributor of many different brands of playing cards and other gaming paraphernalia, such as poker chips. The Company continued independently until it was acquired by playing card giant Cartamundi in 2019.

The Cards

Despite the popularity of transformation cards throughout the nineteenth century, it was not until 1895 that the United States Playing Card Company published its first deck in this style. The present example is similar in some ways to the Harlequin playing cards produced by the Kinney Tobacco Company (see item 111) in that court cards of each suit are assigned a theme: clubs focuses on injuries, diamonds on wealth, hearts on smoking and spades on gardening.

They also draw on humour, with the pip cards showing all manner of bizarre scenes, from a marching band made up of frogs, to the activities of witches. Ominously, the devil is pictured on the joker. The title is found on the Ace of Spades, which reads 'Vanity Fair No. 41'; it would be the final transformation deck published in the nineteenth century.

Vanity Fair
No 41
COPYRIGHTED 1895 BY
THE UNITED STATES PLAYING CARD COMPANY,
CINCINNATI, U. S. A.

Printed in gold for the Tsar

118 [ANONYMOUS]

[Imperial Russian playing cards].

Publication
St Petersburg, Imperial Playing Card Factory, 1896.

Description
52 chromolithograph playing cards, gold and blue printed pattern to versos.

Dimensions
70 by 48mm (2.75 by 2 inches).

References
Van den Bergh p.263.

The Maker

In 1817, Tsar Alexander I founded the Imperial Playing-Card Factory in St Petersburg, intending its proceeds to help fund the Imperial Foundling Hospitals, although it was speculated that his private coffers may also have benefitted. In 1842, French card-maker Paul Bienvenu de la Rue took charge of the imperial playing card monopoly, and under his leadership it went from strength to strength. Decks issued from the factory all bear a stamp showing a pelican nurturing its young, found here on the Ace of Diamonds.

Cards were a popular pastime in nineteenth century Russian society. The long, dark nights would be filled with hours of card games, and they also formed a key parlour activity for upper-class ladies. Russia was the greatest importer of playing cards in Europe, using around one million decks of cards each year.

The Cards

Perhaps the best-known example of the Jugendstil style to come out of Russia, these cards feature the double-figure court cards, with far more abstract designs than those traditionally found on the publications of the Imperial Playing Card Factory. The mirror images blend seamlessly into one another on several cards, for example the Queen of Clubs, Jack of Diamonds and King of Spades.

The golden print gives the present cards an additional sense of luxury which suggests that this deck may have been intended for export, or else for Russian high-society. It was included at the Hermitage, Amsterdam in 2009 and 2010 as part of an exhibition on life at the Russian Court, implying that such cards may even have been produced for the royal family itself.

ВЪ ПОЛЬЗУ ИМПЕР: ВОСПИТ: ДОМА.

Designed by Tiffany

119 **TIFFANY, Louis Comfort**

[Tiffany playing cards].

Publication
Cincinnati, United States Playing Card Company, 1896.

Description
52 chromolithograph playing cards and one joker card, brown printed pattern to versos.

Dimensions
87 by 63mm (3.5 by 2.5 inches).

References
Van den Bergh p.247.

The Maker
Louis Comfort Tiffany (1848-1933), son of the famous jeweler, was a glass artist who played an important role in popularizing Jugendstil (see item 120) in America.

The deck was published by the United States Playing Card Company; for a description of the company, please see item 117.

The Cards
Tiffany designed this set to coincide with the fast-approaching turn of the century. The style of the cards clearly shows Jugendstil elements, an art movement that was very popular fin de siècle.

The double-figure court cards are far less constricted and formal than the standard design, while retaining its common features, such as an axe on the Jack cards and the Kings holding swords. The suit mark is shown twice in both the upper left and lower right corners, one accompanied by the value of the card.

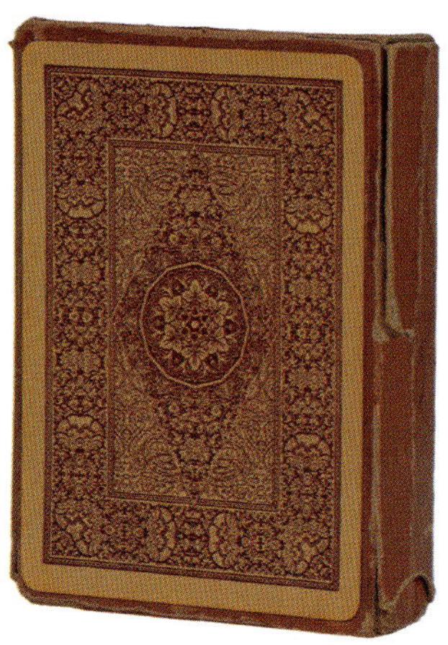

Q
J
Q
K

Organically inspired, representing a transition toward abstraction and functionalism

120 **UNITED STATES PLAYING CARD COMPANY**

[Circus playing cards].

Publication
Cincinnati, United States Playing Card Company, 1896.

Description
52 chromolithograph playing cards and one joker card, red and green panels to versos.

Dimensions
88 by 64mm (3.5 by 2.5 inches).

References
Hargrave pp.355-356; van den Bergh p.208; Yale 424/USA233.

The Maker
For a description of the United States Playing Card Company, please see item 117.

The Cards
The circus features as the theme of the present deck, which shows the influence of the Jugendstil style that developed in Germany while Art Nouveau was taking hold across Europe. Jugendstil, or 'Young Style', tended toward arabesques and was organically inspired, representing a transition toward abstraction and functionalism. These cards show much the same style as those designed by Louis Comfort Tiffany around the same time (item 119).

The double-figure court cards depict a series of familiar characters from the circus, with the Kings pictured as ring-masters, Queens as dancers or Amazons, and Jacks as clowns. The Joker card shows an elaborate mirrored image of a ballerina, surrounded by the ominous faces of jesters in all four corners. The Ace and pip cards are simply identified by the number of suit marks shown.

J
Q
K
J

"X"-rated

121 **UNITED STATES PLAYING CARD COMPANY**

No. 65x The Stage playing cards.

Publication
Cincinnati, United States Playing Card Company, 1896.

Description
52 chromolithograph playing cards with photo-engraving and one joker card, all edges gilt, with blue, green and gold panels to versos.

Dimensions
89 by 63mm (3.5 by 2.5 inches).

References
Van den Bergh p.218; Yale 447/USA256.

The Maker
For a description of the United States Playing Card Company, please see item 117.

The Cards
Depicting famous actors and actresses from the end of the nineteenth century, this deck of card appeals to the new celebrity culture that was beginning to emerge towards the turn of the century. Each Ace and court card shows four photographs of leading stars of the stage, their names identified in the photograph. The joker shows popular actor and comedian Marshall P. Wilder. The influence of the Jugendstil artistic movement (see item 120) is readily apparent in the layout of the cards. The pip cards simply reflect their value in the number of suit marks shown.

The cards are entitled 'No. 65x The Stage playing cards', with the 'x' indicating that the cards have gilt edges.

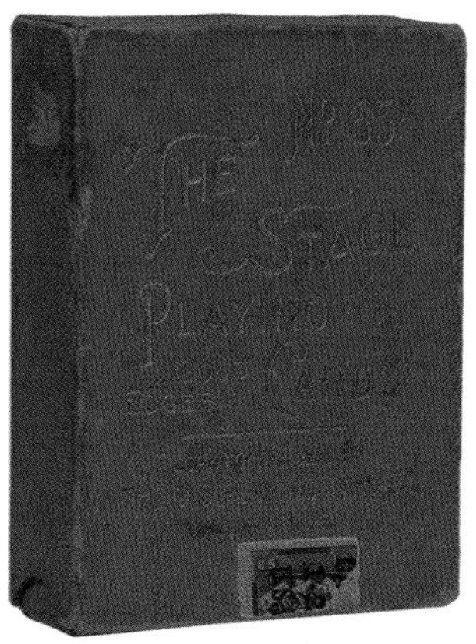

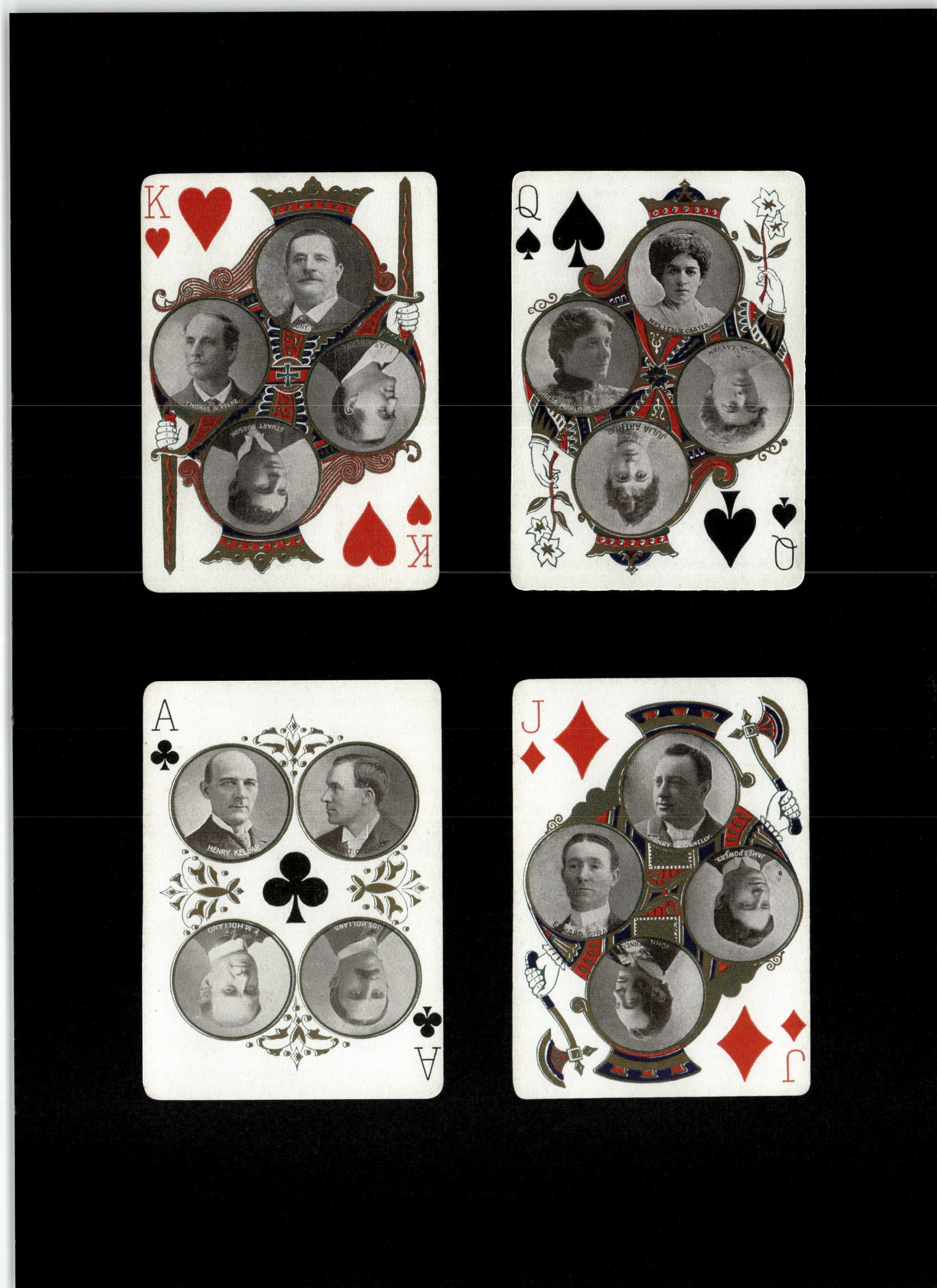

Victorian leading ladies

122 W. D. & H. O. WILLS

[Advertising playing cards].

Publication
[Germany, 1898].

Description
52 chromolithograph playing cards, with advertisement to versos.

Dimensions
67 by 35mm (2.75 by 1.5 inches).

References
Van den Bergh p.192.

The Maker
Founded in Bristol in 1786, W. D. & H. O. Wills was a British tobacco importer and manufacturer which became the first company in the country to mass-produce cigarettes. In 1887, it started adding promotional cards to its products, and then 1897 and 1898, the first series with small playing cards was published. Wills issued dozens of decks in the early decades of the twentieth century, but only a few of them actually functioned as playing cards; the others were simply collectable trading cards designed to appeal to the masculine market, with sports, aviation and women all frequently featured.

The Cards
Wills' second venture into promotional playing cards was preceded, the year before, by a deck that had shown a collection of 'charming ladies' focusing on actresses. Both decks showed the text 'Will's Cigarettes' and 'W.D. & H.O.Wills Ltd Bristol & London' on the back of each card.

Each card of a suit shows a different portrait of an actress, dressed up in the fine garments, jewellery and hats of the day. Their serene faces perfectly fit the mould of the ideal Victorian woman, in a period when actresses were beginning to shed the disrepute often associated with the profession, and win some respect for their talents. The suit mark and value is shown in the upper left-hand corner, while a miniature version of the playing card appears in the upper right.

A caption reads 'Printed in Germany', showing that the British company had opted for foreign manufacture, no doubt due to cheaper costs.

This deck proved extremely popular, and over the following decades W. D. & H. O. Wills would continue to publish cards showing famous actresses, eventually adopting photographic images and captioning each card with the name of the specific woman shown. Despite its success at the time, the present deck is now extremely rare.

WILLS's
W.D.&H.O.WILLS.Ld.
TRADE MARK
Bristol & London.
Cigarettes
Printed in Germany

Playing at grown-ups

123 [ANONYMOUS] [after] Joseph GLANZ

[Children's playing cards].

Publication
[?Austria, c1900].

Description
52 engraved playing cards with fine original hand-colour.

Dimensions
74 by 43mm (3 by 1.75 inches).

References
Van den Bergh p.272.

The Maker
Nothing is known about the origin or the maker of this deck. It is even uncertain whether it was made in Austria, as a German manufacturer cannot be entirely ruled out. It is clear, however, that the maker was inspired by the "children cards" published by Joseph Glanz in Vienna in 1890.

The Cards
The court cards are by far the most interesting aspect of the present deck: the typical double-figure royal characters are here represented as children, little boys dressed up as Kings and Jacks, and young girls wearing the elaborate robes of Queens. The bright primary colours add an equally childish yet charming touch. It is not entirely clear whether the cards were designed with the aim of appealing to children themselves, but the smaller solitaire-sized cards do suggest that they were made for small hands.

"To the Cigarette Connoisseur the name 'Muratti' is a guarantee of Purity & Excellence"

124 MURATTI

[Advertising playing cards].

Publication
[London, Barclay & Fry Ltd., 1904].

Description
52 chromolithograph playing cards, advertisement to versos, lacking joker card.

Dimensions
69 by 37mm (2.75 by 1.5 inches).

References
Van den Bergh p.189.

The Maker

Established in Constantinople in 1821 by Greek tobacco trader Basil Muratoglu, the Muratti tobacco company was transferred to Western Europe after the Ottoman Empire monopolised the industry. In 1885, therefore, Muratti was established in Berlin, and then in London two years later. The company continued to prosper throughout the following century, despite being shut down by the Nazis during the Second World War, and still operates under Philip Morris International.

The printing company of Barclay & Fry Ltd operated first from Cannon Street and then from Queen Street in London, before opening premises in Portsmouth as well. The firm specialised in books and prints, but also produced playing cards. In a somewhat surprising change of direction, it merged with two other companies to form the Allied Tin Box Makers Ltd, which later became Metal Box & Printing Industries.

The Cards

Designed and used as a marketing tool by the London branch of the Muratti tobacco company, these cards centre around the theme of Japan. Although it seems somewhat unrelated to the company's products, it did at least serve to distinguish them from the other promotional decks in circulation at the time, which mainly showed images of attractive women.

Sixteen images appear on the cards, with some designs occuring twice, three or four times on different cards. They show Japanese military personnel and activities, and are particularly notable for their interesting water-colour effect. An advertisement on the back of each card declares the superiority of the brand, with the slogan: "To the Cigarette Connoisseur the name 'Muratti' is a guarantee of Purity & Excellence".

JAPAN
PRESENT DAY
JAPAN
PIONEER
MARCHING ORDER
JAPAN
1870
JAPAN
EARLIEST PERIOD
SERGEANT & PRIVATE
JAPAN
CAVALRY OF THE GUARD
TRUMPETER
TO THE
CIGARETTE
CONNOISSEUR
THE NAME
"Muratti"
IS A
GUARANTEE
OF PURITY &
EXCELLENCE.
JAPAN
1873
JAPAN
ANCIENT ARMY
JAPAN
LINE CAVALRY
MARCHING ORDER
JAPAN
SAILOR
FULL DRESS
JAPAN
GENERAL & OFFICER
1880
JAPAN
EARLY PERIOD
OFFICER & PRIVATE

Rock, Paper, Scissors

125 W. D. & H. O. WILLS

Beauties.

Publication
[?England, 1904].

Description
52 chromolithograph playing cards, advertisement to versos.

Dimensions
66 by 35mm (2.5 by 1.5 inches).

References
Van den Bergh p.194.

The Makers
For a description of W. D. & H. O. Wills, see item 122.

The Cards
One of the oldest brands produced by W.D. & H.O Wills is Scissors. Introduced in 1898, it still exists today and is mainly sold in South-east Asia. In the early twentieth century, a box of Scissors came with a deck of playing cards. These almost always showed images of famous or beautiful women, with decks entitled 'Film Stars', 'Actresses' and 'Beauties'.

The present deck is an example of the latter, with each card showing a portrait of an attractive woman in a series of different outfits or natural environments. In the upper left corner is a miniature version of the playing card, while the suit mark and value appear in the lower right, making the deck a fully functional set of playing cards.

On the back of each card is an advertisement showing a box of Scissors cigarettes, which are described as "special army quality".

SCISSORS

"Resolved! That I will make people laugh if I get a licking every hour. Buster Brown"

126 **UNITED STATES PLAYING CARD COMPANY**

[My Own Playing Cards, Buster Brown 654].

Publication
Cincinnati, United States Playing Card Company, 1906.

Description
52 chromolithograph playing cards and joker card.

Dimensions
62 by 44mm (2.5 by 1.75 inches).

References
Hargrave p.365; Van den Bergh p.190.

The Maker
For a description of the United States Playing Card Company, please see item 117.

The Cards
Buster Brown was a character from a comic book series that emerged in 1902, a young boy who starts every story with good intentions but inevitably ends up in trouble.

Each suit in the present deck contains three of Buster's adventures, with two stories illustrated across four cards, and one across five. The charming comic-book style illustrations have speech bubbles to express the characters' thoughts. The title of each story is found at the bottom of the card, while the suit marks and values are shown in the upper left and lower right corners.

A sign on the Joker reads: "Resolved! That I will make people laugh if I get a licking every hour. Buster Brown". On the box, Buster is shown standing next to his loyal dog Tige, holding a sign with the text "My Own Playing Cards, Buster Brown 654". The subject matter of the cards may suggest that they are an early example of a deck aimed at children.

BUSTER BROWN JOKER
RESOLVED THAT I WILL MAKE PEOPLE LAUGH IF I GET A LICKING EVERY HOUR.— BUSTER BROWN

A
THERE BUSTER IS A NICE BICYCLE FOR YOU
Copyright, 1906, by The U.S. Playing Card Co.
Buster Brown's new bicycle.

2
NOW TIGE OUT TO WESTCHESTER COUNTY FOR A LITTLE TRIP
Copyright, 1906, by The U.S. Playing Card Co.
Buster Brown's new bicycle.

3
WELL, I'LL BE HANGED
ARE THOSE ROCKS AHEAD
Copyright, 1906, by The U.S. Playing Card Co.
Buster Brown's new bicycle.

A
PORTIA I WANT YOU TO BAKE A NICE CAKE
Copyright, 1906, by The U.S. Playing Card Co.
Buster helps bake a cake.

2
I'LL JUST TRY THAT DOUGH
Copyright, 1906, by The U.S. Playing Card Co.
Buster helps bake a cake.

3
SOL, LA, SEE, DOUGH!
DOUGH, RA, ME, FA.
Copyright, 1906, by The U.S. Playing Card Co.
Buster helps bake a cake.

4
TURN OFF THE WATER, BUSTER
Copyright, 1906, by The U.S. Playing Card Co.
Buster helps bake a cake.

Paint me like one of your French girls

127 BRITISH AMERICAN TOBACCO

Beauties.

Publication
[?London, B.A.T, c1908].

Description
52 chromolithograph playing cards, advertisement to versos.

Dimensions
68 by 35mm (2.75 by 1.5 inches).

References
Van den Bergh p.197.

The Maker
Established in 1902, B.A.T (British American Tobacco) was one of the many tobacco companies that issued promotional playing cards along with their products. B.A.T continues to operate today as the second-largest cigarette manufacturer in the world.

The Cards
In 1908, B.A.T published a deck of cards showing a number of charming ladies entitled 'Beauties'.

Each card shows a three-quarter portrait of an attractive woman wearing a variety of adornments. In the upper left-hand corner is a miniature version of the playing card, while the suit mark and value are shown in the lower right. This makes the deck a fully functioning set of playing cards, rather than just a series of collectable trading cards.

It is possible that actresses and go-go dancers modeled for these cards. It would at least explain the somewhat revealing clothes and sultry poses of the pictured ladies. The deck may even have been a response to the cards of the same name published four years earlier by their competitor, W. D. & H. O. Wills (see item 122). The more risqué images could suggest that B.A.T were trying to one-up their rivals with this deck of 'Beauties'.

Commemorating the sixth centenary of the Swiss Republic

128 MULLER, Jean

Vues & Costumes Suisses.

Publication
Switzerland, Jean Muller, [c1910].

Description
52 engraved playing cards with fine original hand-colour, different views to verso of each card.

Dimensions
89 by 59mm (3.5 by 2.25 inches).

References
British Museum Schreiber Swiss 22; van den Bergh p.62.

The Maker
In 1828, Colonel Johann Bernhard Zundel founded a small playing card workshop under the name 'AG Müller'. Two years later, he took on Johannes Müller as an apprentice and in 1838, Johannes bought the business, which was by then producing thousands of decks each year. Under Müller's leadership, machinery was introduced into the process of card-making and the firm experienced huge growth, eventually expanding to produce railway tickets as well. Müller's son, also named Johann, took over the business after his father's death and the firm remained in the family until 1982. Today it continues to produce cards, specialising in tarot cards, which are sold worldwide.

The Cards
Sold under the name 'Vues & Costumes Suisses' ('Swiss views & costumes'), the present deck was designed for tourists in Switzerland. These souvenir playing cards had first appeared in the early nineteenth century. Of the earlier examples, this deck bears the most resemblance to those published by C.L.Wüst in 1860 (item 102). Unusually, however, the Ace cards show only one scenic view, namely:

Club – Glacier de Rosenlaui
Diamond – Montreux
Heart – Chûte-du-Rhin
Spade – Rigi-Koulm

The double-figure court cards exhibit the native dress and coat-of-arms of various Swiss regions, identified by name in the upper right- and lower left-hand corners, opposite their respective suit marks. Each card has a different scenic view on the back contained within an oval, the spandrels decorated with a red floral design. The distinctive nature of the backs makes it unlikely that the present cards were designed to be used in games.

This deck first appeared in 1891, when it was published to commemorate the sixth centenary of the Swiss Republic. A title card was included in this first edition that fails to appear in any of the subsequent versions. The box in which the present deck was originally found bears the imprint of 'J. Muller & Cie', which was used by the firm from 1910 onwards, allowing it to be dated to roughly this time.

Rigi-Koulm
SEELISBERG
Chûte-du-Rhin
Valais
Argovie
Berne
Vaud

Birds of a feather,... play poker?

129 W. D. & H. O. WILLS

Birds of Brilliant Plumage.

Publication
[?England, c1910].

Description
52 chromolithograph playing cards, with advertisements to versos.

Dimensions
62 by 35mm (2.5 by 1.5 inches).

References
Van den Bergh p.193.

The Maker
For a description of W. D. & H. O. Wills, please see item 117.

The Cards
Birds are the theme of this later deck published by W. D. & H. O. Wills, which were often found on insert cards. The company published this deck as an accompaniment to its 'Four Aces' cigarette brand from 1909 to 1912, although many of the same images are also found in decks issued with other brands, such as 'Ogdens', 'Ruler' and 'Cigarettes Copain'. They are distinguished, however, by the advertisement on the back of each card.

The deck certainly lives up to its title, 'Birds of Brilliant Plummage': each card shows a double image of a different bird. From woodpeckers to parrots, the depictions are realistic and coloured in bold hues. In the upper left corner there is a miniature version of the full playing card, while in the lower right the suit mark and value of each card is indicated, making it a fully functioning deck as well as an attractive series of images.

While there is no caption to indicate the manufacturer of the present deck, it may be the case that W. D. & H. O. Wills continued to have their cards made in Germany at this time.

The German navy on deck

130 PETZOLDT, Hermann

[Deutsche einheiskarte].

Publication
[Stralsund, Altenburger und Stralsunder Spielkartenfabrik, c1915].

Description
24 chromolithograph playing cards, stamp to one, cross patteé pattern printed to versos.

Dimensions
101 by 57mm (4 by 2.25 inches).

References
Van den Bergh p.101.

The Maker

Hermann Petzoldt was the designer behind the present deck of cards. The publisher's imprint on Under-Knave of Acorns reads 'Spielkartenfabriken A.G. Straslsund Vereinigte Stralsunder'. Vereinigte Stralsunder was the name the Altenburg printing firm operated under after merging with two other local playing card companies in 1872. In 1832, two brothers named Bernhard and Otto Bechstein established a small company in Altenberg for the manufacture of French and German playing cards. Remarkably, the firm made no profit until 1840 due to the immense competition from larger factories in neighbouring states. From 1840, however, Altenberg cards became well-known for their good quality and value. The business changed hands numerous times throughout the following century, and remains active today as a market leader of German playing cards.

The Cards

The German navy is honoured on these cards, which show its ships, personnel and leaders during the early years of the First World War. The first edition of this deck consisted of 36 cards, the additional cards being the Sevens and Eights, which showed the Navy's most important vessels. The deck is distinguished from the former only by the removal of these cards and the printing of the "K" on the Kings, which is here on the border rather than in the centre.

All the Aces show a portrait of Emperor Wilhelm II, and on the Kings are found the rulers of the various German states:

Acorns – Bavaria
Bells – Baden
Hearts – Württemberg
Leaves – Saxony

The remaining court cards and the Nines and Tens show the images of men who had contributed the German naval efforts during the war thus far, including Graf von Zeppelin and General Hindenburg.

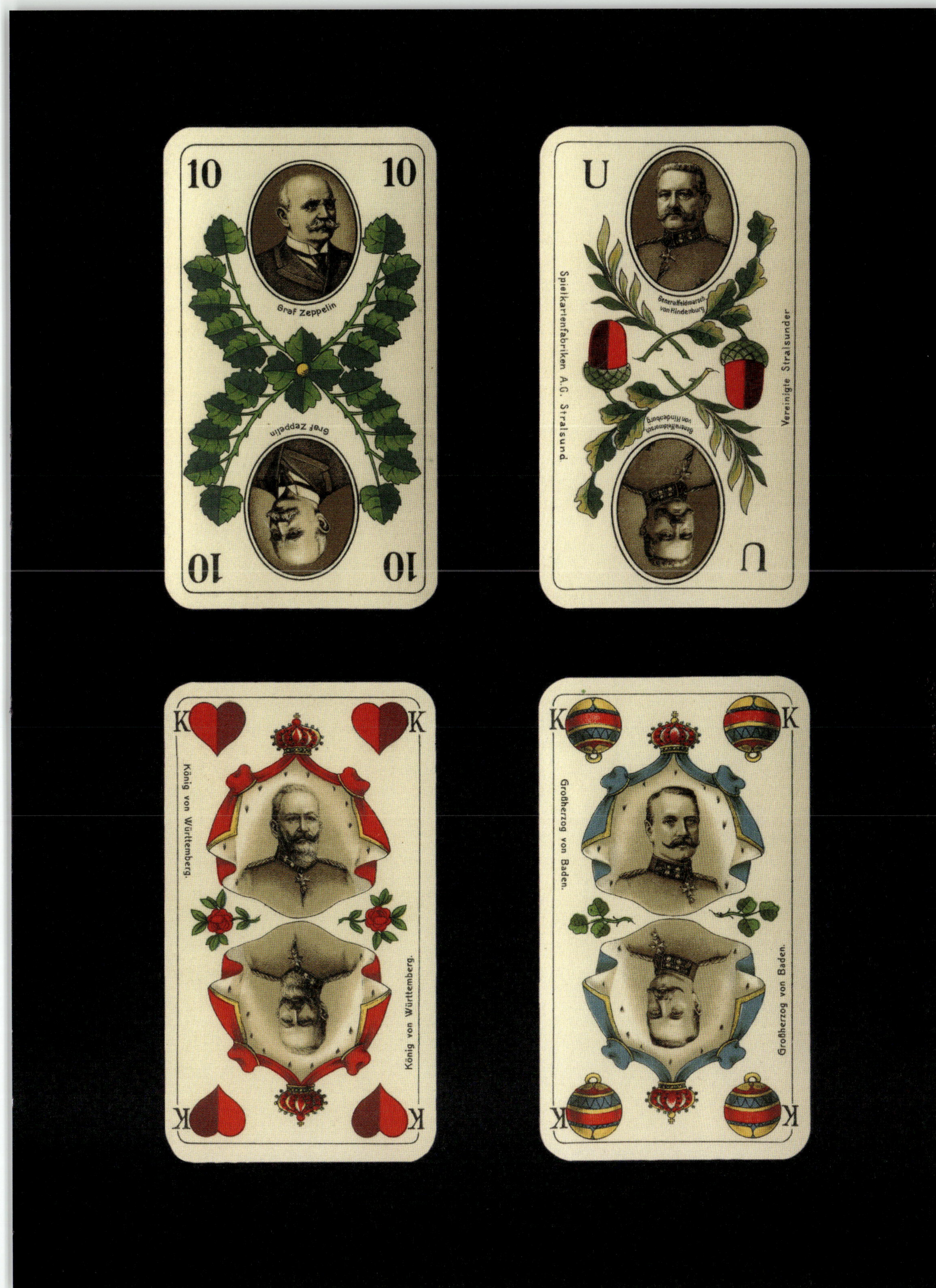
10
Graf Zeppelin
U
Generalfeldmarsch.
von Hindenburg
Spielkartenfabriken A.G. Stralsund.
Vereinigte Stralsunder
K
König von Württemberg.
Großherzog von Baden.

Kaiser Bill – King of Acorns

131 ALTENBURGER UND STALSUNDER SPIELKARTENFABRIK

[German Army WWI playing cards].

Publication
Stralsund, Altenburger und Stralsunder Spielkartenfabrik, [c1916].

Description
32 chromolithograph playing cards, eagle to versos.

Dimensions
101 by 57mm (4 by 2.25 inches).

References
Guiard 19; van den Bergh p.96; Yale 2823/GER420.

The Maker
For a description of the. Altenburger Spielkartenfabrik, see item 130.

The Cards
During the First World War, the Altenburger Spielkartenfabrik firm published propaganda decks to support the war effort. The present deck patriotically uses the German suits of Acorns, Bells, Hearts and Leaves, and each card shows a different image intended to evoke national pride. The court cards show double-figure portraits of the German leaders, the Aces the heraldic arms of the country's kingdoms, and the pip cards various scenes from the war, including two soldiers setting up a huge missile before the cityscape of Antwerp, and armed men marching along the Rhine in Belgium.

The cards proved extremely popular and by the end of the war, 100,000 decks had been published. Interestingly, the design of the cards changed throughout the conflict, reflecting the military and political developments that occurred from 1815 to 1819. The present deck of cards represents an early example, published in the first half of the war. It shows Kaiser Wilhelm as the King of Acorns, reflecting his popularity at this point; by the time the final editions were published, however, he had been replaced by Prince Leopold von Bayern due to general public dissatisfaction with their ruler. This dissatisfaction would, of course, come to manifest itself in the civil unrest that eventually forced the Kaiser to abdicate in 1918.

K
HERZOG ALBRECHT
D
400-499.
TAUSEND
PROVIDENTIAE MEMOR
U
ZEPPELIN
K
KAISER WILHELM

Count Ferdinand von Zeppelin promoted from Under Knave to Knave

132 ALTENBURGER UND STALSUNDER SPIELKARTENFABRIK

[German WWI playing cards].

Publication
Stralsund, Altenburger und Stralsunder Spielkartenfabrik, [c1916].

Description
32 chromolithograph playing cards, blue printed panel to versos.

Dimensions
101 by 57mm (4 by 2.25 inches).

References
Van den Bergh p.97; Yale 27/GER426 or 2828/GER425.

The Maker
For information about Altenburger Spielkartenfabrik, please see item 130.

The Cards
The propaganda cards of the Altenburger Spielkartenfabrik firm attain their final form in the present deck of cards. Dating from the last year of the war, these cards illustrate the developments that had occurred in both leadership and public opinion.

Some small changes are shown on the court cards, including the King of Bells, which shows Duke Albrecht van Württemberg now adorned with the Iron Cross and Pour le Mérite that he had been awarded over the course of the war. Similarly, the rising importance of Count Ferdinand von Zeppelin is mirrored by his promotion from Under Knave to Knave, a higher-ranking card.

Interestingly, the scenes on the pip cards have also been changed, the modifications reflecting the shifting mood within Germany. In early editions, the Seven of Bells showed soldiers marching along the Rhine, but in the present edition this vignette has been replaced with a scene entitled 'Feinde im Lande' ('Enemies in the country'). The illustration suggests that spies, black marketeers, Jews and captains of industry are responsible for Germany's deterioration. Likewise, on the Nine of Bells, which is captioned 'Durchhalten' ('Hold strong'), the ration packs reflect a sense of long-lasting endurance.

K
PRINZ LEOPOLD VON BAYERN

9.
Brotkarte
Durchhalten!

D
900-999.
TAUSEND

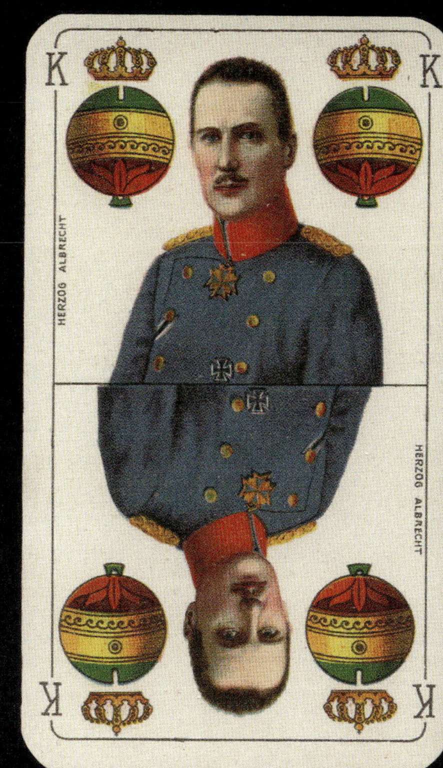
K
HERZOG ALBRECHT

Queens of "technik u wissenschaft"

133 **ALTENBURGER UND STALSUNDER SPIELKARTENFABRIK**

[German WWI playing cards].

Publication
Stralsund, Altenburger und Stralsunder Spielkartenfabrik, [c1916].

Description
32 chromolithograph playing cards, stamp to one, eagle and iron cross to versos.

Dimensions
93 by 61mm (3.75 by 2.5 inches).

References
Van den Bergh p.98; for later edition see Yale 2834/GER432.

The Maker
For information about Altenburger Spielkartenfabrik, please see item 130.

The Cards
Unlike the range of other propaganda cards published by the Altenburger Spielkartenfabrik firm during the course of the First World War, the present deck uses the French suit system and consists of 52 cards.

The Aces represent the most important German kingdoms, with the crest above the central suit mark and their mottos below:

Clubs – Prussia
Diamonds – Württemberg
Hearts – Bavaria
Spades – Saxony

The double-figure court cards show portraits of important German leaders on the King and Jacks, including Commander Hindenburg, Kaiser Wilhelm and renowned aviation pioneer Zeppelin, while the Queens show allegorical representations of valuable pursuits, such as "technik u wissenschaft" ("technology and science").

The present deck is an example from the early years of the war, but by 1918, the design of several cards had been changed to reflect developments in the conflict and in public opinion. For instance, the Queen of Clubs, which in earlier examples had shown Auguste Victoria, the last queen of Prussia, was replaced by a female figure holding a child, captioned "Volkskraft" ("community strength").

K
KRONPRINZ RUPPRECHT
B
TIRPITZ
K
KRONPRINZ WILHELM
D
TECHNIK u. WISSENSCHAFT

The Generals cards

134 WÜST, Conrad Ludwig

[Feldherren karte].

Publication
[Frankfurt, c1916].

Description
32 chromolithograph playing cards, stamp to one, eagle, throne and flag to versos.

Dimensions
92 by 62mm (3.5 by 2.5 inches).

References
Van den Bergh p.100; Yale 2844/GER442.

The Maker
For a description of Conrad Ludwig Wüst, please see item 41.

The Cards
Entitled 'Feldherren Karte' ('The Generals cards'), the present deck of cards was published in 1916 as propaganda in support of the German war effort. The national character of the deck is emphasised by the imagery found on the back of each card: the imperial eagle, the emperor's throne and two military flags.

Each Ace card shows two stylised depictions of the German army in action, with the suit mark in the centre:

Clubs – SMS Emden & a U9 in action
Diamonds – Fortifications on Heligoland & the German territory of Kiautschou
Hearts – German aviators on a reconnaissance mission & Howitzers deployed from a aircraft
Spades – A 42cm Morser in firing position & a Zeppelin flying over England

The illustration of the SMS Emden and her Captain von Müller is likely a tribute to this ship and her crew, after its destruction during the Battle of Cocos in November 1914. Each King displays two German leaders, the Queens show personifications of significant states and the Jacks depict military personnel with their medals and awards:

Clubs – Emperor of Germany/Emperor of Austria, Germany, Beneckendorff/Hindenburg
Diamonds – Duke Albrecht of Wurttemberg/King of Wurttemberg, Turkey, V. Dankle/V. Emmich
Hearts – King of Sachsen/Crown-prince of Germany, Bavaria, V. Moltke/V. Beseler
Spades – King of Bayern/Crown-prince Rupprecht of Bayern, Austria, Archduke Friedrich of Austria/V. Kluck

AUSTRIA
AUSTRIA
v. BESELER
v. MOLTKE
HERZOG ALBRECHT VON WÜRTTEMBERG
KÖNIG VON WÜRTTEMBERG
S.M.S. EMDEN
v. MÜLLER
WEDDIGEN
U. 9. IM VOLLER FAHRT

Alexander I of Serbia becomes King of Clubs

135 **BREPOLS**

[Guerre Mondiale].

Publication
[Turnhout, Brepols, ?1921].

Description
52 chromolithograph playing cards with one joker, red and blue motif to versos.

Dimensions
89 by 53mm (3.5 by 2 inches).

References
Van den Bergh p.99; for first edition see Guiard 38.

The Maker

The King of Hearts bears the name of the manufacturer: "ETABL. BREPOLS Ste Ame TURNHOUT".

In 1795, a printer named Pieter Corbeels moved to Turnhout in Belgium with his assistant, Philippus Jacobus Brepols, in flight from the French army. Corbeels established a small printing firm in the city before his death at the hands of the French army in 1798, forcing Brepols to take over responsibility for the business. He soon expanded the firm by offering bookbinding services and setting up a shop. In 1826, Brepols began printing playing cards and quickly became Belgium's leading card-maker, largely thanks to his early adoption of lithography, and later chromolithography.

Remarkably, after Brepols' death in 1845, the publishing house remained in the hands of his descendants until 1971. During this period, it continued to flourish by incorporating new technology, such as the steam engine, and expanding to open new departments, including wallpaper. Brepols publishing house persists today as one of the largest printing companies in the world, as well as an active publisher of historical material.

The Cards

Following the Allied triumph over Germany in 1918, Brepols published a 32-card deck entitled 'Guerre Mondiale' ('World War'). This deck celebrating the victors of the First World War, with King George V and President Woodrow Wilson, among others, featuring on its King cards.

The present deck is a sequel to this earlier deck, with which it shares a title, and has been expanded to 52 cards. Each Ace shows two scenes or events from the First World War, such as the 'Entrée du Roi à Bruxelles' ('the entrance of the King into Brussels') and the Hôtel de Ville in Reims, which was burnt down in March 1917. The double-figure court cards show portraits of the leaders and commanders who had won significant victories during the war. They are identified by name or title, and accompanied by their national flag; the suit marks are shown in the upper left and lower right corners.

The deck can be dated by reference to the King of Clubs, which shows Alexander I of Serbia. It was not until the death of his father in 1921 that Alexander ascended to the Siberian throne, providing an *ante post quem* for the cards.

Général Pershing
V
J
Entrée du Roi à Bruxelles
AS
Hotel de Ville Reims
Reine de Roumanie
D
Q
Roi des Belges
R
K
Etabl. Brepols Ste Ame
Turnhout
Bagdad
AS
Salonique
Général Leman
V
J

Silly rabbit, these cards were made for kids!

136 LIT INDUSTRIAS MADRIGUERA, S A-BARNA

[Soccer Stars playing cards].

Publication
[Spain, c1925].

Description
40 chromolithograph playing cards, portraits and text to versos.

Dimensions
97 by 60mm (3.75 by 2.25 inches).

References
Van den Bergh pp.198-199.

The Makers
The name of the maker of the lithographs is found just outside the framework of the card. Lit. Industrias Madriguera was a printing firm based in Barcelona during the first half of the twentieth century.

The Cards
The traditional Spanish suit system of cups, clubs and swords, is used, with the exception that instead of coins, there are balls. This was no doubt designed to appeal to children, a fairly rare target market for card-makers of the early twentieth century. The symbols are integrated into playful images of children playing with balls, swinging from swords, balancing cups and toppling wooden skittles.

On the back of the cards are the profiles of famous football players. In the centre is a lifelike image, accompanied by text explaining their name, position and the club they played for. One example is the legendary goal keeper, Ricardo Zamora, nicknamed 'el Divino' ('the divine'). A native Catalan, he played for Espanyol and Barcelona, before later moving to Real Madrid, as listed on the present example. The trophy for the goalkeeper who has the lowest "goals-to-games" ratio in the Primera División is named after Zamora.

The distinct images on the back of the cards effectively make them redundant as a playing deck, and it is more likely that they were designed as trading and collectable items for children.

1

1

1

1

Chocolate film stars

137 CEBRIAN, J.

Baraja Cinematografica.

Publication
[Barcelona, J. M. Arnau, c1925].

Description
48 chromolithograph playing cards, with advertisement to versos.

Dimensions
93 by 57mm (3.75 by 2.25 inches).

References
Van den Bergh p.196.

The Maker
The One, Ten, Eleven and Twelve of each suit shows the name of the maker as 'TIP.LIT. J.M. ARNAUMUNTANER, 66-BARNA'. J. M. Arnau worked on a range of 'chocolate cards' for the Spanish chocolate market. The design for the present deck was the work of artist and illustrator J. Cebrian, and seems to have been his only foray into the world of playing cards.

The Cards
Using the traditional Spanish suits of coins, cups, clubs and swords, the suit symbols are incorporated into the design of each card in this deck.

Entitled 'Baraja Cinematografica' ('Film Cards'), the court cards depict famous movies stars of the day, including Charlie Chaplin, Douglas Fairbanks, Harold Lloyd, and Tom Mix. The pip cards show whismical and humorous scenes, the likes of which would often be seen on the silver screen.

On the back of the cards is an advertisement for 'Chocolates Jaime Boix', along with scenes from various movies accompanied by their Spanish titles. These designs effectively made the deck redundant as playing cards, as they could be roughly identified by the images on the reverse.

1
BARAJA
REGISTRADA CON EL Nº 4.364
SE PERSEGUIRÁ TODA IMITACIÓN
CINEMATOGRAFICA
CHARLES CHAPLIN
TIP. LIT. J. M. ARNAU-MUNTANER 66-BARNA

1
REGISTRADA CON EL Nº 4.364
TIP. LIT. J.M. ARNAU-MUNTANER-BARNA

HAROLD LLOYD (EL)
11
TIP. LIT. J.M. ARNAU-MUNTANER, 66-BARNA

4
BEBE DANIELS
MARIE PREVOST
GEORGE WALSH
WILLIAM RUSSELL

“the thief of Bagdad” steals coins, cups, clubs and swords

138 **MESTRES, Apeles**

Los Ases del Cine.

Publication
Barcelona, [Litografia Bano, c1925].

Description
48 chromolithograph playing cards, blue printed chocolate advertisement on verso.

Dimensions
94 by 57mm (3.75 by 2.25 inches).

References
Van den Bergh p.191.

The Maker
Apeles Mestres was a Catalan painter and illustrator whose career spanned the end of the nineteenth century and the early decades of the twentieth. He designed decks for various card-makers across Europe.

The Cards
1920s movie stars feature in this deck, which uses the traditional Spanish system whereby the suits are represented by coins, cups, clubs and swords.

Some cards show famous figures from the silver screen, including “Charles Chaplin” and Harold Lloyd, while others depict typical scenes from action movies. The Ace of Coins bears the title of the deck: ‘Los Ases del Cine’ (‘The Aces of Cinema’).

The dating of this deck is based on the One of Swords, where Douglas Fairbanks is imaged as “the thief of Bagdad”, after a film that he made in 1924. Fairbanks was co-founder of the ‘Motion Picture Academy’ that hands out the annual Academy Awards to this day. On the Twelve of Cups is pictured Ben Turpin, an actor famous in the early 1920s, but who stopped making films when it became clear that silent movies were a thing of the past.

On the back of each card is shown an advertisement for a Spanish chocolate company, “Chocolates Amatller S. A. Barcelona”, which remains active today.

1
CHARLES CHAPLIN
1

1
Los "Ases" del Cine
1

3
3

4
MYERS
ADOREE
NAGEL
Mc. LEAN
4

Chocolate heroes

139 [ANONYMOUS]

Cine Manual.

Publication
[Valencia, ?Graficas Valencia S.L., c1927].

Description
48 chromolithograph playing cards.

Dimensions
92 by 57mm (3.5 by 2.25 inches).

References
Van den Bergh p.195.

The Maker
While the present deck has been attributed to a printing company based in Valencia, there is no solid evidence for the manufacturer. It has been suggested that the deck is an example of the 'chocolate cards' popular in Spain at the time. Chocolate companies would insert their cards into packages of their products to encourage the consumer to complete the deck by purchasing more.

The Cards
Using the traditional Spanish system, in which suits are categorised as Coins, Cups, Clubs and Swords, the symbols, in this deck, for these suits are incorporated into the design of each image, meaning that the cards can be considered a "transformation deck".

The court cards depict male icons from the 1920s, all portrayed in the contemporary art-deco style. They include movie stars such as Charlie Chaplin and Douglas Fairbanks, explorer Roald Amundsen, aviation pioneer Charles Lindbergh, motorcycle racer Vincente Riera, as well as famous sportsmen. The pip cards show a variety of sports, such as polo, football, cycling, rowing, boxing, skiing and tennis.

On the back of each card is a numbered image.When viewed quickly, one after another, they form a so-called "flick-book", an artificial "movie" starring a cat and several mice.

CHARLOT

7
FUTBOLISTAS

7
TENIS

REMEROS

Dutch Castles

140 **SPEELKAARTENFABRIEK NEDERLAND**

[Dutch Castles].

Publication
[Amsterdam, 1930].

Description
52 chromolithograph playing cards with one joker, brown printed pattern to versos.

Dimensions
93 by 67mm (3.75 by 2.75 inches).

References
Van den Bergh p55.

The Maker
Speelkaartenfabriel Nederlands was established in 1870 and traded from various locations in Amsterdam. It was bought by Van Genechten (now Carta Mundi) in Turnhout in 1970.

The Cards
Playing cards with two Dutch Castles on each ace, together with the publisher's details.

Hearts - Muiderslot Muiden & Kasteel Stapalen bij Boxtel
Diamonds - Kasteel de Doorwerth & Kasteel Croy
Clubs - Kateel Horn & Kasteel Helmond
Spades - Slot Henkenshage & Kasteel Rechteren

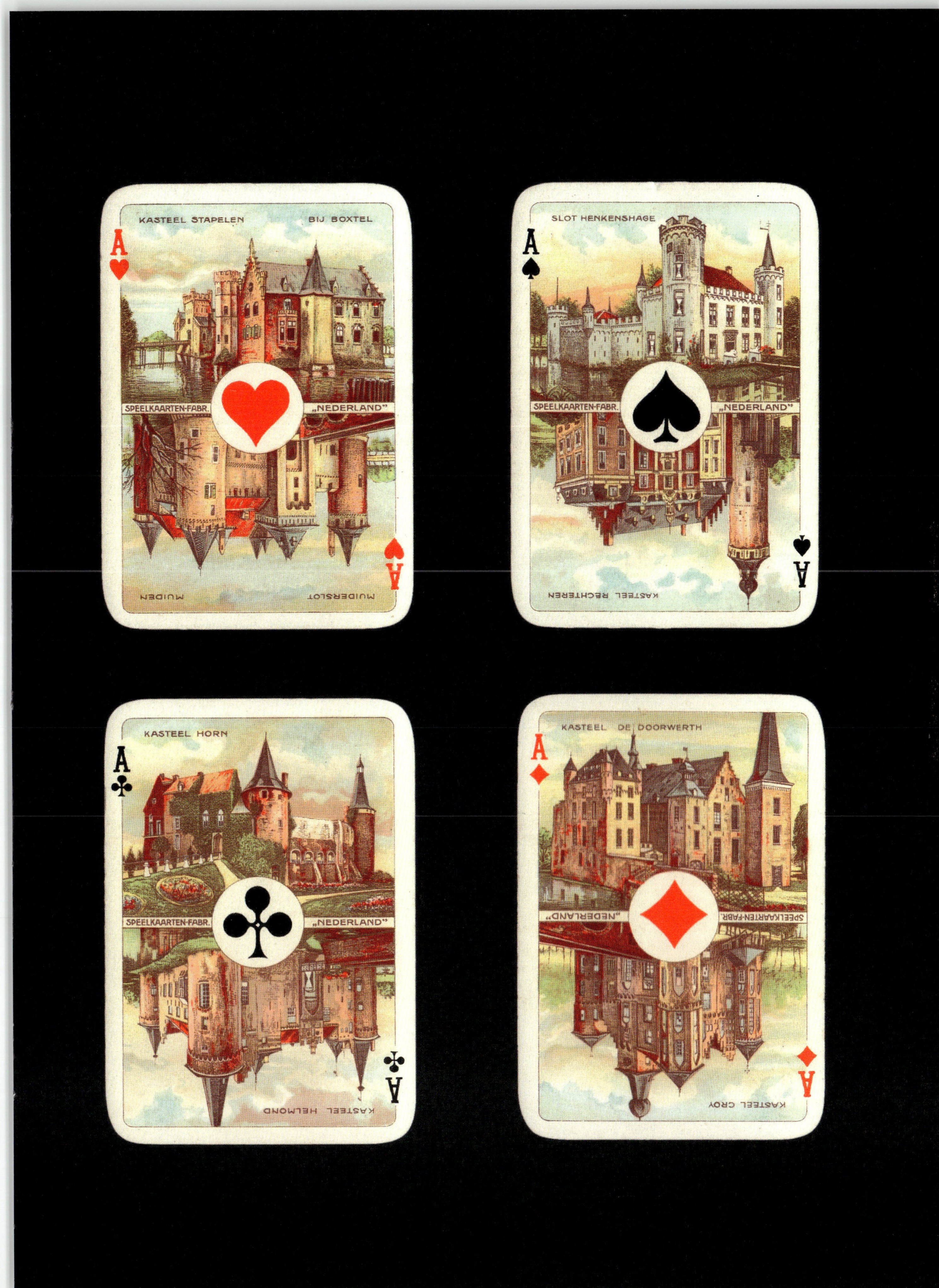
KASTEEL STAPELEN
BIJ BOXTEL
SPEELKAARTEN-FABR.
„NEDERLAND"
MUIDERSLOT
MUIDEN
SLOT HENKENSHAGE
SPEELKAARTEN-FABR.
„NEDERLAND"
KASTEEL RECHTEREN
KASTEEL HORN
SPEELKAARTEN-FABR.
„NEDERLAND"
KASTEEL HELMOND
KASTEEL DE DOORWERTH
SPEELKAARTEN-FABR.
„NEDERLAND"
KASTEEL CROY

The rise of Hitler and Nazi Germany

141 **Elsner & Co.**

National-karte.

Publication
Görlitz, Elsner & Co., 1933.

Description
36 lithograph playing cards, art deco pattern and two eagles to versos.

Dimensions
100 by 56mm (4 by 2.25 inches).

References
Van den Bergh pp.122-23; Yale 2797/GER394.

The Maker
According to the slipcase in which the present deck originally came, they were made by Elsner & Co, at the Kunnerwitzer Strasse 12 in Görlitz, and published under the title 'National-karte'. We have been unable to trace any evidence of other playing cards made by Elsner & Co.

The Cards
The growing prominence of Nazi propaganda throughout the 1930s is reflected on the present deck. Published only one year before Hitler assumed the position of Führer, the cards celebrate his achievements thus far. The Ten of Hearts, for instance, refers to 30 January, 1933, the day that Hitler was appointed Chancellor by President Hindenburg.

The Ace cards show nationalistic slogans and images, while the King cards each depict a different German leader:

Acorns – Frederick the Great
Bells – possibly, von Moltke the Elder
Hearts – Bismarck
Leaves – Hindenburg

The pip cards depict various scenes from Nazi Germany, with soldiers in S.S. and S.A. uniforms a common feature. One of the most striking cards is the Eight of Leaves, which shows a caricature of a Jewish man in a prison cell with the caption "Endlich bin ich am rechten Platze" ("I'm finally in the right place").

SCHLESIEN
Es brennt im Osten !
SIEG-HEIL
FRONT-HEIL
Endlich bin ich am rechten Platze

Evidence of the tense relationship between church and state

142 [ANONYMOUS]

Anti-Religions Cards.

Publication
Moscow, United Socialist Soviet Republics, 1934.

Description
52 chromolithograph playing cards with one joker card, blue and brown image of horned heads to versos.

Dimensions
90 by 58mm (3.5 by 2.25 inches).

References
Van den Bergh p.274, Yale 1388/RUS15.

The Makers
Since the Imperial Playing Card Factory had been established in the nineteenth century, Russian card production had always been monopolised by the authorities. After the fall of the Tsar in 1917, the manufacture of playing cards came into the hands of the state. In true socialist style, the Soviet authorities controlled production of cards throughout the twentieth century, often using it as a means of propaganda, as evidenced by the present deck.

The Cards
This deck embodies the tense relationship between communism and religion in the USSR. Each suit represents one of the four leading religions in Russia at the time:

Clubs – Russian Orthodox Church
Diamonds – Judaism
Hearts – Catholicism
Spades – Buddhism

If religion, according to Karl Marx, is the 'opium of the people', these cards depict the dealers with all their vices. Each double-figure court card shows a religious leader ostensibly fulfilling his or her duty, while in the background their true intentions and desires are shown. The priest, for instance, holds up a cross in the foreground, while behind him stands a table laden with food and wine; a rabbi reads from his holy book with one hand, his other hand open to catch notes and coins. Likewise, a seemingly devout nun holds a candle in reflection, but in the background her true dreams of a romantic relationship are revealed. Most ominously of all, behind a Catholic priest at prayer is the decapitated head of a woman…

The Ace cards show vignettes of various religious buildings and meeting places, satirised with the addition of trivial or commonplace objects, such as musical instruments. On the joker, a capitalist entrepreneur is pictured as the devil, holding leaders from the respective religions on a leash. As if the theme were not obvious enough, the present deck was published under the title 'Anti-Religions Cards'.

Easy on the eye

143 **FAN-C-PACK Co. Inc.**

[Past-L-Eze].

Publication
New York, Fac-c-pack Co. Inc. 1935.

Description
52 lithograph playing cards, plus one joker, plus one blank, scene of horse and carriage to versos.

Dimensions
89 by 56mm (3.5 by 2.25 inches).

References
Dawson, Tom & Judy: The Hochman Encyclopedia of American Playing Cards, U.S. Games Systems Inc., 2000; Segeth, Uwe-Volker: Spielkarten Jugendstil und Art Déco, Edition Christian Brandstätter, Wien, 1994; Van den Bergh p237.

The Maker
An insert card sometimes included (although not present here) reads: "Past-l-exe is our exclusive brand name applied to playing cards. Instead of glaring white, you are faced with a soft, pleasing pastel colour, green or cream. Easy and non-glaring on your eyes." Some of these packs are believed to have been manufactured by E. E. Fairchild because wrappers have been found with the tax stamp cancelled by E.E. Fairchild Corp.

The Cards
Geometric Art Deco designs in pastel colours.

The present single deck is also known to come in a double box, with images of Pan and a goat to the versos.

The insert describes the design as follows: "on Past-l-Eze playing cards Kings, Queens and Jacks are no longer stodgy and conventional but pleasingly reflect suspicion, flirtation and worry."

Issued for the 1936 Olympics

144 HERWIG, Ferdinand

[Olympic playing cards].

Publication
[Baden, Badische Spielkartenfabrik, c1935].

Description
32 chromolithograph playing cards, orange, red and blue pattern to versos.

Dimensions
95 by 62mm (3.75 by 2.5 inches).

References
Van den Bergh p.273.

The Maker

The designer of these cards, Ferdinand Herwig, has left his name on the Ace of Hearts, while the name of the publishing firm, Badische Spielkartenfabrik, is found on the Seven of Hearts.

Herwig (1884-1959) studied at Stuttgart before pursuing his artistic career in illustrations and painting. He is known to have presented pieces for exhibition at the Munich Glass Palace and the Great Berlin Art Exhibition.

The Badische Spielkartenfabrik firm appears to have been a playing card manufacturer based in Baden, with these cards as the only known deck attributed to it.

The Cards

Dedicated to the theme of sport and athletics; it is possible that this deck was published for the occasion of the infamous 1936 Olympic games, held in Berlin under Nazi rule.

Each of the Ace and court cards shows a different sport taking place. The Aces present scenes of cross-country skiing, sailing, flying and motorbike racing, with only the central suit marks and borders coloured. By contrast, the court cards show brightly coloured double-figure images of athletes in action. Both male and female competitors are shown, along with the various accoutrements of their sports, which include tennis, boxing, football and track and field. The athletes on the King cards are crowned.

The pip cards are presented in the traditional style, with the number of suit marks corresponding to the value. Two versions of this deck exist, the present example with 32 cards, and a later edition with 52 cards and a joker. The joker depicts a hapless football player getting hit in the face with the ball.

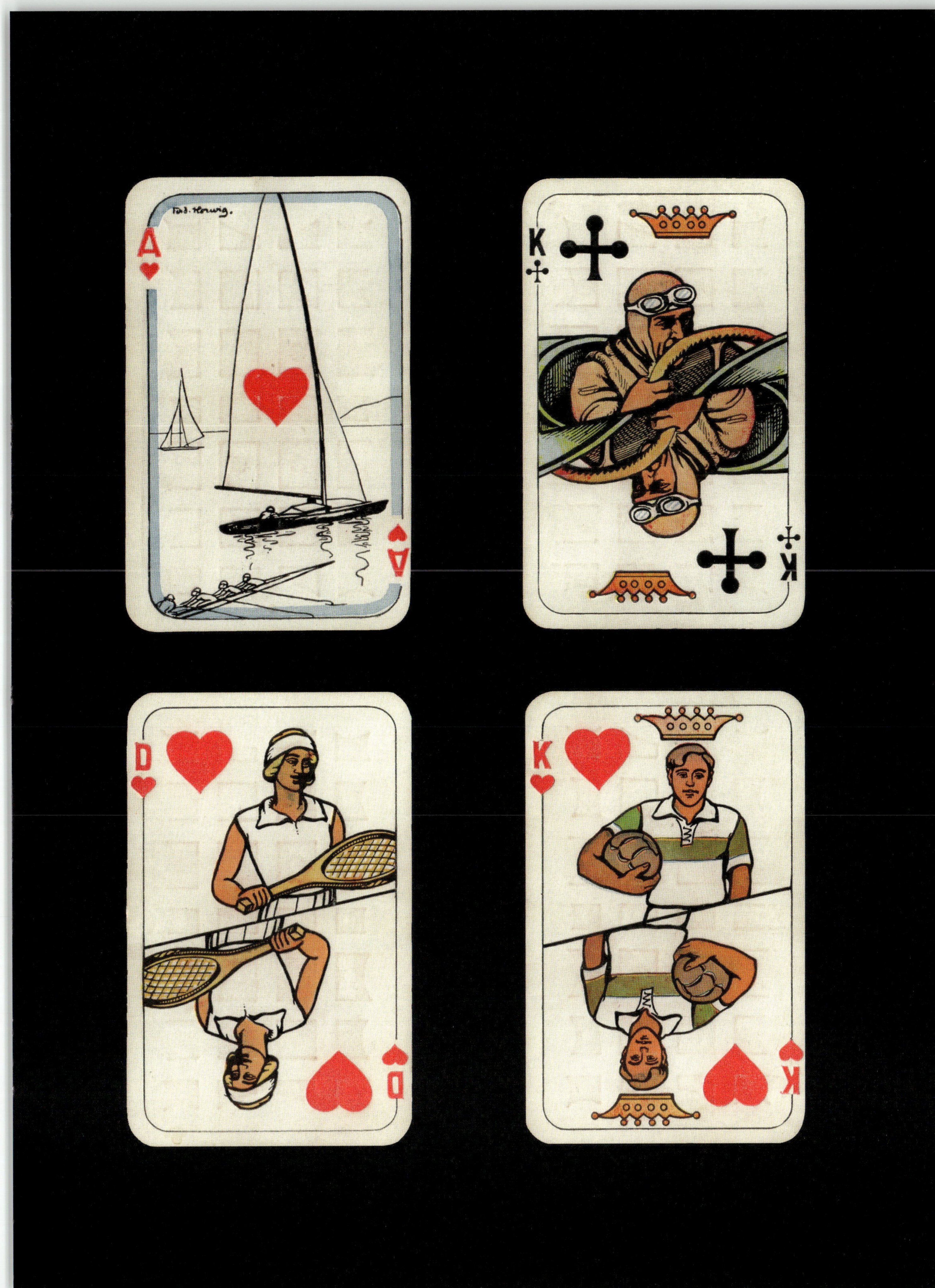
A
K
D
K

Allied Generals

145 SOCIETE ANONYM LIMITE BIERMANS

Jeep.

Publication
[Turnhout, Biermans, 1944].

Description
52 playing cards, plus one joker, housed within printed paper box.

Dimensions
84 by 57mm (3.25 by 2.25 inches).

References
Belgische Speelkaarten, Luc Biebouw(2014), LB17 p.316; Van den Bergh p86.

The Maker

Léonard Biermans had been employed by Brepols from 1871-1874 before opening his own steam-powered playing card factory in 1875. In 1879 he married Marie-Thérèse, daughter of Van Genechten's manager, Charles Poupaert, so playing cards were never far from his attention. Léonard Biermans died in 1896 and the company continued as a limited company, S.A. Léonard Biermans.

Biermans initially built up trade with India and South-East Asia (Burma) and business prospered until the competition became fierce and India became independent. After that Biermans expanded into other markets, winning several exhibition medals and also registering a patent for rounded and gilded corners.

Eventually the firm was merged into Carta Mundi in 1970.

From the beginning Biermans produced a wide range of playing cards which were shipped all over the world. An 1877 export price-list mentions Cartes de Luxe, Impériales, Royales, Italiennes, Belges, Allemandes, Bongoût, Espagnoles, and others. After 1900 Biermans also produced Swiss, Oriental and Congress cards, English packs, Spanish packs, Chinese cards, children's cards and domino cards. In many cases packs contained scenic aces with views of Belgium, Brasil, France, Germany, Switzerland, Portugal or Holland which appealed as tourist souvenirs.

The Cards

One of several decks printed in Belgium at the end of Second World War to celebrate victory over the Nazis. It was printed by L. Biermans of Turnhout in 1945 and is specifically named 'Jeep', probably to honour the famous Willys Jeep which was used extensively by the US army during the war. A picture of the jeep is also shown on the back of the cards.

The Aces all show caricatures of famous military commanders who were instrumental in the defeat of the Nazi.

Depicting famous allied military commanders as aces, with the joker being a caricature of Adolph Hitler. The courts cards are the Belgian, or Genoese, pattern with French indices.

Hearts: General Jean de Lattre de Tassingny, Commander of the 1st. French Army and leader of the Liberations Army from 1943-45. He represented France at the signing of the treaty in Berlin on May 8th. 1945.

Diamonds: General Bernard Law Montgomery, Commander of the British 8th. Army during the Western Desert Campaign & as Commander of the Allied Ground Forces during the Battle of Normandy. He eventually became Supreme Allied Commander of Europe.

Clubs: General Dwight D. Eisenhauer, Supreme Commander of the Allied Expeditionary Force in Europe during WW2. He became President of the United States from 1948 until 1953.

Spades: Secretary General Joseph Stalin, leader of the Soviet Union who remained in power until his death in 1953.

"Victory" cards celebrating U.S. participation in the Allied victory, c.1945.

146 ARRCO Playing Card Company

[Victory Playing Cards].

Publication
[Chicago, ARRCO Playing Card Company, 1945].

Description
52 playing cards, plus two jokers, Stars and Stripes device printed to versos.

Dimensions
88 by 57mm (3.5 by 2.25 inches).

References
Van den Bergh p86.

The Maker
The Arrco Playing Card Company was established in 1927, but initially under the name of Arrow Playing Card Company, and under the leadership of Theodore Regensteiner, inventor of the four-color lithograph press.

Based in Chicago, the company used Chicago's "Century of Progress" World's Fair in 1933-34 to launch under the new name: Arrco. Innovators in the field, Arrco were the first company to developed what they called their "Plastic Coated Duratone Cards" with a special coating that made it possible to clean the cards with a damp cloth. The new finish was billed as follows:

"It's a quick trick to remove soil, candy or ink stains from Plastic-Coated Duratone cards... a damp cloth, a wipe, and presto - they're like new! At this time, not even a magician could supply the tremendous demand for Duratone cards".

As evidence of their popularity and success is the fact that the US government made large orders of the cards with the new Duratone finish for the army. A special deck design was even produced by Arrco for military service members!

Arrco continued to manufacture playing cards into the 1980s, but in 1987 the Regensteiner family decided to sell their operations. The playing card division of their company was taken over by its long term rival USPCC.

The Cards
"Victory" cards issued by ARRCO Playing Card Co soon after VE day celebrating the U.S. participation in the Allied victory. The court cards are Uncle Sam, Lady Liberty repeated in each suit, with the jacks being different at each end, either a saluting soldier or sailor.

JOKER
JOKER

Victors of WWII

147 **MESMAEKERS FRERES**

Cartes de Luxe.

Publication
[Turnhout, Mesmaekers Frères, 1945].

Description
52 playing cards, plus one joker, housed within printed paper box.

Dimensions
88 by 58mm (3.5 by 2.3 inches).

References
Van den Bergh p86.

The Maker
The Mesmaekers firm was established in Turnhout in 1859 by the partnership of Gustaaf Mesmaekers and Louis-François Moentack. In 1862 Moentack withdrew from the partnership, leaving Gustaaf Mesmaekers who then turned to his two brothers for their support to continue the business. From then on the firm was known as Mesmaekers Frères.

The Cards
Depicting the allied victors of World War II, with the joker being a caricature of Adolph Hitler, and each suit representing one of the four major Allied victors, with Ace as a famous building, the King as the wartime leader, the Queen a personification of the flag, and the Jack as a soldier.

Hearts: Russia - The Kremlin (Ace); Joseph Stalin (King).
Diamonds: U.S.A. - Statue of Liberty (Ace); Franklin D. Roosevelt (King).
Clubs: France - Eiffel Tower (Ace); Charles de Gaulle (King).
Spades: Britain - Houses of Parliament (Ace); Winston Churchill (King).

R
R
R
R

Stalin gives Europe a clubbing

148 JACOVITTI, Benito

[Italian political playing cards].

Publication
Spoleto, S. A. Art Grafiche Panetto & Petrelli, 1951.

Description
40 chromolithograph playing cards, blue advertisement to versos.

Dimensions
113 by 72mm (4.5 by 2.75 inches).

References
Van den Bergh pp.180-181.

The Maker

The Three of Swords identifies Benito Jacovitti (1923-1997) as the designer of this deck. He was an Italian illustrator, famed for his controversial designs, which were often themes centred around politics and erotica.

The cards were published by the Panetto & Petrelli printing company. In the first half of the nineteenth century, printer Domenico Bossi and his son Vincenzo ran a small company in Spoleto, Italy. In 1850 it merged with the company of Gherardo Gherardi, and the firm soon expanded its activities to include printing posters, notices and correspondence cards. In 1902, Carlo Panetoo and Gaetano Petrelli took over operations, renaming the company SPA Art Grafiche Panetto e Petrelli.

By 1920, they had a huge lithograph-printing workshop covering 7000 square meters, as well as paper and photography departments. The modernisation of the firm meant that it won notable national commissions. Much of the factory was destroyed during the Second World War, but the owners rebuilt, and celebrated the 50th anniversary of their company in 1952. The current deck was issued only one year earlier, and may have been among the first publications from the newly rebuilt factory.

The Cards

Publicised on the occasion of the 1951 election, this deck reflects an interesting time in Italian politics. In the aftermath of the Second World War, socialist and communist parties in France and Italy had been in the ascendant, but by 1951, the Italians seem to have turned against left-wing policies, perhaps because of the developing Cold War. The cards in this deck echo the public mood with strong anti-communist imagery.

As well as serving as propaganda, the deck is also an example of the transformation style, as the Italian suits of coins, cups, clubs and swords are creatively used to complete the images. On the Seven of Clubs, for example, we see Stalin brandishing seven wooden clubs, which represent some of the Central European countries under the control of the USSR. The Three of Swords shows the dove of peace chained to three Chinese swords, which collectively show the letters "MAO". The lire and ruble are frequently used for the suit of coins, and the cups are often represented as vessels filled with blood.

The cards remained popular throughout the latter half of the twentieth century, no doubt a reflection on the ever-increasing tensions between East and West, and a facsimile edition was released in 1975. The original deck published by Panetto & Petrelli, however, is extremely rare.

PACE
PROPAGANDA
RUBLO
P.C.I.

Provocative Vargas girls

149 VARGAS, Alberto

[Provocative playing cards].

Publication
1953.

Description
52 chromolithograph playing cards and one joker card.

Dimensions
91 by 62mm (3.5 by 2.5 inches).

References
Van den Bergh p.230.

The Maker
The Peruvian artist Alberto Vargas (1896-1982) became world famous for his pin-up images. While he was active in America from 1916, his real breakthrough came in the 1940s when he developed images for Esquire Magazine, which would soon come to be known as "Vargas girls".

According to trade-mark records from the time, the Western World Playing Card Company was owned by Henry Miller of Missouri. The Vargas girls deck was the firm's most successful publication by far.

The Cards
One of the earliest examples of cards showing pin-up girls in explicit, rather than simply suggestive, clothing and poses. Each card shows an attractive woman in either swimwear or lingerie, with the Joker wearing a provocative jester's outfit. The suit mark is shown in the upper left and lower right corners, and the artist's name is shown on each one.

These are the forerunner for a long line of provocative playing cards, but despite its huge popularity, only a single edition would appear during Vargas' lifetime. In the following decades, the cards were reissued multiple times.

vargas

vargas

vargas

vargas

Games of Love and Chance

150 ALBARRAN, Pierre, and Monique ARIETTI

[Cancan cards].

Publication
Paris, Philibert, 1956.

Description
58 chromolithograph playing cards, including two joker cards and four additional aces, blue illustration of pillow to versos.

Dimensions
95 by 64mm. (3.75 by 2.5 inches).

References
Van den Bergh p.203.

The Maker
"Can-can was designed by Pierre Albarran, the world-famous bridge and tennis player. Pierre Albarran played two times in the Davis Cup tennis-team for France, and won a bronze medal in the Antwerp summer Olympics in 1920 (in doubles), but he became much better known as a contract bridge player. At Bridge, he was French champion 19 times and played in 32 international matches for France... For many years he, ranking first, organized and directed the annual bridge tournament held in Monte Carlo. He ranking first in the 1935 Brussels World-tounament for teams. He was a columnist on bridge for several French newspapers and authored several books on bridge. Perre Albarran was referred to as 'The Aristocrat of Bridge'. He died on 24 February 1960, at the age of 66. Pierre Albarran's biggest contribution to the game of Bridge is a theory for a bidding systems that includes the 'Canapé approach' and the convention that was later called "Roman two-suiter". And of course he has designed this beautiful 'Can-can'-deck" (World of Playing Cards).

The deck was drawn by Monique Arietti (pseudonym of Gabriel Garachon, designer at Draeger Frères who printed the cards, and herself a dancer).

The Cards
The gently risqué luxury playing cards, with lots of lace, are designed in the style of the 1900s. The Aces show nude dancers, repleat with suitably arranged suit marks covering their privates. The Jokers show a croupier, and a flower girl.

D
A
A
D

Games of Love and Chance

151 **BECAT, Paul-Emile**

Memoires de Casanova.

Publication
Paris, Philibert, 1960.

Description
52 chromolithograph playing cards, with two joker cards and one title card, blue illustration of pillow to versos.

Dimensions
95 by 64mm (3.75 by 2.5 inches).

References
Guiard 186; Van den Bergh p.233; Yale 2686/FRA386.

The Maker

Between 1954 and 1960, the French publisher Philibert produced playing cards including two decks drawn by painter and engraver Paul-Emile Bécat (1885-1960). The first deck appears in 1955 under the title 'Le Florentin' and the second deck in 1960 with the title 'Memoires de Casanova'. Bécat leaves his mark on this deck with a signature on each card.

The Cards

The subheading for the 'Memoires de Casanova' deck was 'Les Jeux de l'Amour et du Hasard' ('The Games of Love and Chance'), reflecting the amorous, romantic and even erotic imagery shown on the cards. On the Two of Clubs, a woman pines over her missing beloved, while the King of Spades shows a whole host of figures, one completely naked and another dressed in an elaborate theatrical costume.

Certain cards point towards specific places or locations. The Five of Diamonds seems designed to evoke a Venetian atmosphere, with a nude woman reclining on a gondola; the Queen of Hearts bears a close resemblance to Marie Antoinette, an allusion reinforced by the dress and hair of her partner.

The suit marks and values of each card are indicated in the upper left and lower right corners, with both the French and the English index letters on the court cards. The pip and Ace cards also show the corresponding number of suit marks across the image.

5
2
R
K
D
Q

From the creator of "Nose Art"

152 **ELVGREN, Gil**

American Beauties.

Publication
[Saint Paul, MN, Stancraft Products, c1960].

Description
52 chromolithograph playing cards and two joker cards.

Dimensions
88 by 65mm (3.5 by 2.5 inches).

References
Van den Bergh p.231.

The Maker
Just like Alberto Vargas, Gil Elvgren (1914-1980) was extremely popular as an illustrator and painter of pin-ups during the mid-twentieth century. He began his career producing images for calendars, and during the Second World War many of his designs made it onto the bodies of American aircrafts as "nose art".

In 1937, he started working for the publisher Louis F. Dow but in 1944 he transferred to the competitor Brown & Bigelow, where he would be active for almost 30 years. Well-known actresses such as Kim Novak posed for drawings by Elvgren.

Stancraft Products was a subsidiary company of the Brown & Bigelow printing firm and was responsible for several decks of playing cards during the 1960s and 1970s. They were the first company to patent plastic-coated playing cards.

The Cards
An example of one of the many decks published in America in the mid-twentieth century with the raunchy theme of pin-up girls.

The 52 'American Beauties' shown on the cards are all scantily-clad women, many identified by a generic first name, such as Lola on the King of Hearts, and Celeste on the Jack of Clubs, or labelled according to their pose, with a woman adding "The finishing touch" to her nail polish. The woman on the Joker card is dressed in a provocative harlequin costume.

The suit marks and values are indicated in the upper left and lower right corner of each card, making them a fully functional deck as well as the voyeur's delight.

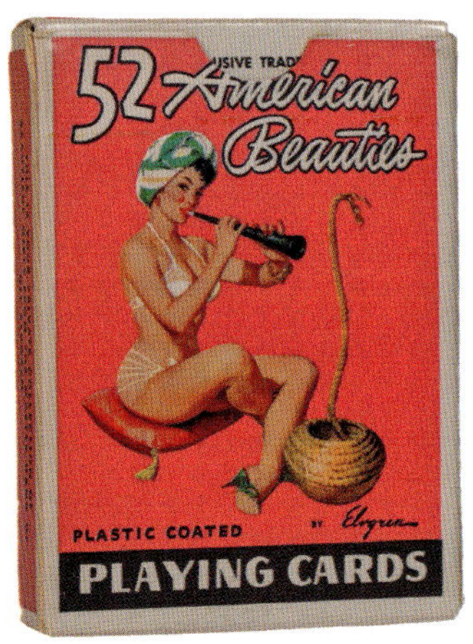

8
THE FINISHING TOUCH
8

10
DENISE
10

J
CELESTE
J

K
LOLA
K

It's coming home!

153 MONTY GUM

[Caricatures of Footballers].

Publication
[Leiden 1961].

Description
52 colour printed cards, plus one joker.

Dimensions
87 by 56mm (3.5 by 2.25 inches).

The Maker
Monty Gum was established in Leiden after World War II. The name Monty is a reference to Field Marshal Bernard Law Montgomery. Monty Gum were regular producers of football cards, beginning with this, their first, set of English cards in 1961, with their last in 1990.

The Cards
Each card features and English football player caricature, including Jimmy Bloomfield, Bobby Charlton, Brian Clough, Jimmy Greaves, Jimmy Hill, and Stanley Matthews. The joker is the French goalkeeper François Remetter.

STANLEY MATTHEWS

BOBBY CHARLTON

JIMMY GREAVES

JIMMY HILL

"JACK of Hearts"

154 HUMOR HOUSE INC

Kennedy Kards.

Publication
1963.

Description
54 playing cards, including explanation card, "Donkey" joker, "democratic" red printed verso, housed withinprinted paper case.

Dimensions
900 by 57mm. (35.5 by 2.25 inches).

References
Van den Bergh p4.

The Maker
Humour House, Inc. appears in the Library of Congress' Copyright Office catalogue of 1963, where it is listed for its caricature playing cards copyrighted on 2nd March 1963. The artist is listed as Henry Allan Hartley. Known professionalyl as Al Hartlet, he was a comic book artist and son of a New Jersey Congressmen, best known for his work on Archie and Atlas Comics during the mid-twentieth century.

The Cards
"The royalty of playing cards has variously represented Adam, Julius Caesar, Charlemagne, Helen of Troy, Pallas Athena and others. Our own national leaders and heroes have been occasionally commemorated on face cards. The Kennedy Kards have been conceived within this tradition and confirm what voters have said in recent elections - we have a new JACK of Hearts.

The White House is now a full house. Long live the King, the Queen and the Jack!"

Produced in 1963, presumably to coincide with Kennedy's re-election campaign, and shortly before his assassination in Dallas on 22 November of that year.

A
© 1963, HUMOR HOUSE, INC.
K
Q
J

Not your ordinary video game

155 ASLAN

Old Suntory Whisky.

Publication
Kyoto, Nintendo, 1978.

Description
52 chromolithograph playing cards and two joker cards.

Dimensions
82 by 56mm (3.25 by 2.25 inches).

References
Van den Bergh p.232.

The Maker

Alain Gourdon was a French painter, sculptor and pin-up artist, better known by his moniker Aslan. He famously contributed to the adult entertainment magazine 'Lui' from its creation in 1964 until the early eighties, providing a monthly pin-up.

Published by Nintendo, established in 1889 as a producer of playing cards, until it became the phenomenon that it now is, creating electronic toys and video games from 1969.

The Cards

Issued to advertise the Old Suntory Whisky brand, established in 1899. The Suntory Beverage and Food Limited is one of the oldest alcohol companies in Japan. During the 1970s, the firm issued promotional decks, both erotic and non-erotic.

Distinctly erotic, the current deck is designed in a remarkably western style, with provocatively-dressed (or undressed!) women adorning each card. The technique of photorealism, which had emerged during the 1960s and 1970s, is used by Aslan to create incredibly lifelike images.

The suit marks and values are given in all four corners, and on the pip and Ace cards, the value is also represented by a corresponding number of suit marks across the image.

K
5
A
5

"Le Jeu des Alliés"

156 VAN DE HOEVEN, Marion

Le Jeu des Alliés.

Publication
[Breda, Breda Art Academy, 1987].

Description
52 playing cards, plus two jokers, green versos.

Dimensions
100 by 70mm (4 by 2.75 inches).

References
Van den Bergh p237.

The Maker
Made for the graduation project of the artist.

The Cards
From an edition of 10 copies. As far as we are aware, this is the only deck of cards made with the silk screen printing technique.

B
V
H
V

"Que Concorde rapproche les hommes"

157 VERAME, Jean

2 Jeux de 54 Cartes.

Publication
Paris, Editions Dussere, 1991.

Description
Two packs each comprising 52 offset lithograph playing cards, plus two jokers in each, unopened in original wraps, housed within original card box.

Dimensions
86 by 62mm (3.4 by 2.4 inches).

References
Van den Bergh p278.

The Maker
Jean Verame (b1936) is a French artist and collector of playing cards.

The Cards
Presented to Concorde passengers on Air France. The Air France motto for Concorde was "Que Concorde rapproche les hommes" (somewhat more in the spirit of the enterprise (although perhaps less catchy) than the British Airways "Arrive before you leave").

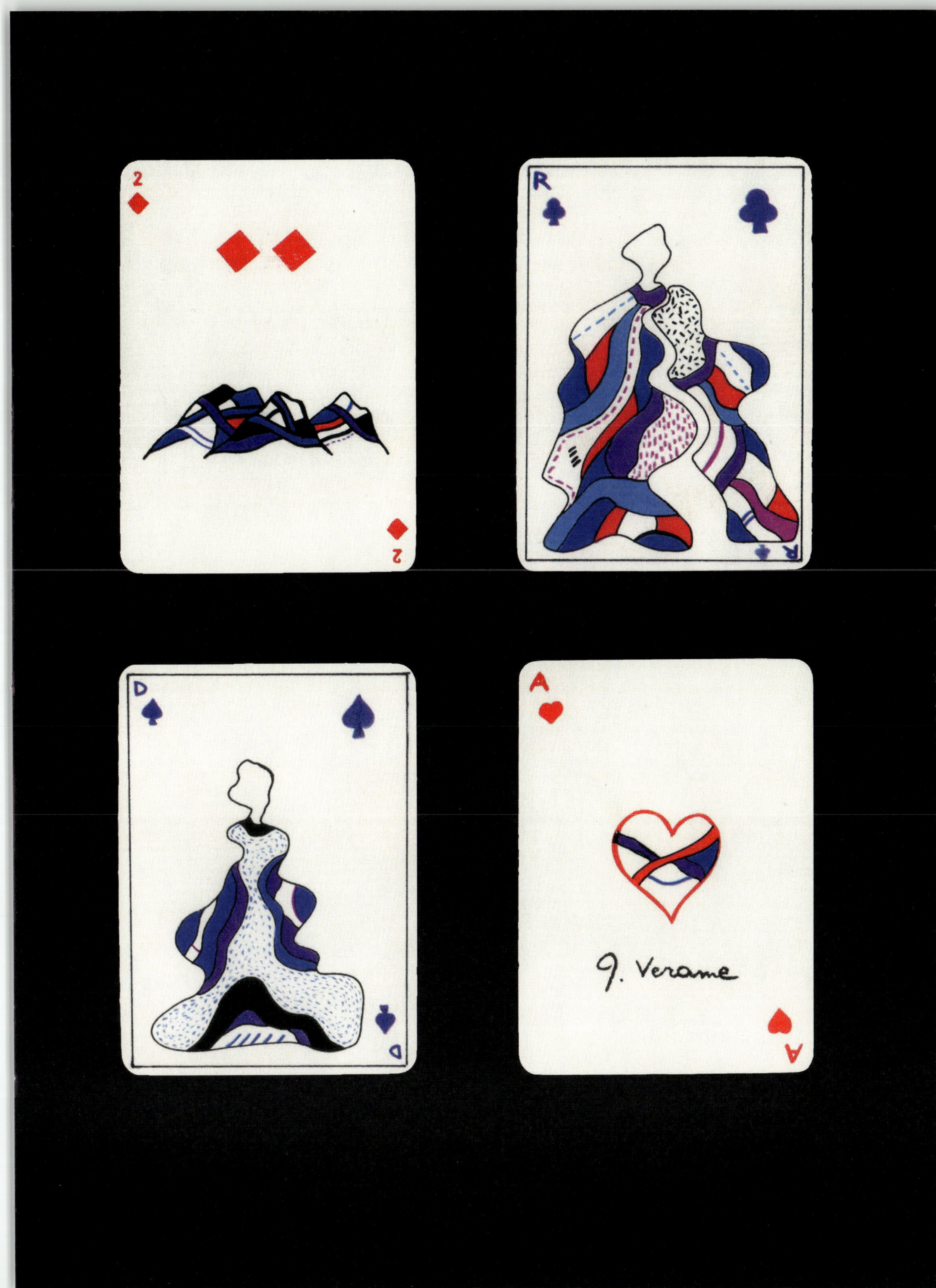
2
R
D
A
J. Verame

158 SCHREIBER, Lady Charlotte Elizabeth

Playing Cards of Various Ages and Countries. Selected from the Collection of Lady Charlotte Schreiber.

Publication
London, John Murray, 1892-95.

Description
First Edition, folio, three volumes, 447 plates, a few printed in colour, generally toned, orinal. gilt-decorated crimson quarter morocco by Leightons (with their ticket).

Comprising: Volume I - English, Scottish, Dutch and Flemish cards; Volume II - French and German; Volume III - Swiss, Swedish, Russian, Polish, Italian, Spanish and Portuguese, together with a Supplement of other countries from the collection of the late Jaime Ortiz-Patino.

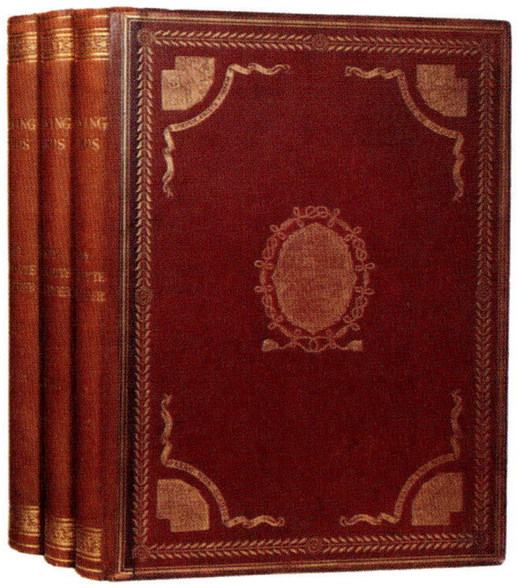

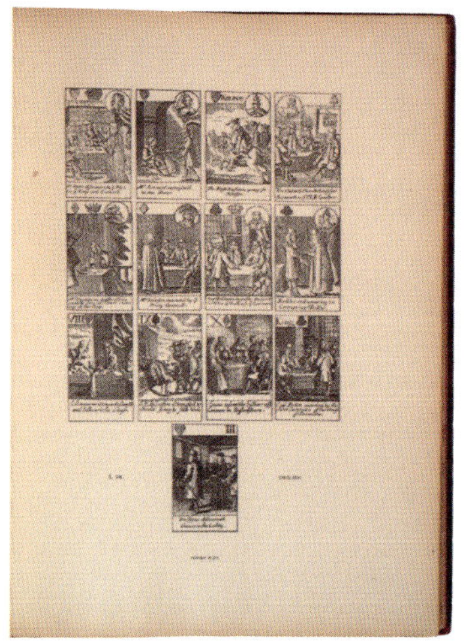

159 D'ALLEMAGNE, Henry Rene

Les cartes à jouer du XIVe au XXe siècle.

Publication
Paris, Librairie Hachette, 1906.

Description
4to, Two volumes, Frontispiece, with illustrations throughout, blue cloth boards.

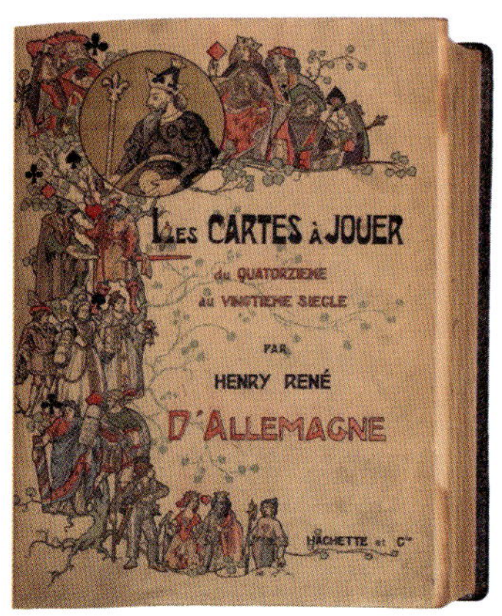

160 HARGRAVE, Catherine

A History of Playing Cards and a Bibliography of Cards and Gaming.

Publication
Boston and New York, Houghton Mifflin Co., 1930.

Description
4to, colour printed frontispiece, illustrated with colour and black and white plates, publisher's red cloth, worn.

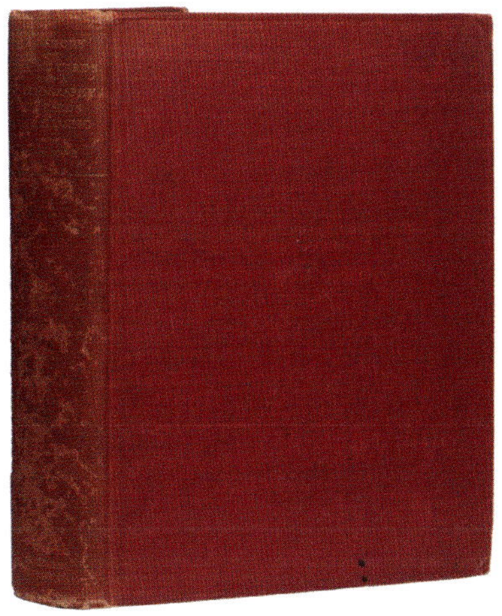

Bibliography

Freeman, M. O'Donoghue. *Catalogue of the collection of playing cards bequeathed to the trustees of the British museum by Lady Charlotte Schreiber.* Longmans & Co., 1901.

Hargrave, C. P. *A history of playing cards and a bibliography of cards and gaming.* Courier Corporation, 2000.

Million. *Cartes à jouer et Tarots. Collection Claude Guiard.* Million, 2011.

Van den Bergh, F. *Verzamelde Speelkaarten, de Frank van den Bergh collective,* 2018.

Yale University Library. *The Art of the Playing Card, the Cary Collection.* Yale University Library, 1973.